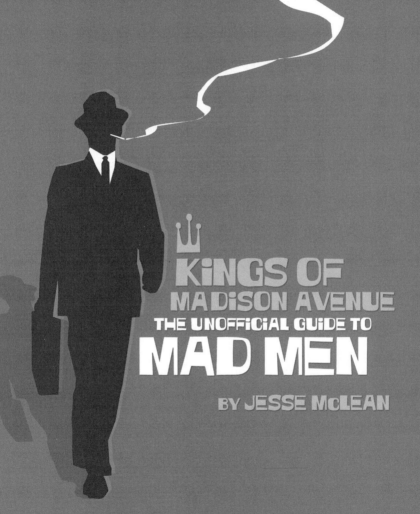

KiNGS OF MADiSON AVENUE
THE UNOFFICIAL GUIDE TO
MAD MEN

BY JESSE McLEAN

ECW Press

Published by ECW Press, 2120 Queen Street East, Suite 200,
Toronto, Ontario, Canada M4E 1E2
416.694.3348 / info@ecwpress.com

LIBRARY AND ARCHIVES CANADA CATALOGUING IN PUBLICATION

McLean, Jesse
Kings of Madison Avenue : the unofficial guide to Mad men / Jesse McLean.

ISBN 978-1-55022-887-8

1. Mad men (Television program). I. Title.

PN1992.77.M33M35 2009   791.45'72   C2009-902549-3

Editor: Jennifer Hale
Cover design: Keith Berry
Text design: Tania Craan
Typesetting: Mary Bowness
Printing: Transcontinental 1 2 3 4 5

The publication of *Kings of Madison Avenue* has been generously supported by the Ontario Arts Council, by the Government of Ontario through Ontario Book Publishing Tax Credit, by the OMDC Book Fund, an initiative of the Ontario Media Development Corporation, and by the Government of Canada through the Book Publishing Industry Development Program (BPIDP).

Canadä   ONTARIO ARTS COUNCIL
          CONSEIL DES ARTS DE L'ONTARIO

PRINTED AND BOUND IN CANADA

ECW PRESS
ecwpress.com

For Darlene, who keeps me mad in the best possible way

How the Kings Roll: What You Can Expect 1

Smoking, Drinking, Selling:

    It's Don Draper's World and We Just Live in It 5

CAST BIOGRAPHIES

JON HAMM – "DON DRAPER" 15

ELISABETH MOSS – "PEGGY OLSON" 19

JOHN SLATTERY – "ROGER STERLING" 22

VINCENT KARTHEISER – "PETE CAMPBELL" 26

CHRISTINA HENDRICKS – "JOAN HOLLOWAY" 29

JANUARY JONES – "BETTY DRAPER" 32

ROBERT MORSE – "BERTRAM COOPER" 34

EPISODE GUIDE — SEASON ONE

1.01   SMOKE GETS IN YOUR EYES 37
    Gender Politics and Helen Gurley Brown's *Sex and the Single Girl* 42

1.02   LADIES ROOM 49

1.03   MARRIAGE OF FIGARO 53
    Doyle Dane & Bernbach's "Think Small" Campaign for Volkswagen 57

1.04   NEW AMSTERDAM 63
    Money Part One — Inflation from 1960 to Now 68

1.05   5G 68

1.06   BABYLON 72

1.07   RED IN THE FACE 77
    What Are They Smoking? 82

1.08   THE HOBO CODE 82
    Before Sterling Cooper — Recommended Viewing:
      Delbert Mann's *Lover Come Back* 87

1.09   SHOOT 90
    How Tall Is the Mayor? 94

    Before Sterling Cooper — Recommended Reading:
      Betty Friedan's *The Feminine Mystique* 94

1.10   LONG WEEKEND 99
    Before Sterling Cooper — Recommended Viewing:
      Billy Wilder's *The Apartment* 103

1.11   INDIAN SUMMER   105

1.12   NIXON VS. KENNEDY   110
      Nixon, Kennedy, and the Changing Face of American Politics   110

1.13   THE WHEEL   123
      Redskins Presidential Prediction Record   126

EPISODE GUIDE — SEASON TWO

2.01   FOR THOSE WHO THINK YOUNG   129

2.02   FLIGHT 1   134
      Before Sterling Cooper — Recommended Viewing: David Swift's
        How to Succeed in Business Without Really Trying   138

2.03   THE BENEFACTOR   142
      Money Part Two — What They Made Then and What They Make Now   146

2.04   THREE SUNDAYS   147

2.05   THE NEW GIRL   151

2.06   MAIDENFORM   156

2.07   THE GOLD VIOLIN   161

2.08   A NIGHT TO REMEMBER   166
      Before Sterling Cooper — Recommended Reading:
        Richard Yates's *Revolutionary Road* and *Disturbing the Peace*   171

2.09   SIX MONTH LEAVE   176

2.10   THE INHERITANCE   179
      Civil Rights Movement — Dr. Howard Thurman's *Jesus and the*
        ***Disinherited* and its Influence on Dr. Martin Luther King**   184

2.11   THE JET SET   189
      Guest Stars — I Know That Face . . .   193

2.12   THE MOUNTAIN KING   194
      Notable Writers and Directors from *Mad Men*   199

2.13   MEDITATIONS IN AN EMERGENCY   200
      Before Sterling Cooper — Recommended Reading:
        Frank O'Hara's *Meditations in an Emergency*   203

APPENDICES

How to Party Like the Mad Men   209

The Perfect Manhattan Rendezvous: An Itinerary for Touring Locations
      Highlighted in *Mad Men*   218

Sources   223

Acknowledgments

Writing a book of any kind is a solitary experience, but preparing it for publication is clearly another matter. I'd like to take a moment to thank everyone at ECW Press who helped, including but not limited to: copy editor Emily Schultz and proofreader Crissy Boylan, who kneaded the lumps out of my prose; Tania Craan, who designed the interior; Jen Knoch for sourcing the photos; typesetter Mary Bowness; publicists Sarah Dunn and Simon Ware; co-publishers Jack David and David Caron; and my editor Jen Hale, an early champion of this project and an unflagging supporter, without whom this book would not have been possible or half as much fun.

I'd also like to thank my good friend Keith Berry for designing the cover and making me look classy and James Salisko for his keen advice and relentless cheerleading.

Last but certainly not least, I'd like to thank the one who stood by my side while I toiled on this book from the first day to the last — my dog Bear. You were right about Frank O'Hara. I'm glad I listened.

How the Kings Roll: What You Can Expect

For my money, watching an episode of *Mad Men* provides the pleasure of a well-written show set in a fascinating era (close enough for current-day relevance, far enough removed to feel exotic) but also inspires a confidence not unlike Don Draper himself — cool, patient, methodical, and always with an eye on the big picture. No matter where the story goes, no matter how seemingly oblique or digressive the drift, as a viewer I've always felt secure. Much like Don describes advertising in the pilot episode, I've always felt that everything is going to be okay.

I had only felt that way once before when I gave myself up to a television show — Michael Mann's *Crime Story*, created by Chuck Adamson and Gustave Reininger. As I watched *Mad Men* I couldn't help but compare the two. They both take place in a similarly glamorous, stylized universe; both are concerned with the struggles of a conflicted protagonist as well as those of the surrounding characters. And while both were critical darlings, *Mad Men* reaped the rewards (and longevity) that the other could not manage past two seasons.

Crime Story carved out a peculiar place in the prime-time schedule of 1986. Sleek, violent, and historically canny, this epic tale of a Chicago cop's battle to bring a rising mobster to justice always felt out of place in the quick-cut mentality of '80s television. But audience members willing to invest time in the series not only enjoyed a satisfying entry in the police procedural genre, they also saw subtler dramas unfold, like the cost of career dedication, alcohol abuse, and the strain of interracial romance against the backdrop of the Civil Rights movement.

An even greater correlation between the two TV shows is an infinite patience in pacing; both reveal the larger narrative and allow delicately observed moments room to breathe. In this, both series feel more like one-hour movies than episodic television, and relate a sure-handedness that allows for storytelling sidesteps that enhance the overall viewing experience instead of detracting from it.

It is there, however, that the similarities end. *Crime Story* received a

1

great deal of acclaim for the glitzy yet gritty approach (and derision for a pervasive violence that many thought bordered on exploitation). The show struggled in the cutthroat major network atmosphere, steadily losing the audience it reaped from a post–*Miami Vice* debut. A benefit of airing on a boutique network like AMC is that *Mad Men* has never had to worry much about Nielsen ratings, an allowable indulgence provided that the shelves in the award cabinet continue to buckle. The list of laurels granted to *Mad Men* is extensive, while *Crime Story* only managed three Emmy nominations, one for cinematography and two for "outstanding achievement in hairstyling." And while history has treated *Crime Story* well (cited by *Time* magazine as one of the best television shows of the '80s), the cultural impact of *Mad Men* was immediate and profound.

I suppose that is why I felt I had to write this book. A show as well written and steeped in historical detail as *Mad Men* demands further discussion. The investigation of shifting societal mores are more than a framing device; they actually inform every episode in a way that current events inhabit our own daily lives. When you watch a program that builds historical events into a story with a sly confidence — like the Volkswagen ad campaign or the American Airlines crash in Jamaica Bay — then it can only enhance the viewing as that context is explored more fully. *Mad Men* is a show that asks profound questions — such as the very nature of identity or the role of gender in determining status and success — and it benefits the show's fans who examine those questions not only with regard to the characters and the times of the show but in a comtemporary context as well.

As a fan of *Mad Men*, I sought out a single volume that would combine all of these questions and concerns but also celebrate the show and augment the viewing experience, a book that looked behind the scenes at the forces that conspired to create the show, and the people who brought it to life; a book that assessed the literary and cinematic antecedents that helped inspire this amazing show. I looked high and low, but I couldn't find the book I wanted.

So I wrote it.

After unearthing interesting information in biographies of *Mad Men* cast members (including who started their acting career in a stage production of *Winnie the Pooh* and which actor spent high school as a socially outcast Goth), we'll move on to the episode guide. I will examine the thematic aims of each installment, discuss what I have seen, and reflect on what the fans are talking about around the water cooler (or online, this century's version of the water cooler). Included in each episode's assessment will be sidebar observations and historical footnotes, including a "Period Moment" (a quick look at one of the many cultural signposts that populate each episode), "Ad Pitch" (a review of the campaigns created by the Sterling Cooper group and how close they are to actual promotions of the time), "Manhattan Real Estate" (the history of the city's geographical landmarks and which of them still stand in the New York of today), "The Philosophy of *Mad Men*" (dialogue that reveals the characters and their philosophies, and, more often than not, provides sound words to live by), and "Cocktail of Note" (a perfect drinking guide complete with recipes and suggested servings).

Fans of history — just about every *Mad Men* fan I know — will enjoy the chapters devoted to historical context. Interspersed throughout the guide, these are more detailed examinations of the events and movements that serve as a more than just background throughout the series. Historical evaluations in these Context entries include Helen Gurley Brown and her bestselling book *Sex and the Single Girl*, the contentious presidential campaign between John Kennedy and Richard Nixon, the changing face of "New Advertising" as spearheaded by the Doyle Dane & Bernbach agency, and an often overlooked influence on the Civil Rights movement, Dr. Howard Thurman.

Also peppered throughout the book are reviews of influences and the direct and oblique connections to *Mad Men*. Whether literary (Frank O'Hara's *Meditations in an Emergency*, the Age of Anxiety fiction of Richard Yates, Betty Friedan's *The Feminine Mystique*) or cinematic (*How to Succeed in Business Without Really Trying, The Apartment, Lover Come Back*), the impact from various sources on Matthew Weiner's show is ascertained and debated.

And lest you think this a dry history lesson, the appendix will contain fun and lively guides detailing how to party like the Mad Men and how to plan the perfect Mad Men Manhattan weekend.

What you won't find between these covers is a substitute for the series itself. My aim is for this book is to inform and supplement the already enjoyable viewing experience that is *Mad Men*. The episode guides are not simply breakdowns of plot points fans of the show will already know

3

by heart. Also, you won't find any nitpicking about typographical anachronisms and the like (e.g. the "Sterling Cooper" font used a whole year before it existed — the horror!). When a show like this gets so much right, the occasional lapse is forgivable.

What you will find is a fun, informative addition to one of the finest television shows of this new century. So sit back, drink up, and enjoy. It's Don Draper's world, and we just live in it.

Smoking, Drinking, Selling:
It's Don Draper's World and We Just Live in It

On July 19, 2007, at 10 p.m, AMC aired the inaugural episode of their first original drama, *Mad Men*. This debut airing garnered a 1.4 share in the Nielsen ratings (approximately 1.5 million viewers), an increase of 75 percent in viewership for AMC in that time slot. Viewership increased with each successive episode along with a groundswell of critical appreciation, a cultural impact unlike any television program in recent history, including two Golden Globe wins (for Best Drama and lead actor Jon Hamm), the prestigious Peabody Award, and six Emmys for the first season.

Drawing inspiration from many cinematic predecessors (*A Guide for the Married Man, The Apartment*) as well as literary (the collected fiction of John Cheever, J. D. Salinger, Betty Freidan's *The Feminine Mystique*, and Helen Gurley Brown's *Sex and the Single Girl*), *Mad Men* creator Matthew Weiner crafted a show that fulfills an audience's hunger for intelligent drama about complex characters, all delivered with an irresistibly slick layer of dramatic irony.

In theory, this show should have filmed once Weiner typed the final Fade Out on the pilot script. Why, then, did it take five years from the initial writing before *Mad Men* aired to such a receptive audience? How could a show with this high-quality pedigree not find a home on original programming standard-bearer Home Box Office (HBO), particularly one created by a writer/producer on their signature hit *The Sopranos?*

Whether a result of myopia or laziness, this stumble from the once

5

and long-thought future home of peerless television drama missed a chance to harness one of this century's first breakout hits. And when it comes to that kind of top-drawer original cable programming, they should have known better.

They invented it.

Matthew Weiner
Portrait of the Writer/Producer as a Young Man

The reverence for New York's 1960s heyday is an important element to the success of *Mad Men*. All the more interesting in that Matthew Weiner was born and raised in Baltimore, Maryland.

The love of all things Manhattan came, indirectly, from Weiner's parents. His mother grew up in the Bronx, while his father spent his formative years in Manhattan proper. Julia Weiner studied law but never practiced, and Leslie Weiner forged a career for himself as an eminent neuroscientist. But once they made the decision to start a family, they left the guys and dolls of Forty-second Street for the safety of Maryland.

"Once my parents left New York, they had nothing nice to say about

The cast gathers for a Golden Globe win. From left to right: Jon Hamm, January Jones, John Slattery, Matthew Weiner, Elisabeth Moss, Christina Hendricks, and Vincent Kartheiser. (AP Photo/Reed Saxon)

it," Weiner said in an interview for the *New York Times*. "But I loved going to visit my grandparents, going past the Empire State Building and trying to crane your head out the window."

The third of four children, Weiner grew up in a household that placed a premium on debate.

"My family is made out of argument. There is argument, there is discourse, you better stick up for yourself. My sister is a journalist, my other sister is a physician, my little brother is a physician, my mother is an attorney. There is direct conversation of the deepest, most profound, intellectual sort."

This appetite for rigorous intellectual discourse has served Weiner well. After his family moved to southern California, Weiner began an educational path that led him to a combined program of philosophy, history, and literature at Wesleyan University. It was an invaluable education that directly affected the influences on *Mad Men*, which are as literary as they are cinematic.

Weiner not only flourished under the deft touch of Wesleyan film and television department head Jeanine Basinger, he also discovered a kindred spirit in fellow student and Basinger acolyte Joss Whedon (*Buffy the Vampire Slayer, Firefly, Dollhouse*). Word has it that while at Wesleyan, Weiner and Whedon often engaged in a friendly academic rivalry, where one's highly regarded project countered with another's even farther reaching entry. And even though their professional lives have never crossed, there is an unmistakable correlation between their arcs: talented writers who toiled on other people's shows before launching their own, medium-changing efforts.

While Wesleyan is one of the highest ranked colleges in the United States, success in the program Weiner attended was not gauged by a traditional grading system. As a result, Weiner could only pursue his MFA in Film Studies at University of Southern California after strong lobbying on his behalf by his father — a task more easily completed due to Dr. Weiner's esteem in the academic community (culminating in the dedication of a neurological research center at the University of Southern California in his name).

Weiner hit his academic stride in the Film Studies program. His personal life also took flight when, after graduating from University of Southern California, he married architect Linda Brettler. This union with an established professional provided the financial support Weiner required during his early attempts to find employment as a screenwriter — other than winnings from a stint on *Jeopardy!*, those first years saw Weiner contributing little income to the marriage.

During this process, Weiner made an independent film at his wife's urging, and while the final product never saw a commercial release, private screenings did land him work as an uncredited joke writer for the short-lived 1996 FOX sitcom *Party Girl*. This, in turn, resulted in work as a writer/producer on subsequent sitcoms *The Naked Truth* and *Andy Richter Controls the Universe*. While neither of these shows had a long shelf life, Weiner did parlay his experience into a staff position on the long-running if critically dismissed sitcom *Becker*.

Finally making a living as a writer, Weiner encountered a career crisis when he realized that penning formulaic plots and lock-step setup/punch line japes failed to fulfill his artistic yen. And while the dismal prospects of such a career may have darkened his days, it ultimately inspired him. He tried to write his way out of the professional doldrums when he spent his off hours working on a story, a character, and a moment in time that had always intrigued him.

"There's too much smoking," was the response Weiner received when he pitched his show idea to a select few. Those who heard Weiner explain his intentions for the show felt the era too remote, the protagonist inscrutable, the environment toxic and bereft of empathy. Undaunted, Weiner proceeded to write his pilot. Already a veteran of the television game, Weiner no doubt realized that an audience hungry for intelligent drama would vault past their distaste of any profession. Nobody likes lawyers, but how many hit shows have detailed their exploits?

David Chase, creator of HBO juggernaut *The Sopranos*, read Weiner's pilot script as a piece of sample writing and responded immediately. The distinct voice, point-of-view, and respect for the audience dovetailed with his own sensibilities. Chase offered Weiner the opportunity to join his show as a writer/producer.

Weiner wrote or co-wrote twelve episodes over the following five years, won a Writer's Guild of America award and two Emmys for his work as producer. All the while, his pilot script for *Mad Men* sat in the desk drawer and waited.

Once *The Sopranos* concluded and relinquished its stranglehold on the critical and cultural imagination, Weiner dusted off his beloved script. After his years at HBO, Weiner understandably felt that he would find a welcome home at the network for his whip-smart take on a pivotal moment in American history.

This would prove an equally pivotal moment in Weiner's history.

From Made Men to *Mad Men*

In 1965, a man named Charles Dolan won the rights to create a cable system in lower Manhattan. He knew that the key to success in this tough market was as much a matter of geography as programming; while the crowded Manhattan skyline impressed, the tall buildings hampered television reception. Mr. Dolan conquered this obstacle with a new system that snaked miles of cable beneath the streets of New York, the first urban underground cable system in America. He called the system Sterling Manhattan Cable.

Dolan received investment from Time Life Inc. and by 1972 launched the cable channel Home Box Office. Initially a pay-TV service offering uncut motion pictures and top-line sports events, HBO soon expanded its mandate and began producing original programming in 1977. Movies and series produced under the HBO banner took advantage of the loosened standards of basic cable and created programming that brimmed with adult themes, violence, and profanity that could never find a home on network television. For a number of years, HBO became synonymous with the R-rated nature of its content rather than a standard-bearer of quality.

All that changed on January 10, 1999, when HBO aired the first episode of *The Sopranos*. An unlikely critical and commercial hit about a New Jersey mob boss who struggles with violent usurpers, a controlling mother, and anxiety attacks, *The Sopranos* became the yardstick by which all other television dramas were measured. Creator David Chase's passion project became the first cable series to win the Emmy for Outstanding Drama, garnered a number more for acting, citations from every major entertainment guild, as well as the prestigious George Foster Peabody Award.

When *The Sopranos* came to an end on June 10, 2007, HBO found itself in a curious position. After building an empire through original programming that won over audiences and critics alike, they faced the prospect of a pale schedule that had once been robust. Not only had *The*

Sopranos finished its run, audience favorite *Sex and the City* had concluded in 2004, the award-winner *Six Feet Under* expired in 2005, and epic Western odyssey *Deadwood* shuddered to a stop in 2006. Other highly touted shows like *The Wire* and *Rome* exhibited a complexity and overwhelming narrative scope comparable to *The Sopranos*, but they never wooed a sizable audience despite bouquets of lavish critical notices. And while ratings performer *Entourage* continued to build momentum and win over initial skeptics, David Milch's *Deadwood* follow-up *John from Cincinnati* stalled out of the gate. *Big Love* was framed as the heir apparent to Tony Soprano's HBO throne (signaled by the series opener following *The Sopranos'* season 6 premiere in March 2006), and while it has since evolved into a critical and audience favorite, it started slowly and left many wondering if the patriarchal polygamist did not have the frame required to fill Tony's seat at the head of the HBO table.

Fresh off his successful writing/producing stint on *The Sopranos*, Matthew Weiner saw an excellent opportunity to jump-start his gestating pilot for *Mad Men*. David Chase delivered Weiner's script to HBO executives with enthusiasm and approval. "It was what you were hoping to see," Chase remarked about Weiner's pilot script. "[It] was lively and had something new to say. Here was someone who had written a story about advertising in the 1960s and was looking at recent American history through that prism."

What better place for the exploits of advertising house Sterling Cooper than at the cable company founded on the Sterling Manhattan Cable system?

Unfortunately, HBO executives did not seem to appreciate the symmetry. More accurately, it is difficult to know *what* they thought; despite early rumors of a rejection from HBO, they did not pass on the project. They simply did not respond.

On October 10, 2007, *Variety* TV critic Brian Lowry moderated a Q & A at the Paley Center for Media with *Mad Men* cast and creator Matthew Weiner. During the discussion, Weiner confirmed that HBO did not respond to his pilot script, or his phone calls. A baffling response from such a seasoned player in the high-quality original programming game it invented.

Even stranger is the disregard for personal relationships. "All I can tell you is that it was very disappointing to me," Weiner said of the situation. "Because I was part of the family."

Mad Men rakes in Emmy awards in 2008. (AP Photo/Reed Saxon)

When Charlie Collier assumed stewardship of the cable network AMC (formerly standing for American Movie Classics) in 2006, his intention was to dramatically alter its course. Primarily known for airing movies from the 1950s and earlier, Collier hoped to change the stuffy image of the network by providing audacious, original programming. After the success of Robert Duvall's miniseries *Broken Trail*, Collier knew that the time had come to plunge into a continuing series. He read a pilot script from a former writer of *The Sopranos*, liked what he saw, and jumped on the chance for a daring first series.

"When the creative community sees a *Mad Men*," Collier said later, "They know we're willing to take risks."

A notorious perfectionist, Matthew Weiner found the perfect home for his pet project. "They completely trusted me . . . With the exception of three lines, the pilot was the script I had written five years before that."

While HBO might have seemed the natural place for *Mad Men* to flourish, further inspection suggests otherwise. HBO's original programming not only takes full advantage of the creative freedom their cable status provides, it also exploits this independence from the strict censorship of the public airwaves. Marketing for *The Sopranos* relied almost as heavily on its violence and language as it did its quality. *Mad Men*, while a supremely adult show, features no violence and only PG 13–level language (the kind often heard in FX series such as *The Shield or Nip/Tuck*). True, there is a long history of quality original programming on HBO, but there isn't the same kind of connection to history shared by AMC and *Mad Men*. What better home for a series with allusions to the 1947 film *Gentleman's Agreement*, 1956's *The Man in the Grey Flannel Suit*, 1960's *The Apartment* and 1967's *How to Succeed in Business Without Really Trying* than a network founded on airing those kinds of films?

And while HBO may be home to critical acclaim, *Mad Men* has already surpassed any expectations for a successor of *The Sopranos*. In the show's short run it has already eclipsed Emmy nominations for any single season of *The Sopranos*, and, in fact, any other drama in television history.

The cultural impact of Weiner's series is already more profound than the mafia series he worked on. Advertising agencies have harkened back to the glory days depicted in *Mad Men*, with Philadelphia-based agency Red Tettemer redesigning their website in honor of the series, and dressing their entire staff in era-appropriate pomade-laden hair and conical bras.

Speaking of fashion, Weiner's mania for accuracy in 1960 period details affected the runways in 2008. Celebrated designer Michael Kors launched a *Mad Men*–inspired clothing line in February of that year, complete with wool cardigans and short-brimmed fedoras. And while *The Sopranos* can lay claim to a strong influence on the cultural zeitgeist, nobody wore nylon track suits or loud short-sleeved Burma Bibas shirts in deference to the show.

The Soprano crime family may have cast a long shadow during its six season run, but Don Draper and the men and women of Sterling Cooper stepped into the limelight before the end of the first season. Some might say they cast an even longer shadow.

The Road Behind and the Road Ahead

Matthew Weiner has charted a long, crooked road to success with his pet project. Through the prism of self-made man Don Draper's adventures in the advertising world of 1960s New York, Weiner allows the audience to view the many facets of American culture that experienced overwhelming metamorphoses in that exhilarating time, from gender politics and the first cracks in the glass ceiling, to presidential politics during the

Kennedy/Nixon campaigns. There also emerged a mainstream accept-ance of psychoanalysis, and a revolutionary change in notions of race via the Civil Rights movement. As well, a growing social consciousness changed the role of American youth in society, and, along with the cul-ture, advertising itself underwent a seismic change.

Mad Men provides a fizzy cocktail of crackerjack writing, intoxicating costume and set design, along with a splash of sweet irony that provides as much insight into the distant past as it does into our current world.

CAST BIOGRAPHIES

I was forced to grow up very early . . . that tends to take
a lot of childhood out of the equation and you
become very aware of adult things.

— Jon Hamm

JON HAMM – "DON DRAPER"

Born in St. Louis, Missouri, on March 10, 1971, Jon Hamm was to know the solitude of an only child. He also came to know heartache at a very young age, with his parents' divorce when he was only two years old. He lived with his mother, only seeing his father every other weekend. He struggled to find happiness in this lonely and fractured existence, and in some measure succeeded.

"I do have very good memories of being a kid running around, but that all pretty much got lost."

When he was ten, Hamm's mother developed a stomach ache that would not subside. What she first thought an inconvenient malady turned out to be advanced cancer that spread quickly to her internal organs. A radical surgical procedure removed two-thirds of her colon and along with it, doctors hoped, the cancer that ravaged her body. She did not survive the surgery.

Hamm moved in with his father who also lived in St. Louis, and while this saved him a geographical upheaval he still had to grapple with an emotional one.

"I loved my dad and [until then] would see him every other weekend," Hamm noted in an interview with *The Observer*. "It wasn't like he was this guy I didn't know."

Hamm's father had two other children from a previous marriage, one

"I appreciate alcohol. I love the place that alcohol holds in our society, but I'd never attempt to drink as much as Draper." (AP Photo/Matt Sayles)

of whom he lived with at the time. Also at the house was Hamm's eighty-year-old grand-mother. Despite the surrounding blood relations, one can only imagine the isolation a ten-year-old Jon Hamm endured in such a situation.

The time spent with his father did help inform the character that would bring Hamm to the spotlight. A successful businessman in the 1960s, Hamm's father bears much surface resemblance to a certain Madison Avenue ad man.

"My dad would have been twenty-seven or twenty-eight in 1960 . . . he would have had a Don Draper–type sway over things."

Early exposure to theater (Hamm starred as Winnie the Pooh in a grade school production of the bear's adventures) led to a life-long interest in acting, which resulted in his attendance at the University of Missouri to study theater on a full scholarship. Hamm's desire to immerse himself in another person may well have sprung from his truncated formative years.

"Acting is sort of an extension of childhood," Hamm has said. "You get to play all of these roles and have so much fun . . . I wouldn't turn down any of that."

While a theater major, Hamm eked out a living in unrelated fields like so many of his fellow actors. Instead of making his way exclusively as a waiter or bartender however, Hamm opted for a role as educator. Immersed in his studies, Hamm worked at a daycare center where he led his students in "after-school stuff." And for a short while after graduating, Hamm returned to his high school alma mater, John Burroughs School in

The *Saturday Night Live* parody of *Mad Men* featured host Jon Hamm and special guest John Slattery. (Dana Edelson/NBCU Photo Bank/AP Images)

Ladue, Missouri, to teach drama. But the siren call of professional acting continued and in 1995, it lured him to Los Angeles.

Work in his chosen discipline did not come easily. Once again forced to make ends meet, Hamm took work where he could get it, at one point working as a set dresser on a soft-core porn shoot for $150 a day.

A phone call from New York provided the lifeline Hamm desperately sought. He had been introduced to writer/actress Jennifer Westfeldt through mutual friends at a birthday party. They did not immediately hit it off ("She thought I was a cocky asshole," says Hamm of the meeting), but while workshopping a sketch idea, Westfeldt thought of Hamm for a role. Eager to distance himself from the least glamorous work of his professional life, Hamm left the porn set, scraped together enough money for airfare, and made his way east.

Eventually, the sketch took life as an independent movie with Hamm taking on a supporting role. *Kissing Jessica Stein* was a critically acclaimed same-sex romantic comedy that gained notoriety for snappy dialogue and a fresh take on relationship foibles in a bi-curious context between Jessica

(Jennifer Westfeldt) and Helen (Heather Juergensen).

Jon Hamm could have cared less for the acclaim, happy as he was to nurture his working relationship with Westfeldt into a romantic one that continues to this day.

Acting roles slowly materialized, including small parts in movies such as *Space Cowboys* and *We Were Soldiers*, along with parts in television shows like *The Hughleys, Charmed, The Sarah Silverman Program,* and *Numb3rs*. He landed recurring roles in programs like *Providence, The Division, Gilmore Girls, What About Brian,* and *The Unit*, which helped increase Hamm's visibility in Hollywood. But despite his professionalism, humble demeanor, and movie star looks, Hamm could never break out of the "working actor" mold.

Once he received a pilot script for a show about advertising executives in the 1960s, Hamm sensed an opportunity for greater success and artistic fulfillment. The network behind the production had other plans. AMC wanted an established star to lead their first foray into original dramatic programming. Show creator Matthew Weiner was inclined to give the role to Hamm, but faced resistance from the network. Hamm weathered seven auditions in total for the role of Don Draper and finally persevered.

As Hamm stated in an interview, "People really needed convincing that they wanted me."

After an Emmy nomination and Golden Globe win for Best Lead Actor in a Drama Series for Jon Hamm, it is clear that the audience did not need persuading.

> It wasn't that much of a leap for me to become an actor. Had I
> wound up as a doctor, now that would have been surprising!
>
> — Elisabeth Moss

ELISABETH MOSS – "PEGGY OLSON"

For some, the call to an artistic life provides an avenue of escape from an expected way of life — whether working on the production line or taking over the family business. For others, it is the only sensible road to travel. Elisabeth Moss had no choice but to walk the latter path.

Her home life was dominated by music — her British father manages jazz musicians, and her Chicagoan mother is a professional harmonica player, who has performed with many of the biggest names in blues, including icon B. B. King.

"I grew up going to gigs, watching rehearsals, touring on the road," Elisabeth Moss said in an interview with the *Toronto Star*.

Born in 1982 in Los Angeles, Moss took quickly to acting. Her first professional gig was at the age of eight. She filmed a pilot called *Bar Girls* in 1990 and hasn't stopped working since.

In between acting jobs, she attended a small, private school and graduated early at the age of fifteen. The accepted route of training and apprenticeship usually applies to actors as well as the rest of workforce, but Moss rejected further schooling for real world experience.

"I just kept working, kept acting. I've done everything. Big parts in indie films, small parts in big films, TV movies, one or two commercials. I've been acting for twenty years."

The lack of formal training has never hindered Moss, as she set about creating a career for herself on the small and big screens. "I never had a single day of training," she has said of her background. "And I have nothing against it, but my acting school was working with some of the best actors, writers, and directors in the business."

Along with the requisite résumé-building television work, Moss also found a niche for a while providing voices in animation — from *Animaniacs* to *Frosty Returns* and *Batman* to *It's Spring Training, Charlie*

Brown! Moss also voiced a character in the big-screen ecological adventure *Once Upon a Forest*.

She might have continued on in a quietly successful acting career if not for two developments in 1999. In that one year, she appeared in a film with one of the biggest stars in Hollywood, and landed a recurring role on one of the smartest shows on television.

In *Girl, Interrupted*, Moss played Polly, a troubled girl scarred by a self-inflicted burn on her face. She acted alongside Academy Award–winner Angelina Jolie in the adaptation of Susanna Kaysen's memoir.

Of the role, Moss has said, "It's very rare for an actress of my age to be offered a role of such substance . . . I had to go through three hours of makeup every morning. Once the makeup was on, I wouldn't have to do a lot. I would immediately walk and talk differently."

Moss also first appeared as presidential daughter Zoey Bartlet in Aaron Sorkin's *The West Wing*. What was to become her trademark display of innocence coupled with inherent intelligence was used to great effect in playing a young girl pushed to maturity through an attempted assassination of her father, a widely publicized interracial romance, and a kidnapping by a group of homegrown terrorists.

"Working on *The West Wing* prepared me for anything I might have to face in the business. You had to work fast, and well, and be ready for changes at the last minute," she said of the experience. "Of course, with Aaron doing the scripts, your job is that much easier when the writing is that good."

Once the run on that watermark series ended, Moss returned to parts in independent films (*Day Zero*) and television appearances (*Invasion, Ghost Whisperer, Medium, Grey's Anatomy*). However, she soon caught wind of a pilot script that was generating interest throughout the industry and decided to audition.

"I just went and auditioned for it because I thought it was a great script . . . and a great part . . . and I was kinda like, 'Wow . . . a '60s advertising agency . . . on *what* network? Don't they just show movies?'"

Moss had to audition twice for the part, but her view of Peggy Olson as an identifiable everywoman rings so true that it is hard to imagine show creator Matthew Weiner ever having a moment of doubt.

"She's Jack Lemmon, she's Ernest Borgnine in *Marty* . . . you want her to succeed, you want her to do well. She's definitely very ambitious . . . but the last thing she would do is trample anyone to get to the top."

"I grew up going to gigs, watching rehearsals, touring on the road."
(AP Photo/Chris Pizzello)

The constantly developing aspects to the character of Peggy Olson are largely attributable to the high caliber of writing, but Elisabeth Moss's endless energy and verve investigating these corners (sometimes flattering, other times not) is contagious. Her artistic exploration is not limited to her portrayal of Sterling Cooper's first female copywriter, but to her career as well. In 2008, Moss jumped into her first Broadway production in a revival of David Mamet's *Speed-the-Plow*. She received glittering reviews, and not just for surviving the media roller coaster that resulted from the mid-production withdrawal of cast mate Jeremy Piven (*Entourage*).

"Ms. Moss [brings] a naked clarity to her unvarnished, tinny-voiced Karen that makes the play hang together in ways it didn't before," wrote Ben Brantley in the *New York Times*.

In her best known pieces, there is a common thread to Elisabeth Moss's work. *Mad Men*, *The West Wing*, and *Speed-the-Plow* feature her as a smart, principled young woman in a world dominated by men. That she plays characters that succeed and flourish in such a setting without sacrificing femininity is one thing; that she plays them with such conviction and believability is quite another — a tribute her talent.

People are always asking me what it was like back then.
I'm like, "How the fuck old do you think I am?"

— John Slattery

JOHN SLATTERY – "ROGER STERLING"

For the record, Sterling Cooper's resident silver fox John Slattery was not present at the time of Kennedy's presidential run, or for the Volkswagen Lemon campaign. In fact, he was born the year in which *Mad Men*'s second season is set. As for the cultural upheavals of 1962, he doesn't remember much.

Born in Boston and the second youngest of six siblings, Slattery was by all accounts an average student at Saint Sebastian's in Newton, a small suburb ten miles east of Boston. While strong in subjects that he liked, his academic ranking suffered from a competing desire to hang out with his friends.

Salvation of a kind came when he developed an interest in acting. "I would stay up all hours by myself watching movies and then couldn't get up for school in the morning." He enrolled in Catholic University of America in Northeast Washington, D.C., and emerged in 1984 with a degree from their theater program.

The Slatterys were not an artistically inclined family and John's decision to attempt a career in show business did not align with his siblings' view of their brother.

"He wasn't a theater guy," said older sister Julie. "He wasn't the kind of kid who was at home putting on shows for you or anything."

And like most families and friends without a theatrical tradition, the notion of a sustainable acting career challenged what was acceptable or even possible.

"People always told me it was impossible, where I went to school ... it's certainly difficult and the competition grows every day, but it is not impossible."

Slattery's first professional job on-screen was as Private Dylan Leeds in an ill-fated series based on *The Dirty Dozen*. His crisp gray hair and debonair profile made him a natural for the Second World War–set adventure and marked him as a default casting choice for stories of that era.

"I think I probably have a fairly cynical sense of humor." (AP Photo/Bebeto Matthews)

Once again, Slattery's timeless looks and straight-shooting demeanor won him a role in a series set well outside of his experience. Slattery played Al Kahn in 1991's *Homefront*, a post–World War Two drama that critics and ardent fans loved but one that failed to gain a wide audience during its two-year run. Slattery made an impression in the Golden Globe– and Emmy Award–nominated series, and his work as the clear-eyed, level-headed union organizer helped the show win the People's Choice Award for Favorite New TV Dramatic Series. But one can only wonder if Slattery feared that he might find himself stuck in a bygone era for the rest of his working days.

While pigeonholing might be detrimental for artistic growth, it can be good for a career. But Slattery managed to occupy a second distinct stereo-type in the minds of casting directors in Hollywood — the aloof, caustic supporting player, perfect for pinning down the antagonistic corner of a romantic isosceles.

Slattery dented the public consciousness playing exactly that on two hit television shows. He played the aloof, caustic principal who threatens the unrequited love of lead character Ed, in the series of the same name (starring

Thomas Cavanagh and Julie Bowen), and an aloof, caustic older brother who threatens the unrequited love of the lead characters on *Will & Grace* (starring Eric McCormack and Debra Messing). Both roles played to Slattery's easily identifiable acting strengths — facility with a devastating shrug and a discouraging word.

If screen casting has slotted him into two distinct archetypes for the majority of his career, Slattery has shown a deft hand for subtle character-ization onstage. While he made a strong impression in Neil Simon's *Laughter on the 23rd Floor*, Slattery impressed with his subtler turns in a revival of Harold Pinter's *Betrayal*, and in particular his role as a grieving father in David Lindsay-Abaire's Pulitzer Prize–winning *Rabbit Hole*. In the *New York Times* Ben Brantley referred to Slattery's "stunning resource-fulness and economy," while *Variety* referred to his "emotional explosion" at one point as "wrenching."

Yet it is easy to take Slattery's work for granted. Cast mates are often singled out for reward (Juliette Binoche and Liev Schreiber for *Betrayal*, Tyne Daly and Cynthia Nixon for *Rabbit Hole*), without a similar nod for him. But many "experts" still mistake the appearance of effortlessness with artlessness, or just simply good luck.

In fact, Slattery's surface is at odds with the true nature of the actor. Colleagues often refer to him warmly, or how "wickedly smart and wickedly funny" he is, but this kind of fealty would not be inspired by someone as remote as Slattery often appears on-screen. In this, Slattery shares a similar burden with another iconic, prematurely gray actor. Steve Martin demonstrated an abstract wit and a penchant for surreal slapstick in his stand-up routines, yet managed to become Hollywood's first phone call when looking to fill an amiable father role (*Parenthood, Cheaper by the Dozen, Father of the Bride*).

While Slattery's dashing looks and silver hair place him out of time, there is also a taciturn unflappability in his approach to acting that would suit him well as the hero in an Alfred Hitchcock thriller. But show creator Matthew Weiner has used this persona to *Mad Men*'s advantage. Roger Sterling is very much that kind of man, as comfortable with a clever line as with a vodka-and-milk. And yet the foundation of Sterling's character betrays that affability. When a health crisis fells him, Sterling becomes a vulnerable, haunted man and what looked like a ring-a-ding *joie de vivre* cloaked a wounded man forever running. Who better to approach that character from an oblique angle than an actor known for just that sort of façade?

Nobody, according to Weiner. He cast Slattery just as the actor started a recurring role on *Desperate Housewives*. "We shot his episodes out of order so that we could have him because I didn't want to do the show without him . . . he inhabits the guy," Weiner declared.

As a result, the "experts" have started to see the light. In 2008, John Slattery was singled out with an Emmy nomination as Outstanding Supporting Actor for his work as Roger Sterling. While he didn't win (but did share in an Ensemble award with the rest of the *Mad Men* cast), the nomination is encouraging. And there is time for him to receive further accolades, after all — it's not like he's old enough to have voted for Nixon.

> I think Pete is less of a man than me. The difference in the visual
> is that Pete had a finishing-school upbringing. I'm an actor, so
> part of my job is looking like a bum.
>
> — Vincent Kartheiser

VINCENT KARTHEISER – "PETE CAMPBELL"

"What drew everyone to the show was the dialogue and the era and the subtleties of it." (AP Photo/Shea Walsh)

A sartorial schism isn't the only separation between Vincent Kartheiser and Pete Campbell. But while they couldn't have traveled more divergent paths, the case could be made that the actor's life as a journeyman performer at the young age of thirty was the perfect training to play such a conflicted man — a privileged scion of Manhattan elite who still wants desperately to prove his worth.

Vincent Kartheiser was born on May 5, 1979, in Minneapolis, Minnesota. The youngest of six children to parents Marie and James, this final child of the Kartheiser clan was named after Vincent van Gogh, and grew up surrounded by paintings from the post-impressionist master.

Or did he? "Not true." Kartheiser planted the red herring himself in an interview with Backstage.com. "I like to throw noodles on the wall and see where they stick. Most people never know who I am."

This puckish attitude toward biographical truth may please the artist in him and confound his fans, but it signals another stark difference between the actor and the part he plays. The fudging of historical facts is the sort of thing one expects from Don Draper, not Pete Campbell.

While any accounts of Kartheiser's background should therefore be viewed with a jaundiced eye, there are a few facts about his formative years that can be clearly seen. He was homeschooled for most of his life but attended the University of California to study history. His father made a living as a tool salesman but from a young age, Vincent envisioned a different career for himself.

His professional acting career took root early, starting at the age of six. In his teens, Kartheiser worked onstage at the Guthrie Theater in Minneapolis and made his on-screen debut in 1993's *Untamed Heart*, starring Christian Slater and Marisa Tomei. Featured roles in kid-friendly movies such as *Little Big League* (1994) and *The Indian in the Cupboard* (1995) followed, which led to a co-starring role in director Fraser Heston's family adventure story *Alaska* (1996), alongside Thora Birch and Charlton Heston.

A lead role in a Hollywood film came next, with Kartheiser taking second billing to Patrick Stewart in *Masterminds* (1997). A fluffy piece of tween action/adventure hokum, the film features Kartheiser as Oswald "Ozzie" Paxton, a rebellious student at a prep school who stumbles across a total *Die Hard* situation, a ridiculous plot underscored by Kartheiser having to utter dialogue like, "This is a total *Die Hard* situation."

The dilemma most young actors face is how to modify their career arc as their voice changes, but that wasn't a problem for Kartheiser. "Too many actors are able to break the mold. It becomes a bad excuse for those who don't." At the age of nineteen, Kartheiser managed an impressive about-face from the G-rated fare he was becoming known for by winning a role in director Larry Clark's *Another Day in Paradise*. A rough independent film about a "family" cobbled together through petty crime and drug addiction, this film co-starred James Woods and Melanie Griffith and takes its seedy place alongside the transgressive Clark's other guerilla-style explorations of America's grimy underbelly (*Kids, Bully, Ken Park*). Kartheiser's performance as the smack-addled Bobbie generated interest around the actor (with Roger Ebert likening his performance to that of Martin Sheen in *Badlands*) and it is safe to say that the free-wheeling, improvisational spirit of the film appealed to the artist. Reportedly, an improvised scene between Kartheiser and Woods led to the elder actor unexpectedly slapping the younger, whose surprise is genuine and noticeable on-screen; after shooting finished, Kartheiser approached director Clark and said, "I didn't know that motherfucker was going to hit me."

Kartheiser appeared in other Sundance darlings *Crime and Punishment*

in Suburbia and *Dandelion*, building a reputation as an indie stalwart. Before long, he managed another career pivot by entering the pop culture consciousness as a conflicted young man grappling with secrets and an overwhelming antipathy toward his father.

In 2002, Kartheiser joined the cast of *Angel* as Connor, the teenage son of the eponymous vampire. As if growing up with the knowledge that he was sired by two dead people wasn't enough, Connor's simmering anger toward his father could also be attributed to the early estrangement from Angel or the fact that he spent his formative years growing up in an alternate hell dimension. Suddenly, Pete Campbell's emotionally distant father seems like a bargain.

Another featured role in Nick Cassavetes's *Alpha Dog* may have contributed to his rising stock within the industry. But it did little to elevate him in the public eye considering his established cast mates like Bruce Willis and Sharon Stone, as well as other burgeoning young actors such as Ben Foster (*X-Men: The Last Stand, 3:10 to Yuma*), Anton Yelchin (TV's *Huff, Charlie Bartlett, Terminator Salvation*), and Justin Timberlake.

That all changed when he landed the role of Pete Campbell on AMC's first foray into original dramatic programming. And while he auditioned for roles in a number of high-profile pilots that same year (*Jericho, Heroes*), Kartheiser held out hope for landing a job within a certain Madison Avenue ad agency.

"*Mad Men* was one of those pilots where I read it and after I was done I wanted to read it again. There was this swagger about the script that was different from so much I had read in the last few years. I knew it was something I could do."

While Vincent Kartheiser may enjoy the high quality of the scripts and the peers he encounters each day on the set, the journeyman actor can't help but find the pragmatic silver lining in his role.

"This is like the Ari Gold [Jeremy Piven's character on *Entourage*] of the show — he gets all the dialogue — and I don't have to sweat out the fifteen-hour days that Jon Hamm does."

But given Kartheiser's penchant for embroidering the truth, who can say he really means it?

> I had the worst high school experience ever. People literally
> spit on me. I was a Goth girl and, in preppy
> Fairfax County, that did not go over well.
>
> — Christina Hendricks

CHRISTINA HENDRICKS – "JOAN HOLLOWAY"

While few might have envisioned Christina Hendricks as a glum Goth girl with purple hair and black lipstick, even more might be surprised to discover that her speaking voice is much higher than that of her television character; or that, even more startling, her trademark five-alarm fire hair comes out of a bottle. That's right — TV's most vivacious redhead is a natural blond.

"When they meet me, people say, 'Oh my God, you seem so young and you don't seem mean.'"

One thing Hendricks and her character Joan have in common is a public preoccupation with her body. This is hardly a new development for women, and somewhat understandable given the nature of the character. But Hendricks has received a great deal of praise for her influence on mainstream media. In a world populated by toothpick-thin ingénues, many women are pleased to see a successful actress celebrated for her curves instead of punished for them. "You look like what a real woman is supposed to look like," fawned one red-carpet interviewer. And while the sentiment is noble, it can only be a cold comfort that women now have two media-fuelled body types to choose from — anorexia chic and hourglass elegance.

Pleased by the accolades, Hendricks still wearies of the obsession over her body. "I feel like everyone talks about my bust in public."

Hendricks has dealt with strangers fretting about her proportions before. She worked as a model in her teens, first staking her claim in New York and London. At nineteen, Hendricks stood five-foot-nine and 115 pounds, only to have her agency tell her to shave off ten pounds because her ankles were a little large. Still, she enjoyed the life of a model, and the perks that went along with the long hours and hard work. "I really took advantage of the travel and learning about different cultures."

"I feel like the luckiest actress in the world to be on what everyone, including our cast and crew, thinks is the smartest show on television." (AP Photo/Lisa Rose)

The itinerant life of a professional model came naturally to Hendricks. Born on May 3, 1975, Hendricks grew up all across the map due to her father's career in the U.S. Forest Service, with stops in Portland, Oregon; Twin Falls, Idaho; and Fairfax, Virginia. Making new friends with each move was increasingly hard for Hendricks and her older brother, so their psychologist mother suggested they join a community theater in an effort to meet people and fit in. This failed on the second count for Hendricks ("My friends and I were all weird theater people . . . everyone just hated us"), but did provide a direction for her life.

She has referred to her modeling career as "freeze-frame acting" and "good boot camp" for an acting career. While stationed in London, Hendricks received a phone call from her recently single mother asking if she would join her in a move to a warmer climate: Los Angeles. Within two weeks of landing, Hendricks' freeze-frame training landed her a Visa commercial with Pierce Brosnan. A long line of commercial work followed, which culminated in a lead role in producer John Wells's pilot *The Big Time*. That show never went to series, but Wells spotted Hendricks's undeniable star quality and offered a three-year contract. This led to increased visibility for Hendricks with appearances on Wells's *Presidio Med* (2002) and a four episode arc on *ER*.

"He gave me a career," Hendricks recalls of her early days. "He's my fairy godfather."

She followed these with stints as a series regular on the short-lived show *Kevin Hill* and the cult favorite *Firefly*. The rigors of television production and the long-lasting camaraderie that sixteen-hour days can inspire were a great experience, but the frustration of such hard work not translating into a broad commercial success might have scared Hendricks off serialized drama forever.

Until a certain woman named Joan Holloway entered her life.

Matthew Weiner's original vision of the Sterling Cooper office manager was much different. As written, Joan Holloway was smaller, mousier, and with a much sharper tongue — a prune Danish instead of Roger Sterling's "drop of strawberry jam in a glass of milk."

But to his credit, when Hendricks presented him with an alternative take on the character, he kept an open mind. Hendricks dove into her wardrobe for the appropriate clothing ("You never want to go to audition dressed in character, but you do want to get to the essence"), and apparently the tight black sweater with a big bow on the front, to say nothing of the really tight black skirt, made Weiner think twice.

Once on set, Hendricks unleashed the devastating pendulum-swing of her hips. While a definitive statement on the public persona Joan Holloway creates, Hendricks's physical inhabitation of the character is not a result of method acting but method wardrobe. Once in the period-accurate clothing, the strut simply happened.

Perhaps more surprising than Christina Hendricks's true hair color and dour teen years is that, in total, she was in contention for three roles in the *Mad Men* roster, at one point receiving dialogue for the part of Peggy Olson and actually auditioning for the role of Midge Daniels, Don Draper's mistress from the first season. In hindsight, it is difficult to envision her as anyone other than Joan Holloway. And even more astonishing, Weiner meant for the Joan Holloway character to appear as a guest role. Once he saw Hendricks stalk the Sterling Cooper office, he quite rightly changed his mind again. It's not often one catches lightning in a bottle . . . or in an hourglass.

> I really like her but I don't have anything in common with her . . . if something isn't going my way or there is someone holding me down, I will say something.
>
> — January Jones

JANUARY JONES – "BETTY DRAPER"

January Jones on Betty Draper: "She's a mystery to me." (AP Photo/Dan Steinberg)

January Jones may not have much in common with the character that has brought her fame and acclaim, but the independent streak the actress displays is not unlike the burgeoning strength and sense of self Betty Draper develops over the course of the series.

She may be known for her interpretation of suburban housewife angst, but Jones is equally well known for keeping the details of her life out of the spotlight. "I don't have a lifestyle where I'm going out and getting wasted all the time."

Jones was born in Sioux Falls, South Dakota in 1978, and named after a character in Jacqueline Susann's chest-heaving bestseller *Once Is Not Enough*. She attended Roosevelt High School and worked at the local Dairy Queen until, one assumes, she decided that her name was too fabulous to continue pulling soft ice cream for a living.

By eighteen, Jones moved to New York and started her career as a model, at least one other biographical detail she shares with Betty Draper. She landed recurring work as an Abercrombie & Fitch clotheshorse where she met a then-unknown fellow model named Ashton Kutcher. They dated for a few years while both embarked on their acting careers, but ended their relationship before one of them developed an interest in "punking" Hollywood stars.

The cool, Grace Kelly–style looks that helped Jones make her way as a model led to roles in lightweight comedies that called on her to do little other than look pretty and titter at the leading man. She appeared in movies such as *Anger Management, American Wedding,* and *Love Actually.* Jones clearly had an eye on career longevity, however, and expanded her range by appearing in more serious fare like *We Are Marshall, The Three Burials of Melquiades Estrada* (under the direction of star Tommy Lee Jones), and noticeable television appearances in *Law & Order* (where she played a calculating con artist), and Showtime's *Huff* opposite lead actor Hank Azaria.

The desire to keep her personal life away from public scrutiny must have arisen out of the relationships she entered while in Hollywood. After Kutcher, Jones counted among her paramours famous men like Seann William Scott (co-star from *American Wedding*), Jim Carrey, and, most notably, opera-lite crooner Josh Groban.

Jones's involvement with *Mad Men* began when she auditioned for a different part on the show, up-and-coming copywriter Peggy Olson. She read a number of times and was told by her agent that at one point it was between her "and one other girl." Show creator Matthew Weiner ultimately chose Elisabeth Moss because he felt that Jones wasn't innocent enough. But Weiner had another character in mind for Jones.

In the early stages of development, Weiner planned for audiences to see little of Don Draper's home life (a thought that seems impossible in retrospect), but thought to cast an unknown in the role of his wife in the final scene of the pilot. Sensing an opportunity, Weiner wrote an audition scene for Jones that required her to take Betty Draper through a swing of emotions, from "nattering to melancholic to pleadingly lustful." Weiner said later, "I made her do it twice, she did it so well. She just knew who this woman was."

The upside of understanding a character so well is obvious, resulting in widespread acclaim and Emmy and Golden Globe nominations. The downside is the inevitable typecasting that follows. Since her stint on *Mad Men,* Jones has been offered "a lot of dramatic roles as a sadder, more neglected housewife."

Jones hopes to find more interesting, challenging roles in the future but is in no rush. "I have always been so picky about what I do," she has said. "I might be getting offered more roles, but they are not the roles that I want. Yet."

I think I'm the oldest of the group — the only one
who has lived through this period.

— Robert Morse

ROBERT MORSE – "BERTRAM COOPER"

The casting of Robert Morse in the recurring role of savvy agency head and office oddball Bertram Cooper succeeds not only in matching a part to an actor's talents, but also benefits from the iconic weight he brings to the screen. Who better to helm an advertising firm that features a lowly secretary's swift ascension through the ranks than the man who played a lowly window washer who jockeys up the corporate ladder to the vice-president of advertising?

While movie audiences may know Morse best as J. Pierpont Finch from *How to Succeed in Business Without Really Trying* (1967), he made his presence known on Broadway in *The Matchmaker* twelve years earlier, co-starring with theater luminary Ruth Gordon. He won the role after studying acting under the G. I. Bill at the prestigious American Theatre Wing in New York. A year later, Morse garnered interest from a theatrical agent while making ends meet as a game show contestant stand-in on *Name That Tune*, which led to his first screen role in *The Proud and the Profane* (1956).

In 1958, Morse recreated his role as Barnaby Tucker in the film version of Thornton Wilder's *The Matchmaker* (this time opposite Shirley Booth) and also appeared on Broadway again in *Say, Darling*. This stage production gave Morse a few firsts — working with the renowned writer/director Abe Burrows (*Guys and Dolls, Can-Can, Cactus Flower*) and his first of five Tony Award nominations. However, Morse's initial run-in with Burrows at the audition was not favorable.

"When Julie Styne saw my head beginning to shake negatively, he whispered to me, 'I saw the kid in *The Matchmaker*. He's really great,'" Burrows wrote in his autobiography *Honest Abe*. "So I took another long look at this kid. Morse eventually stole the show."

Next appearing onstage in *Take Me Along*, Morse not only shared the spotlight with Jackie Gleason and Walter Pidgeon but he also shared Best Actor nominations with them, with Gleason crowned the winner at the 1960 Tony Awards.

"I'm grateful to be here with all of these people and, at my age, to be part of something that is absolutely magnificent."
(AP Photo/Chris Pizzello)

There would be no sharing of awards when the curtain rose on *How to Succeed in Business Without Really Trying* on October 14, 1961. As J. Pierpont Finch, Morse made the most of his gap-toothed fecklessness and won the Tony Award for Best Actor in a Musical. An adaptation of the bestselling satirical handbook written by Shepherd Mead and published in 1952, the show went on to win an amazing eight Tony Awards and the 1962 Pulitzer Prize for Burrows and Frank Loesser, one of only seven musicals to receive such an honor.

Before he knew it, Robert Morse had become a breakout star and started to fill out his film résumé. Between his Tony win and reviving that role for the big-screen adaptation in 1967 he appeared in five major films. These movies can be divided between the earnest (*The Cardinal*), the lighthearted (*Quick Before It Melts*), the forgettable (*Honeymoon Hotel* with Robert Goulet), the offbeat (an adaptation of Evelyn Waugh's *The Loved One*), and the disastrous (the notoriously wrongheaded black comedy *Oh Dad, Poor Dad, Mama's Hung You in the Closet and I Feel So Sad* — filmed in 1965 and held back by the studio for two years, only releasing it after filming more palatable "comic" interstitials with Jonathan Winters and interpolating them in the already finished film).

By the time a film adaptation of his signature Broadway role was offered, Morse might have worried that he wouldn't be able to reprise the part faithfully. But when the critics saw the big-screen debut of *How to Succeed in Business Without Really Trying*, they could not have been more emphatic.

"Entertaining," a *Variety* review raved. ". . . Fast-moving in tracing the rags-to-riches rise of Robert Morse within Rudy Vallée's biz complex."

The following years Morse kept busy, paying the bills with appearances in television shows (*Night Gallery; Love, American Style; One Day at a Time;*

The Fall Guy; Murder, She Wrote) and the occasional voice work for animated specials (*Jack Frost, The Stingiest Man in Town, Pound Puppies*). He appeared on Broadway during the mid-'70s in the musicals *Sugar* (which gave Morse another Tony nomination) and *So Long, 174th Street* (which closed after sixteen performances).

One more trip to Broadway gave him another signature role. In the 1989 one-man play *Tru*, Morse assayed the life of Truman Capote with such all-encompassing power that nowhere in reviews for his performance were there references to him as "pixie-like" or a "chipmunk." Morse won a Tony for Best Actor in a Play, a Drama Desk Award for Outstanding One Person Performance, and an Emmy for a PBS recreation in 1992.

At just over sixty years of age, Morse could well have looked forward to a comfortable if uneventful late career, voicing characters on television cartoons (*Superman, The Wild Thornberrys*) and guest-starring on the occasional sitcom (*Suddenly Susan*).

Matthew Weiner thought differently. While immersing himself in culture that reflected and commented on the period of his show *Mad Men*, Weiner found himself watching Morse a few times. Not only in the role of Finch who takes the Worldwide Wicket Company, but as a philandering husband alongside Walter Matthau in 1967's *A Guide for the Married Man*. While notoriously open to suggestions for his characters, Weiner seemed to have his heart set on who he wanted to play the germaphobe with an adoration of Japanese design: "Other producers have said, 'What a great idea to have Robert Morse play the head of the company. I say, 'Yes, it is.'"

Morse hasn't missed the full circle of winning the role of Bertram Cooper and seems to accept it as a graceful way for an actor to age.

"I'm very happy and very fortunate I'm able to go to work and have a job at my age — one could call it the Rudy Vallée CEO part."

For now, Morse is happy not only to have a job, but a place to go on his days off.

"I even come to work when I'm not working, because I don't belong to a senior club. So I feel this is my club, and I come down to the set sometimes just to get the free lunch and hope that I'll be in next week's show."

Nice work if you can get it.

EPISODE GUIDE SEASON ONE

Notable guest cast in season 1: Rosemarie DeWitt (Midge Daniels), John Cullum (Lee Garner Sr.), Darren Pettie (Lee Garner Jr.), Darby Stanchfield (Helen Bishop), Anne Dudek (Francine Hanson), Maggie Siff (Rachel Menken), Marten Holden Weiner (Glen Bishop), Christopher Allport (Andrew Campbell), Alison Brie (Trudy "Tweety" Campbell), Jay Paulson (Adam Whitman), Joel Murray (Fred Rumsen), Talia Balsam (Mona Sterling), Ian Bohen (Roy Hazelitt), John Walcutt (Franklin Newcomb), Megan Stier (Eleanor Ames), Alexis Stier (Mirabelle Ames), Mark Moses (Herman "Duck" Phillips)

1.01 SMOKE GETS IN YOUR EYES

Original air date: July 19, 2007
Written by: Matthew Weiner
Directed by: Alan Taylor

> "With the IBM Correcting Selectric Typewriter, typing errors, erasures, strikeovers, and messy corrections can be a thing of the past."
> — IBM Correcting Selectric Typewriter Operating Instructions

It is 1960. We are introduced to Don Draper, creative director at a prestigious boutique advertising agency on New York's Madison Avenue. We also meet the voluptuous office manager Joan Holloway as she introduces Peggy Olson (Draper's new secretary) to the treacherous waters that roil beneath the ordered desk rows of Sterling Cooper. Ambitious account executive Pete Campbell considers the pros and cons of his impending marriage as he prepares for his bachelor party.

What makes you happy? Many viewers find the opening credits of *Mad Men* enough to overjoy one before the show even begins. Not only does the bold graphic design of the animated introduction grab the attention, it also establishes the advertising milieu that provides the setting for the series. Even more important is the thematic resonance — the ordered world of this mysterious figure falls away around him before he plummets down the side of a crisscrossed high-rise that is a nod to the opening credits of Alfred Hitchcock's *North by Northwest* (interesting because the film stars Cary Grant as a suave advertising executive caught up in forces beyond his control, but also because the film's opening credits were designed by beloved artist Saul Bass, also renowned for his work in advertising and in particular for creating the long-standing AT&T logo).

Just as thrilling is the music by British DJ RJD2. His composition is a tribute to an elegant orchestral swing ending its popular reign in 1960, but one propelled by a modern-day drum machine beat. Not only do the ostensibly opposing currents complement each other well, the music swiftly anchors the dramatic irony of one point in history viewed from a current vantage point.

All this information and style delivered in thirty seconds — no wonder the first episode made so many viewers so happy.

Achieving happiness is more difficult for Don Draper. Even more distressing is the ensuing dilemma: what if you have everything you want and still feel empty?

From the outside looking in, Draper has the tiger by the tail. He works in the prestigious Sterling Cooper Agency where he holds a position of power and sway. Despite fretting from the opening scene over a creative block for the new Lucky Strike campaign he's toiling on, everyone around him is convinced that he will perform his standard ninth inning miracle and bowl over the clients. Whether it is Midge, the sexy artist in the Village he visits late one night; Roger Sterling, co-owner of the agency and fellow veteran; Pete Campbell, the young executive angling for Draper's office: they are all convinced of his genius.

Don isn't so sure. While he appears to be thriving in the wake of the post–Second World War prosperity boom, there is clearly something missing. He is certain that he will fumble the Lucky Strike account, be found out as a fraud, and open himself to a full-fanged attack from the punk executives nipping at his heels.

"Smoke Gets in Your Eyes" set the tone for *Mad Men* — sleek and deliberate, with an eye on complex human emotions. (AP Photo/Kevork Djansezian)

Even though he struggles with the profound emptiness brought on by his stature, Don can't help but use this knowledge to put Pete Campbell in his place. A hallway encounter in which Don sketches out the dire final act for the life Campbell so strenuously maneuvers to achieve is a priceless bit of office warfare and a stunning example of projection. When Don Draper draws a portrait of Pete Campbell as a pathetic schlub in a lonely corner office who manages only to bed new "office girls" because they feel sorry for him, one can't help but wonder how much Don's own fears are cracking through his granite-smooth façade.

There is also a generational schism at play. Both Don Draper and Roger Sterling have served in the war (Draper winning a Purple Heart in the process, a medal that he relegates to a bottom drawer in his office desk) and are perplexed by those of Campbell's generation, wet-eared whelps who are the first in decades to make their way in the business world without battlefield experience. As much as elders always dismiss the youth their naiveté and myopic world-view, this lack of foxhole familiarity breeds a contempt from the veterans that is as thick in the office as the cigarette smoke that hovers over the desks.

The Drapers and Sterlings of 1960 nurture this scorn at their own peril. Hindsight is always eagle-eyed, but those who fought not in Germany or Italy but in Korea straddled an irregular divide in 1960. Before long, the very values they fought for overseas and the respect it brought them at home would vanish. By the end of the decade, army service would become a badge of shame worthy of hiding. The youth movement gathered steam once students realized the political, cultural, and economic power they held, and would soon question the knee-jerk respect expected of their parents. Pete Campbell may want that corner office above all else, but the world he and his brethren are set to inherit will have undergone a fundamental change, and once again another generation will be forced to ask if the trappings of a perfect life are really worth it.

Whether Pete Campbell senses this change in the world he seeks to usurp is up for debate; any sense of unease may be the result of this impending wedding. But in this first episode, we see Pete as the brash frat boy who expects everything that he wants when he wants it. And if he can't get it with charm, he's not above using whatever power he has for coercion. He would be quite unlikable if not for the vulnerability on display in his final scene, where he arrives at the doorstep of Don's new secretary with his hair tussled like a sheepish schoolboy and a plaintive plea ("I wanted to see you tonight . . . I *had* to see you"). New girl Peggy Olson might not have expected that sort of excitement in her new Manhattan job . . . but that doesn't mean she'll back away from it.

Peggy Olson's world changes quickly as she is introduced around Sterling Cooper by office manager and resident vixen Joan Holloway. This geographical shift pushes her to grow up a fair bit even in this first episode: a breathless naïf rendered wide-eyed at Joan's effortless charting of the professional and sexual landscape of the office; an awkward girl playing at adulthood when she places her hand on Don's (and receives a stinging rebuke); and finally a young woman more sure of herself when a boy from the office shows up at her door from his bachelor party, drunk and vulnerable. At this point, the audience is getting used to complex, multidimensional characters. But in Peggy we already see a kindred spirit of Don, one with a knack for reinvention despite the upheaval in the world around her.

By the end of this first episode however, Don has a handle on his world. He pulls inspiration out of thin air and wows the Lucky Strike clients. The approbation of those around him is proven to be well earned.

Yet Don takes little joy in his triumph. He is clearly a dashing man and does not hurt for female attention. But whether he is with his mistress in the Village, flirting with a potential client, or arriving at home to his wife and children, there is no joy in his actions, particularly romantic. He never appears happier than when he is crafting a new advertising campaign, but his personal life is shadowed by a sense of constantly running after something . . . or perhaps he's running away. Even when he pulls inspiration out of the ether, once the moment is over Don once again appears haggard and haunted. It almost seems that he is bound by his victory, as if further success equals greater efforts to protect it.

The Philosophy of *Mad Men* — Don Draper: "Happiness is the smell of a new car . . . a billboard at the side of the road screaming that everything you're doing is okay . . . you are okay."

Period Moment: Joan shows Peggy the latest in office technology, the IBM Selectric, "so easy a woman can use it." Some have claimed that this is an anachronism as this model of carriage-free typewriter did not hit the market until 1961, after the time of this episode. Others have claimed that while this is true, it is quite possible that an esteemed Manhattan ad company might have a test model before it was released to market.

Ad Pitch: Did the Hail Mary Don pulls off for the Lucky Strike account actually exist? It did, but long before 1960. Since 1917, Lucky Strike used the slogan "It's toasted" along with the signature acronym L.S./M.F.T. (Lucky Strikes/Means Fine Tobacco). Examples of era-specific advertising for Lucky Strikes include lines such as "Get the Honest Taste of a Lucky Strike" and "Lucky Strike Separates the Man From the Boys . . . But Not From the Girls."

Cocktail of Note: During this episode, Don orders a Whiskey Neat. He also orders an Old Fashioned, of which there are numerous recipes, but here is one:

> 2 ounces Bourbon
> 1 cube sugar in just enough water to dissolve
> 2 dashes bitters
> Place sugar, water, and bitters in an old-fashioned glass.
> Add 2–3 cubes of ice and Bourbon. Garnish with a twist.

Gender Politics and Helen Gurley Brown's
Sex and the Single Girl

"In a couple of years, with the right moves, you'll be in
the city with the rest of us. Of course, if you really
make the right moves, you'll be out in the country
and you won't be going to work at all."
— Joan Holloway, "Smoke Gets in Your Eyes"

It is widely held that the publication of Betty Friedan's *The Feminine Mystique* launched the "second wave" of feminism in America, while Margaret Fuller's *Woman in the Nineteenth Century* stirred the current that bore the "first wave." One figure stands in a curious place between the two, a breaker between the two waves, a woman who proselytized female emancipation in the workplace and in the bedroom while advising women to use them with the aim of catching a man. This pink-collared suffragette considered it fair game to harness a married man for sexual pleasure but, once married, remained faithful for the fifty years of her union. While she is a vocal supporter of the National Organization for Women and steadfastly pro-choice, she famously made light of sexual harassment, believing that "a little sexual tension in the office never hurt anyone."

While it is easy to criticize *Cosmopolitan* editor Helen Gurley Brown for her crotch-level take on feminism, it is just as difficult to imagine modern feminist theory without her. In her 1962 bestseller *Sex and the Single Girl*, part thinly veiled autobiography, part dating guide for women prowling the singles scene, Brown cleared the path of sexual inequities and lit a fuse on the sexual revolution by writing a book that celebrates women who pursue a career for advancement and sex for enjoyment without demanding that they choose one over the other. Critics (at the time and today) find her thesis nothing more than justification for the objectification of women (a sort of perfumed *Protocols of Zion*), but this fails to understand how the notion of sexual gratification for women was an upheaval in and of itself. And while detractors of *Sex and the Single Girl* rightly cringe at the bald-faced superficiality ("One of the paramount reasons for staying attractive is to have someone to go to bed with") and tiger-trap domesticity ("Spic-and-span the apartment. He does notice, if only subconsciously"), her battle cry of personal fulfillment ("You don't have to get your identity by being someone's appendage . . . You're your own person, go out there and be somebody") never goes out of style.

The cultural effect of Brown's single girl manual echoes throughout the years, from the sassy career-girl in search of love *(That Girl!, Mary Tyler Moore)* to the sardonic career girl in search of love *(Sex and the City).* Matthew Weiner's use of Brown's book in researching *Mad Men* carries something more than a style or attitude, in particular the buxom office manager Joan Holloway who is unafraid to use her brain or wiles to get what she wants. In the arc of her character, however, there is not only a celebration of her power but a critique of it too.

Other than her writing, Brown's biography appears to have affected the show as well, most notably in the career rise of copywriter Peggy Olson. Weiner seems to have woven elements from Brown's life into the tapestry of *Mad Men*, and sometimes in the oddest of places. But her role as breaker between the first two waves of feminism also puts her squarely between Joan Holloway and Peggy Olson, two currents charging in opposite directions but toward a similar destination.

The future savior of *Cosmopolitan* magazine and embodiment of chic sophistication could not have come from more humble roots. Born into meager means in Green Forest, Arkansas, in 1922, the family fortune took an unexpected dive when her father died in an elevator accident when Brown was only ten years old. She graduated high school a valedictorian but after one year at the Texas State College for Women, Brown joined the workforce and became the one and only breadwinner for her family (which included her polio-afflicted sister, Mary). This abundance of responsibility at age eighteen not only soured her on children of her own, but fostered a desire for a better life. Rejecting the world's anticipation that she would remain "ordinary, hill-billy, and poor," Brown left her hometown, moved to the big city, and reinvented herself.

Sound familiar? The correlation between Brown and master of reinvention Don Draper is unexpected but telling. Brown may not have gone to the same lengths to shed her past for a brighter future, but the work required to attain higher status along with an unmovable belief in her talents are little more than the Draper ethos in a tight dress.

One could argue that the acquisition of another identity would have benefitted Brown more than Don; both had to overcome the stigma of low rank in a society that pretends to see beyond class, but as a woman Brown was twice

Sex and the Single Girl author Helen Gurley Brown occupied a unique position between the first and second wave of American feminism. (AP Photo)

cursed. Don takes full advantage of the opportunity to create the man he wants to be and step into his shoes, but after going through this transformation Brown also has to make a place for herself in a male-dominated world. For all his glum existential ponderings, Don is a lesser form of the self-made person when compared to Brown.

The young Helen Gurley Brown worked her way through seventeen secretarial positions before landing at the desk of advertising executive Dan Belding. A letter she wrote for her boss caught the eye of Mrs. Alice Belding who suggested that her husband give his "new girl" the chance to write copy. He resisted (she was just a secretary, after all), but when Brown placed in a "Ten Girls with Taste" essay contest in *Glamour Magazine* (where she claimed that once grown up she wanted to be a "copywriter") and when he received a call from the personnel director at Condé Nast echoing his wife's sentiments, Belding relented.

From 1948 to 1958, Brown served with distinction at Foote, Cone and Belding, passing each rung on the corporate ladder with a confidence that resulted in two Francis Holmes Advertising awards, and security as one of the highest paid copywriters in the country. During this period, Brown would have worked on campaigns for FCB's biggest clients, including Pepsodent, American Tobacco's Pall Mall cigarette, Dial Soap, Clairol hair color, Frigidaire, and Kool-Aid.

In 1958, Brown leapt to a position as copywriter and account executive for Kenyon & Eckhardt, a Hollywood advertising agency. Perhaps she sensed the difficulties ahead as FCB lost two of their biggest accounts in the early '50s, Pepsodent and American Tobacco. Most thought things looked bright for FCB as they won a prestigious new campaign from Ford Motors Company, securing the "E" (for "experimental") account after long and exhaustive competition from almost every major advertising shop in the country. The team at FCB labored to craft a compelling creative for this new car, but despite their best efforts the product and campaign came to represent one of the largest commercial failures at that time.

They had won the campaign for the Ford Edsel.

For those who may not know, the Edsel has attained legendary status as a commercial failure of epic proportions. Not only did Ford introduce the car at the start of a recession in 1958, the company hoped for a spot in the mid-sized car market, which was dwindling even before the financial contraction began. The car was also haunted by reports of mechanical failures, perceived design flaws (in the trademark "horse collar" grille), and a name rife with negative connotations (with some focus group members stating that the name "Edsel" reminded them of either "weasel" or "dead cell," as in a battery). But from a marketing perspective, it stands as a cautionary tale for anyone hoping to roll out a new product. Students in the art of persuasion have learned from the mistakes of FCB, who tried to arouse prerelease interest in the car through a peekaboo approach that included blurred product shots and ads featuring the entire car under paper or tarpaulin wraps.

On a number of fronts, Brown was wise to jump from the FCB ship just before it started to take on water.

Her timing was even better on a personal front. Once she met the man of her dreams through the Hollywood channels of her work at Kenyon & Eckhardt, Helen Gurley went about sinking "her hooks" into him. No tactic was off-limits — flattery, culinary skills, sexual satiation, emotional blackmail — in her campaign to land him as her husband. Film producer David Brown (*The Sting, Jaws, A Few Good Men*) may not have known what hit him, but he knew what was good for him and married this firebrand in September 1959.

A Book

During a period when Brown thought she was headed for unemployment, her husband suggested that she write a book about her days as a single woman working hard for professional and romantic success. He thought she was like no other single girl he'd ever met, in large part because she was never home. Little did he know that she was home, but had the phone locked in the refrigerator so she wouldn't hear the ringing, wouldn't feel tempted to answer, and he wouldn't wise up to the fact that she was home and not fabulously popular.

Sex and the Single Girl appeared in 1962 from obscure publisher Bernard

Geis. The central argument of the book — that a single woman could very well have it all, in the office and the bedroom — struck a chord that many were surprised to hear. When Brown appeared on the morning talk show *Today* she could not say the word "sex" without violating the moral strictures of the time, a problem she solved by simply holding up her book for the television camera to capture.

Despite the number of women inspired by the book (who wrote volumes of fan mail, all of which the author replied to personally), Brown also weathered criticism from people who blanched at the thought of women enjoying sex outside of the marital bond, with that disagreement often taking the form of boos and hurled tomatoes at public functions. But her conviction that women had an appetite for this kind of desire affirmation was proven when Hearst Industries named Brown editor of the failing *Cosmopolitan* magazine. Before her stewardship, it looked like most women's publications with pot roast recipes and advice on how to host the perfect barbecue. She transformed it with sexual instruction pieces, relationship quizzes, and knockoff fashions. Brown steered the magazine from a total of 250 ad pages sold in 1964 to over 2,500 ad pages twenty years later, all under the motto "Land that man, ace your job, and look your sexiest!"

Sterling Cooper and the Single Girls

While she doesn't subscribe to Brown's pre–Second Wave rallying call, Peggy Olson fits into the *Single Girl* mold with a striking similarity in personal biography to the *Cosmopolitan* editor. And even though Peggy hasn't struggled with a doomed product like the Edsel (although the Relaxacisor comes close), her rise through the ranks of Sterling Cooper hits many of the same points as Brown's FCB ascent.

Also plucked from the steno pool for her astute observation and crisp prose, Peggy succeeds by dint of hard work and guileless office comportment (a fact not lost on Joan, and one that causes her ceaseless discomfort). A pronounced difference between the two women is less the professional side than the romantic; it was during her time at FCB that Brown snatched and kept a married lover, who in turn put her up in an apartment and lavished her with travel and gifts. Peggy would never consider such a course of action (and in fact seems willing to surrender any serious dating life for the sake of her craft).

Not that she suspends a social life entirely. If we gage from the hangovers she has suffered in church, Peggy likes (or is compelled) to blow off steam through drinking, dancing, and general after-hours revelry. In this dichotomy perhaps Peggy demonstrates what Brown lived: that a woman needn't choose between being a Marilyn or a Jackie (or in this case, a Joan or a Peggy), but that, in both a social and career context, she could just as easily be both. Whereas Peggy is more like Brown the person, Joan Holloway is clearly more emblematic of the *Single Girl* philosophy Brown espoused. One can imagine Joan chanting the *Cosmopolitan* mantra in the bathroom mirror every morning. Her ideas on romance and fidelity are skewed but definite; she has no compunction engaging in a long-term dalliance with the married Roger Sterling, and sees no hypocrisy in her claim to have been exclusive with him during their time together. In this schism Joan is the quintessential Gurleyean single girl, as unapologetic about her sexual drives as any man in the office and yet fiercely protective of her feminine prerogatives. And when she does land the perfect man — dashing, handsome, and a doctor — the independent city girl titters as she shows off her ring.

She is also an exemplar of Brown's insistence that women make their own mark in the world. As office manager, Joan rules over the women of Sterling Cooper with an iron fist in a lace glove and is quick to correct anyone who dismisses her as a "secretary." The brief stint she spends vetting television scripts for conflicts ("A Night to Remember") augments her stellar client relations with an untapped talent for strategic advertising placement, which makes her pain at her callous replacement all the more heartbreaking.

Joan is no stranger to looking her sexiest, either. In the first episode, she tells Peggy to evaluate her body for her strongest assets and to not shy away from showcasing them. Joan certainly does, her clothing deployed to hug every curve, and displayed with a walk that seems to alter the air current in the office. And yet she manages to elude the coarse sexism of the times and turn it into a powerful weapon. She knows the potency of her looks and the use of it avoids turning her into an objectification of men's fantasies so much as a beacon for them. Granted, she has a strong will, a quick wit, and the readiness to back up her words, and that goes a long way to keeping the unruly "boys" of Sterling Cooper in line. But it is her very belief that she can be both beautiful and powerful that gives her stature, for as Helen Gurley Brown once stated, "You don't have to look like a mud fence in order to be made executive of General Motors."

Perhaps the passivity of her sentiment contains the weak link in that philosophy; it is "to be made" and not "becoming" a person of prestige, and while

Brown couldn't mean anything other than a woman *can* earn such a place, the source of her attitude comes from a defeatist stance. Men are men and women are women, she seems to say; we didn't make the rules, we can sure as hell use them to our advantage.

In this, Brown affirms her place in between the two waves of feminist thought. No wonder those who came after her detected a sour note in her song. To feminists who followed, the idea of accepting a patriarchal system, faults and all, was tantamount to surrender. And yet those who walked after perhaps could not have done so if she hadn't forged a path. Yes, she wrote about womanhood in a way that confirmed entrenched stereotypes that defined a gender by housework and the fulfillment of men's desires, but perhaps she started the dialogue about these issues so that a more profound conversation might follow. She produced a work of sociological importance (more powerful in impact than content, to be sure) that threw a bucket of cold water on the collective assumptions of a society. Betty Friedan may have dismissed Brown's work at *Cosmopolitan* as "quite obscene and horrible," but she wouldn't have been a fan of the magazine before 1965 (see page 94). And Friedan might not have had the opportunity to blow the patriarchal door off its hinges with her magnum opus if *Sex and the Single Girl* hadn't cracked it open first.

1.02 LADIES ROOM

Original air date: July 26, 2007
Written by: Matthew Weiner
Directed by: Alan Taylor

> **Don Draper:** Let me ask you something — what do women want?
> **Roger Sterling:** Who cares?

Don evades an attempt from boss Roger Sterling to open up about his back-ground. Peggy misses Pete, who is on his honeymoon. She ducks advances from other men at Sterling Cooper and runs into crying women in bathroom stalls wherever she goes.

While the place of women in *Mad Men* and the shockingly offhanded sexism they must contend with are on full display in the debut episode, "Ladies Room" seeks to calculate the true cost of it and seek for the harbingers of change.

The "problem" of women in the post–Second World War landscape of America was profound. The suffragette movement had taken hold long before the catastrophic march of war across Europe, but the tenets of it were born out by housewives forced to assume responsibility in spheres thought best left to men. Their daughters watched as they worked in all manner of factories — munitions, vehicles, weaponry — and kept the home fires burning as well. These young girls also watched as the men returned home and expected women to resume their "womanly duties." These daughters would carry out the first true assaults on the frontline of equality in the workplace as they came of working age around the time of *Mad Men*.

Along with the suffragettes' early efforts to recalibrate gender inequality, there was also an equal befuddlement among men with regard to a woman's desires. Famously quoted in Ernest Jones's *Sigmund Freud: Life and Work* (1955), the father of the "talking cure" said, "The great question that has never been answered, and which I have not yet been able to answer, despite my thirty years of research into the feminine soul, is 'What does a woman want?'"

The very dumbfounded nature of the question bespeaks a glaring blind spot in Sigmund Freud's view of women, one easily attributed to the temper of his times. This acknowledgment of ignorance, however, marked a change in his thinking and, almost unbelievably, an improvement.

In 1925, Freud published his paper "Some Psychological Consequences of the Anatomical Distinction between the Sexes" and wrote at length about his notion of "penis envy." In particular, and in contrast to his standard belief, boys were the least aggressive in the curiosity and investigation of the genitalia of the opposite sex. He stated that boys showed a "lack of interest" in girls' nether regions. However, upon laying eyes on a boy's equipment "a little girl behaves differently . . . She has seen it and knows that she is without it and wants to have it."

Understandably, there was adverse reaction to Freud's theories in later years, but he also encountered criticism in his own time. In particular, German psychoanalyst Karen Horney (a whopper of a Freudian name if not pronounced hor-NAY) took exception to his theory. Horney posited that men suffered from "womb envy" and suffered from it even more sharply than the distaff version. In turn, Freud surmised that Horney's theory was the very definition of penis envy.

Don Draper suffers from his own Freudian knowledge envy when it comes to the opposite sex. Charged with creating an ad campaign for Gillette's Right Guard, Don is at a loss for an angle. Members of Don's creative team pitch a hackneyed concept for the campaign — copywriter Paul Kinsey is particularly proud of the space-age setting for the aerosol deodorant spray. Don shoots the idea down and states that it is women who will buy the product for their husbands, so that must be the focus of the campaign.

While Don ruminates on the wants and needs of women, it is clearly a personal project as well. His wife Betty has started suffering from anxiety attacks, trembling hands that result in a mild car crash and cause Betty to worry about her health. She mentions the myriad of doctors who can find nothing physically wrong with her and then suggests psychiatry. No wonder that Don dismisses the notion — a man so secretive about his past (deferring Roger Sterling's inquiries into his childhood so that he will have something left for "the first half" of his novel, and even keeping his wife in the dark) would see little value in the talking cure.

Meanwhile, Peggy Olson deals with the vagaries of being a woman in the workplace. There is no such thing as a free lunch, as she learns when three of the Sterling Cooper boys take her and Joan out for a meal, which ends in an ugly come-on from account executive Ken Cosgrove. Even Phil Kinsey, who shows an interest in Peggy's potential and even invites her to review some of his copy, believes that a decent conversation during a tour of the Sterling Cooper office should later entitle him to a quickie ("We can push the couch in front of the door," he suggests romantically). While Peggy is anxious to make good on her job in a big Manhattan office, and perhaps harbors grander intentions, she feels no need to take the route of least resistance apparently favored by office siren Joan Holloway.

The subtlest approach to the changing roles of women in this episode concerns Don's mistress Midge, the Greenwich Village artist with forward-thinking notions of domesticity. She wears a number of wigs during the episode, a different one each time she appears, trying them out, it seems, as women try on different roles and occupations in this heady time.

No surprise that Don's breakthrough for the Right Guard campaign hits him in Midge's company. His answer to the question that haunted Freud? A woman wants any excuse to get closer.

Don's breakthrough doesn't help Betty. While Don finally relents and arranges for her to see a psychiatrist, any relief the viewer might feel at this development is short-lived. At episode's end, Don speaks with Betty's psychiatrist, who has a funny notion about doctor-patient confidentiality. Things may be changing for women, but there is still a long way to go.

The Philosophy of *Mad Men* — Don Draper: "You think they want a cowboy. He's quiet and strong; he always brings the cattle home safe . . . what if they want something else? Inside, some mysterious wish that we're ignoring?"
Period Moment: Betty Draper and Francine squawk about their new neighbor and divorcée Helen Bishop. And while they voice concerns about the nine-year-old boy and a baby she has to raise on her own or the effect her appearance in the neighborhood will have on property values, it's clear that the women see her as a threat, without even meeting her. They complain about their husbands or the quality of their marriages, but they (like many women of the time) may feel stuck in their situations, while she managed to get out. And let's not even consider the impact a freshly divorced woman might have on their husbands.

More women may have wanted divorce in the early 1960s, but it was a difficult thing to negotiate before California introduced the idea of "no fault" divorce in the Family Law Act of 1969 (with South Dakota the last to introduce such legislation in 1985). Before the appearance of laws which allowed "irreconcilable differences" as a reason to dissolve a marriage, a spouse petitioning the court for divorce had to present evidence that the respondent was guilty of a "sin" or "crime" such as adultery or abandonment. The relative ease of reaching a divorce settlement (provided both parties were willing) certainly spiked the divorce rate throughout the following decades, but other factors cited include strides in pay equity for women, increased political and social consciousness of women, and advancements in contraceptive production and availability (diminishing the need for a man to "make an honest woman" out of his mate). The divorce rate among American first-time marriages in 1963 was 9.6/1000 which rose to 19.3/1000 by 1974. This figure reached a plateau during the 1980s with almost 500/1000 of first-time marriages ending in divorce.

Ad Pitch: Gillette is introduced in this episode as "the only company on earth that can spray deodorant out of a can," thanks to a patent from Robert Abplanalp's Precision Valve Corporation. He filed a patent for the first mass-produced aerosol valve in 1949; the United States Patent and Trademark Office issued certification on March 17, 1953.

The slogan Don creates for Right Guard does not appear to have a foot in reality. During the time of this episode, Right Guard was best known for a television commercial created by the firm BBDO, which featured the line, "One shot and I'm feeling fresh all day!"

Manhattan Real Estate: The diner the boys from the office take Joan and Peggy to for lunch and sexual badgering bears a strong resemblance to the diner where Don meets the mysterious Adam Whitman in a later episode. This greasy spoon "three blocks west" of Sterling Cooper could very well be a D-Lite Coffee Shop (West Fortieth Street and Broadway, New York), according to the travel blog Gridskipper.com.

Cocktail of Note: In the opening scene, Betty Draper loosens up at dinner with her husband's boss and wife over a few Vodka Gimlets.

> 1 ounce of vodka
> 1 ounce unsweetened lime juice
> 1/2 ounce sugar syrup
> Shake with ice cubes, strain into a chilled cocktail glass, and finish with a slice of lime.

1.03 MARRIAGE OF FIGARO

Original air date: August 2, 2007
Written by: Tom Palmer
Directed by: Ed Bianchi

> "And now I begin to learn the foolish art of being a husband."
> — *The Marriage of Figaro*, Act IV, scene vii

While examining the Volkswagen "Lemon" ad in Life *magazine, an old army buddy of Don's greets him on the train but calls him "Dick Whitman." Despite a prickly first encounter, Don and Rachel Menken get a little bit closer. Don builds a playhouse for his daughter's birthday, but disappears halfway through the party much to the consternation of his wife Betty. Pete returns from his honeymoon determined to be a good husband.*

An episode devoted to the nature of character does well to invoke Mozart's famous sequel to *Barber of Seville* about star-crossed lovers, infidelity, and mistaken identities. Based on the play by Pierre Beaumarchais (with a libretto by Lorenzo da Ponte), the action takes over one day at the castle of Count Almaviva in Seville in the late eighteenth century. The philandering count has soured his marriage to Countess Rosine, and hopes to bed the countess's maiden, Susanna. The count's valet, Figaro, intends to marry Susanna, despite the count's designs. The count, however, detects interest in the countess by the young page Cherubino, and awards him an officer's commission in an effort to rid him from the castle. Figaro hatches a plot to use Cherubino (dressed as a woman) to expose the count and his adulterous ways. An old rival of Figaro's (Bartholo from *The Barber of Seville*) descends on the castle with his own plan of revenge for stealing a woman from him. Identities are mistaken, people jump through windows, and it all ends with a wedding.

Unlike the raucous joviality of this opera buffa, the deceptively placid façade of suburban life splinters under the weight of Don Draper's dissatisfaction. Even more startling is a first scene development so jaw-dropping that the remainder of the episode can only stagger while dealing with the ramification of an old army buddy of Don's bumping into him on the train, and calling him "Dick Whitman." Don does not correct the man and has a short conversation with him as if (despite a quick gulp at first) it were

53

the most natural thing in the world.

The very nature of America as haven of the "huddled masses yearning to breathe free" is up for subtle examination in this episode. While the presence of African-Americans in subservient roles has featured in previous episodes, direct reference to Jews occurs in a hushed, disparaging tone. While critiquing the Volkswagen "Lemon" campaign, Roger Sterling mentions that the ad man responsible (Bill Bernbach) is the least likely to contribute to the reindustrialization of Germany, as he was a Jew. When Don woos Rachel Menken in the boardroom after a disastrous pitch session, Pete Campbell refers to the display as "Don and Molly Goldberg." And Pete's remark about the "Chinamen in my office" does little to confirm the American dream of equality in the search for life, liberty, and the pursuit of happiness.

On a sunnier note, Pete returns from his honeymoon and appears amazed at his own commitment to the union. He mentions to his colleagues in the morning elevator bull session that something came over him during the ceremony, particularly the "new baptized" sentiment. The boys are less concerned with his epiphany than with the seedier details of his vacation, but Campbell seems genuine in his transformation. Even when discussing his transgression with Peggy, he refuses any further involvement with her out of a sense of honor to this newly minted role as husband.

Helen Bishop makes her first true appearance in this episode, Betty having invited her to Sally Draper's birthday party out of a sense of obligation. There has been much clucking among the women in the neighborhood about the "poor" divorced woman with two children; in fact, they spend as much time talking about her unusual habit of walking without a destination as the Sterling Cooper men did about the vw advert. Helen appears unfazed by the housewives' whispers she can certainly hear, to say nothing of the oblique advances made by their husbands. She is intent on making a new life, recreating herself in that uniquely American manner. And maybe even enjoys the attention.

All notions of character and secrecy pale next to Don Draper. In fact, the audience gets a good look into the importance of Don's last name. While discussing the vagaries of marriage with Pete Campbell, Harry Crane (Rich Sommer) puts his finger on the very elusiveness of Don, stating that "no one has looked under that rock" and that "he could be Batman for all we know." Harry doesn't know how right he is when invoking that haunted vigilante warring with two sides of his personality.

This is the first episode where the viewer can see past actor Jon Hamm's almost bland movie-star good looks and witness the true torture going on beneath that handsome visage. Draper is the epitome of the self-made American man and despite the ennui he suffers after achieving everything he wanted, the moment that picture-perfect life is threatened he panics. Much was made of the revelation at the end of the first episode that Don was married, but many fans believe the opening scene in this episode beats that handily.

At first blush, the time spent on something as mundane as Sally's birthday party seems an odd dramatic choice, but the creative team behind the show realizes that the audience needs time to recover from the rabbit punch they delivered in the opening scene. The consequences of it are more profound as we see additional scenes of Don's home life. When Don goes AWOL after picking up the birthday cake, he reels as much as the audience. And when he finally returns after the party has broken up, the only act of contrition he can muster is an addition to the suburban picture he's painted. The present of a dog to run along their white picket fence is the only missing piece of this perfect slice of Americana.

This has to be the most inscrutable episode of *Mad Men*, and in that case, it is a perfect reflection of Don Draper. When a character you've come to know is suddenly referred to by a different name, it throws you for a loop. Like the vw ad (and the car), and the blithe divorcée who walks for the sake of walking, it is clear that nothing in this series will be like any show we've seen before.

The Philosophy of *Mad Men* — Don Draper: "Yep. This is it." (This is Don's response to a neighbor's observation that "We've got it all.")

Period Moment: Joan and a few of the other office ladies coo over a dog-eared copy of *Lady Chatterley's Lover*, the story of a young wife married to an older, crippled man, and her erotic awakening in the arms of working-class gamekeeper. The novel, D. H. Lawrence's last, gained immediate notoriety not only for the explicit depictions of the sexual act but also due to unvarnished language of the four-letter variety.

Lawrence wrote the novel in 1928, despite Joan's emphatic statement that she didn't care if it was written "five hundred years ago." But other than a private run in Florence, the novel was so scandalous that it did not receive a commercial publication until 1960 in the United Kingdom, when Penguin

Books underwent a trial under the Obscene Publications Act. Lawrence's smutty epic was also one of three books (along with *Tropic of Cancer* by Henry Miller and *The Life and Adventures of Miss Fanny Hill* by John Cleland) banned in the United States. The British case returned with a verdict of "Not Guilty" and the American ban was soon overturned. Both were watermarks in the fight for freedom of expression.

Manhattan Real Estate: While not visited during the course of this episode, the famed Gotham Book Mart would have been the only place where one of the ladies could pick up a copy of *Lady Chatterley's Lover*. Opened in 1920 and residing at a few addresses, the longest location called home was at 41 West Forty-seventh Street in Manhattan's storied Diamond District. Proprietor Fanny Steloff built a business catering to an avant-garde sensibility by selling literary outlaws, often in defiance of bans. The store also hosted the James Joyce Society, the Finnegan's Wake Society, and a North American answer to the "café culture" of Europe. Authors as varied as E. E. Cummings, Theodore Dreiser, and Woody Allen shopped there; Edward Gorey owed much of his success to Gotham's support in his name; and Fanny Sterloff even employed future writers such as Allen Ginsberg and Tennessee Williams.

Sadly, the store was evicted from its final home on East Forty-sixth Street in 2007, with the bulk of the inventory sold off (including many signed copies and rare first editions) for $400,000, despite evaluations of two or three times that value.

Ad Pitch: The "Volkswagen: Lemon" debuted in 1960. The second in what became a long-standing campaign for the car that continued nearly untouched for ten years, it was part of a shift to "New Advertising" that highlighted the quirky humor and bold graphic design that came to dominate American advertising for decades to follow.

Sterling Cooper is a different kind of agency, classic and "glamorous." But Don and the boys are mystified at the ad, both in the presentation and the product it's selling. They remark upon the year's previous vw campaign, Think Small, which featured a nearly microscopic still of the car in question, a "half-page ad in a full page buy" as copywriter Harry Crane sniffs (see page 57). Created by Doyle Dane & Bernbach, the Volkswagen campaign signaled a shift in American culture, away from the post-war boom mentality of "bigger and bigger is better." While the Sterling Cooper men can't fathom a car without fins, Don Draper notes that love it or hate it, they can't stop talking about it. And that's with it appearing in an issue of *Playboy*.

Cocktail of Note: At Sally Draper's birthday party, Betty haphazardly pours Bourbon into a glass jug, stirs and serves as Mint Julep. Below is a more exacting recipe.

2 or 3 fresh mint sprigs

1/2 teaspoon sugar

1 teaspoon water

3 ounces Bourbon

Place one mint sprig into a highball glass with sugar and water. Stir and then add 2 ounces of Bourbon. Fill glass with shaved ice and stir. Float remaining Bourbon and garnish with remaining mint sprigs.

Doyle Dane & Bernbach's "Think Small" Campaign for Volkswagen

In post-war America, the advertising industry in general and automotive marketing in particular exuded a sleek swagger emblematic of the 1950s. The celebration of success (and excess) made sense; after emerging victorious from an honorable war, the following years of unparalleled prosperity felt like a suitable outcome of a long and punishing conflict. In the United States the outward displays of this affluence took many forms — from the rocketing skylines of major cities launched by the hum of industry to the suburban sprawl fuelled by that urban upswing — but there was perhaps no greater exhibition of opulence than in car designs of the day. Jet age–inspired wings and tails, after-burner taillights, and glistening chrome on every available accent announced the technological and aesthetic dominance of the American Dream.

But then, a funny thing happened. Or more accurately, a funny car happened. An oddly shaped yet resilient vehicle from Germany (originally produced with financial backing from the Third Reich) began production as part of a post-war reinvigoration program to battle unemployment. A German engineer named Heinrich Nordhoff was appointed managing director of Volkswagen in 1948 and his stewardship of the company led to the beginning of a worldwide automotive phenomenon.

By the late 1950s, Volkswagen moved beyond European markets and had sold tens of thousands of cars in the United States without the help of an advertising campaign. When they decided to engage in a nationwide market-

Lemon.

This Volkswagen missed the boat.

The chrome strip on the glove compartment is blemished and must be replaced. Chances are you wouldn't have noticed it; Inspector Kurt Kroner did.

There are 3,389 men at our Wolfsburg factory with only one job: to inspect Volkswagens at each stage of production. (3000 Volkswagens are produced daily; there are more inspectors than cars.)

Every shock absorber is tested (spot checking won't do), every windshield is scanned. VWs have been rejected for surface scratches barely visible to the eye.

Final inspection is really something! VW inspectors run each car off the line onto the Funktionsprüfstand (car test stand), tote up 189 check points, gun ahead to the automatic brake stand, and say "no" to one VW out of fifty.

This preoccupation with detail means the VW lasts longer and requires less maintenance, by and large, than other cars. (It also means a used VW depreciates less than any other car.)

We pluck the lemons; you get the plums.

ing effort, they made the decision to avoid the more established agencies and their conventional thinking. The elegance and glamour of the gold standard agencies (creators of graceful yet humorless ads like those often seen in the offices of Sterling Cooper) did not feel like a proper fit for this hunched workhorse of a car. Volkswagen executives searched for an imaginative agency that could sell a different kind of car in a different way, and ultimately chose New York's Doyle Dane & Bernbach.

What they got was not only an unorthodox and arresting campaign that lasted over a decade and survived multiple DDB creative teams with nary a change in approach, the upstarts from this boutique agency also delivered Volkswagen a place in the pop culture that signaled a seismic shift in the face of advertising.

The agency also benefited, and not just in the form of an impressive client roster. "Think Small" earned DDB a vaulted place in history when *Advertising Age* magazine declared the campaign to be the single best of the twentieth century.

William Bernbach would not have been anyone's choice as the face of "New Advertising": conventional in dress and behavior, Bernbach would have looked like an accountant who strayed onto the creative floor of any large agency. But his approach to advertising, and emphasis on the creative impulse, was nothing less than the bleeding edge.

Publicity material Bernbach wrote for the 1939 New York World Fair garnered interest and led to the mention of his name to William H. Weintraub, an ad man who created one of the first "ethnic" agencies in New York as counterbalance to the predominantly WASP flavor of Madison Avenue. Bernbach competed for a position with several veterans, but the copy he produced at Weintraub's behest was original enough to land him the job despite having no direct advertising experience.

Essential to Bernbach's later success was his exposure to the industry while at the William H. Weintraub Advertising Agency, but even more pivotal in his development was his exposure to the artist Paul Rand. The iconoclastic artist and graphic designer (who, at twenty-seven, demanded complete control of the Weintraub art department . . . and got it) had created arresting work for Dubonnet, Dodge, Coronet, and Air Wick with a style that took inspiration from cubism and constructivism as well as the brash composition of Paul Cézanne and the innovative typographical work of Jan Tschichold. Rand may be best remembered for his work with corporate branding (he designed the logo for IBM, a triumph of typography that transcends language), but his impact was also felt on Bernbach's approach to advertising layout.

Copywriter Bernbach was paired with artist Rand, and they often worked in tandem on campaigns. The prevailing wisdom at the time was that art should follow copy: the visual subjugated to the written word. The pairing of writer and artist didn't just even the playing field; it necessitated a free and open exchange of ideas, and struck Bernbach as a natural method to creating the fresh and unexpected idea.

This shift in creative hierarchy had to wait as Bernbach took a copywriting position at Grey Advertising. The change from "ethnic" agency to Madison Avenue stalwart must have been a shock, but it didn't stop Bernbach from scaling the steps at Grey, taking the mantle of creative director four years into his tenure. But he felt there was faulty reasoning behind Grey's reliance on research, used not to support the creation of campaigns but to modify and weaken the final result. It chafed Bernbach's belief that the best ideas were untried and untested, but the experience helped him define his advertising philosophy.

"I'm worried," Bernbach famously wrote to his superiors at Grey in 1947, "that we're going to worship techniques instead of substance. Advertising is fundamentally persuasion and persuasion happens to be not a science, but an art." His penchant for pungent aphorisms affirmed (along with his rank as champion of the artistic community within advertising), Bernbach no doubt caused his bosses their own worry that their creative director wanted to diverge from their tested path.

It was no surprise then that Bernbach eventually left Grey to set up his own shop. Along with James Doyle and Maxwell Dane, Bernbach struck out to prove that following the artistic inclination — created in concert between writer and artist — could lead to original and effective advertising. When Doyle Dane & Bernbach opened in 1949, they had but one account to prove their argument.

Citizens of New York and New Jersey knew Ohrbach's department store as a second-tier, cut-rate dress shop. Founder Nathan M. Ohrbach believed in trimming costs in an effort to offer deep savings to the customer, but in the late 1950s he wanted to change the store's image so he could cater to a higher level of clientele (shades of Menken's department store anyone?). He opted to follow Bernbach from the Weintraub Agency to the newly formed DDB. The collaboration between Bernbach and art director Bob Gage produced a type of advertising that would become the hallmark of the "new" style.

The team created a full-page ad with four-fifths devoted to the jarring sight of a cat wearing a bonnet and clasping a cigarette holder in its mouth, with the line "I found out about Joan" beneath. Draped around the department store name was copy that detailed the revelations of a catty woman who discovered that her neighbor managed to *look* well-to-do because she bought her "divine" clothes at Ohrbach's. "A business in millions, a profit in pennies."

Not only did the bold graphic layout of the ad impress, but the humor of the ad also made it a winner. The line between hat-wearing cat and snide neighbor is not a direct one, but DDB left it to the viewer to make the connection, assuming a level of intelligence that engaged the consumer but also flattered them on their ability to be "in" on the joke. The campaign also managed to appeal to a different type of customer without betraying the economic nature of the goods on sale, in effect turning what could have been a detriment (or at least a fact to disregard) into an asset.

The campaign was a success and many other customers followed, including Polaroid and the Israli airline El Al. Polaroid also employed a strong photographic element to highlight the simplicity of the product, while El Al built a campaign on humor, including one ad that featured a sketch of Noah's Ark with the line "We've been in the travel business a long time." The skills at work in DDB's bullpen were in place to affect a dramatic shift in advertising, but all they needed was a product as singular and unorthodox as their technique.

German automotive designer Ferdinand Porsche (yes, *that* Porsche) designed luxury cars for Mercedes, but longed to design a more utilitarian, affordable car for the common man, a "people's car." He embarked on designs in 1927 and six years later attracted the interest of Adolf Hitler who ordered the construction of prototypes. This new kind of car, which in its affordability aligned with Hitler's notion that all Germans should own vehicles, was supposed to roll off the Wolfsburg assembly line in 1937. Hitler's concern for the German military took precedence, and Porsche accepted the commission, which resulted in the design and construction of Panzers, the Elefant tank destroyer, and a jeep called Kubelwagen plus an amphibious version known as Schwimmwagen.

Following the war, Ferdinand Porsche was summoned to Baden-Baden by the French government to discuss launching production of the Volkswagen in their country. This deal fell apart and ended with the arrest of Porsche and two others as war criminals. Porsche served twenty months in a Dijon prison without ever facing trial, while the family labored to carry on the Porsche name as a designer and manufacturer of high-end luxury cars.

The Volkswagen might have expired then, but for a few strokes of luck. First, the deal to move production of a revised VW would have required the relocation of the entire Wolfsburg plant, which France would claim as war reparations. When French automakers wanted no part of a new VW built in their country the car might have died with the arrest of Ferdinand Porsche. Instead, Major Ivan Hirst of the British Army became a guardian angel of the VW. First, he was responsible for the removal of an unexploded bomb in the Wolfsburg plant that, if exploded, would have meant a premature end to the car. Hirst then became an ardent supporter of the vehicle and pressed for a British automaker to take over production of the reliable car he'd seen throughout his post-war efforts to rebuild Germany. When no United Kingdom–based automaker would touch the "unattractive" vehicle, Henrich Nordhoff was named head of the Wolfsburg plant and started producing the VW. By 1950, 19,000 cars per year rolled off the line. By 1970 that number increased to 1.6 million.

This jump in production can be linked almost directly to the work of DDB, although they initially struggled with how to sell the VW, only known colloquially as the "Bug" though the proper name has always been Volkswagen. The first thought was to Americanize it, drape it in as much bunting needed to disguise the fact that it was a uniquely *foreign* car. The accepted thinking was that while the Second World War was in the past, it wasn't far enough to quell the moral dyspepsia the American public would suffer at the thought of buying a German car.

Before making a decision, a team from DDB traveled to the Wolfsburg plant to observe the production of the vehicle. They spent three weeks in Germany, following the construction of the car from start to finish, and interviewing workers on the line. They came away from the trip with an admiration for the stringent quality control, which could end with an entire car rejected as "unsellable" for a defect that wouldn't raise an eyebrow on an American auto line.

Bernbach discarded all earlier ideas in favor of a straightforward approach: each ad to feature a single advantage to the car, concise copy, an oblique sense of humor, and austere black-and-white photography (no matter how colorful the magazine it might appear in). This "honest" approach — as translated by art director Helmut Krone and copywriter Julian Koenig — celebrated the "handicaps" of this bulbous foreign car and announced the bottom-line benefits with style. Like the Ohrbach's ad, it assumed a high level of intelligence in the consumer, and, along with an equal focus on visual impact and snappy copy, simultaneously brought the viewer in, included them in the fun.

DDB went on to bag other big-game clients like Lever Brothers, Gillette, Bristol-Myers, Mobil Oil, and Avis (with the "We're number two, we try harder" campaign that not only broke ground in the realm of comparative advertising but also entered a phrase into the pop culture lexicon). The VW ads continued with other memorable shadings on the original ("Lemon," "Some shapes are hard to improve on") and many creative minds who worked at DDB cycled out of the agency to start their own, often producing ads with the same mixture of innovative layouts and crisp copy.

Ex-employees were not the only ones to feel the impact of DDB — and creative director Bill Bernbach in particular — on advertising. The spirit of creativity and dismissal of accepted norms and formulas set the tone for advertising in the coming decades. Bernbach shepherded the industry into a new era where a level of sophistication in creation and execution became synonymous with good advertising.

1.04 NEW AMSTERDAM

Original air date: August 9, 2007
Written by: Lisa Albert
Directed by: Tim Hunter

> "The following tale was found among the papers of the late Diedrich Knickerbocker, an old gentleman of New York, who was very curious in the Dutch history of the province . . . and now that he is dead and gone, it cannot do harm to his memory to say that his time might have been better employed in weightier matters."
>
> — Washington Irving

Pete cannot afford the Park Avenue apartment his wife, Trudy, wants, and is uncomfortable accepting financial help from his in-laws. At Sterling Cooper, Pete discovers the importance of his "Dyckman" family name. While babysitting her neighbor's son, Glen, Betty forms a curious connection with him.

What is in a name? For New Yorkers, everything. From Edith Wharton's brutal aristocracy of *The Age of Innocence* to Tom Wolfe's new-money stratification in *Bonfire of the Vanities*, jockeying for prestige in this teeming Gotham is a blood sport and there are no points awarded for tact.

Possibly the oldest New York name is Knickerbocker. Washington Irving wrote *A History of New York — from the Beginning of the World to the End of the Dutch Dynasty* under the pen name of Diedrich Knickerbocker. A satire on pompous blowhards who value lineage and haughty local history over true accomplishment, this book gave rise to the Knickerbocker name as the epitome of old-money prestige. The fact that this hallowed name is fictional has not stopped people from staking a claim to heredity.

Over time, the impact of the name seems to have been lost and has become an example of the very status-seekers Irving sought to lampoon. In fact, Irving is also responsible for applying New York's nickname of "Gotham," and not without tongue in cheek. In his *Salmagundi Papers*, Irving tagged Manhattan with this epithet in reference to *Merrie Tales of the Mad Men of Gotham* and the inhabitants who were famously both foolish and wise. Despite this (and the Anglo-Saxon translation meaning "Goat Town"), New Yorkers appropriated the name Gotham and robbed it of its power.

The prospect of living up to a name looms large for Pete, and, for the first time, he becomes a figure worthy of pity. The impossibility of gaining respect from his father leads him to churlishly defend the quality of his ideas to Don. The necessity of staking his claim in the world becomes even more important with the pricey apartment his wife, Trudy, desires. That all of this prompts him to try to usurp Don's place in the creative hierarchy when dealing with the Bethlehem Steel account is understandable, but in no way mitigates the consequences of his folly. Pete has the Dyckman name, but doesn't have the income to match. The apartment is out of their price range but, at Trudy's insistence, Pete approaches his parents for help with the down payment. The privileged patois of his father is punishing enough ("Boat's in the water. . . . Your cousin Sarah had a baby and named it after your Uncle Skip"), but that Mr. Campbell assails his son's line of work while wearing shorts, deck shoes, and a yellow seersucker blazer only grinds salt to the wound.

When rebuffed for his request of help with the down payment (ostensibly for no other reason than undesirable geography), Pete is rightly upset. He wonders why it is so difficult for his parents to give him anything, to which his father replies that they've given him everything. They've given him his name.

Pete Campbell comes from imperial Dyckman stock. Farmer William Dyckman built a farmhouse on what is now Broadway and 204th Street, which anchored hundreds of acres of land owned by the family that cemented their place in New York's firmament as the city grew to assume the place of a global capital. The farmhouse still stands in an Inwood neighborhood park as a reminder not only of New York long since come and gone, but also as a classic example of the Dutch Colonial style of architecture.

In a home of similar style, albeit alongside the Drapers, divorcée Helen Bishop houses the solemn and creepy young Glen Bishop, who memorably

Pete and Peggy (pictured here with Maggie Siff, who plays Rachel Menken): star-crossed lovers or workplace rivals? (AP Photo/Matt Sayles)

bursts in on babysitting Betty Draper during this episode, and requests (and receives!) a lock of her golden hair.

The fact that Betty awards Glen a sample of her silky mane is one of the more memorable yet left-field moments of shock in the series. It seems that Betty joins the chorus of tacit disapproval the neighborhood women sing behind Helen's back, and if asked directly Mrs. Draper would aver that the divorcée of the community is jealous of her picture-perfect family life. Betty's surrender of a blond ribbon to Glen doesn't play like a woman trying to placate an oddball child, but a connection with the isolation this boy feels, and even a sense of longing for the freedom Helen's divorce provides.

Helen Bishop struggles with the title of "divorcée" like a crimson A on her blouse, and Pete grapples with the expectations foisted on him by the status his family name engenders. Don is the pivot between the two, but his anger is reserved for the young account executive in his office. When Pete pitches his own creative for the Bethlehem Steel account, Don plays it smooth in front of the client. Behind closed doors, Don's cunning is never

65

clearer than when he summarily fires Campbell for stepping over the line with the Bethlehem Steel executive. He quickly drafts Roger Sterling's backing but finds that Bertram Cooper's notion of "marquee value" trumps his own bruised ego. The great irony is that the name Pete labors under is the very thing that, without his knowledge, saves his job at Sterling Cooper.

The Philosophy of *Mad Men* — Bertram Cooper: "New York City is a marvelous machine, filled with a mesh of levers, and gears, and springs, like a fine watch, wound tight . . . always ticking. . . ."

Period Moment: Pete Campbell and the other junior execs listen to the landmark 1960 comedy album *The Button-Down Mind of Bob Newhart*. This was Newhart's debut recording and it landed at number one on the *Billboard* chart, surpassing both a cast recording of *The Sound of Music* and a new Elvis Presley release. The Sterling Cooper juniors take great pleasure in noting that Newhart was once an accountant, providing hope for all the failed artists in the room. Oddly, the routine they listen to is "The Driving Instructor" and not "Abe Lincoln vs. Madison Avenue," a classic sketch wherein Newhart imagines the great Civil War president consulting an advertising man before his address at Gettysburg ("You changed 'four score and seven' to 'eighty-seven'?" "Abe, that's meant to be a 'grabber'. . . .")

Ad Pitch: The Bethlehem Steel account that provides so much friction between Don and Pete does not appear to have an immediate historical reference. Founded in 1857 and once the second largest producer of steel in the United States, Bethlehem Steel had an internal advertising and marketing department, but that may have served industry-specific publications alone. Bethlehem Steel did provide much of the skeleton for that magnificent city of New York, as Don states in his first pitch to the company executive. In the 1940s, someone suggested that if all the steel provided by Bethlehem were to disappear from New York, eighty percent of the skyline would have fallen.

A giant of American industry, Bethlehem Steel still could have been looking for an improved public image at that time. In 1960, the United States imported more steel than it exported and no company bought more of this cheaper steel than Bethlehem, a fact that could not sit well with the American public. The company also weathered a tough steelworkers' strike in the latter half of 1959, negotiations of which continued even after President Dwight Eisenhower granted an injunction to force the steelworkers back to the foundries. A young politician took an interest in the labor strife (which revolved around wages and the "past practices" stipulation favored by unions in an effort to halt rapid change in the workplace), and set about negotiating an agreement between the workers and management. As many as ten marathon meetings were held at this politician's home, the last of which stretched over twenty-two hours. A contract was hammered out that not only solidified the union's primary concerns, but also provided sizeable insurance benefits and increased pensions. The steel manufacturers claimed the deal would cost them $1 billion, but the young politician who spearheaded the negotiations claimed that a deal reached independently would be more desirous than one forced upon them by a Democratic Congress.

This politician gained some much-needed traction in his bid for the presidency in 1960. And while the unions benefited, it may have been the last time labor found an ally in a Republican candidate. As a *New York Times* headline proclaimed following the deal: NIXON, MEDIATOR GAIN STATURE.

Manhattan Real Estate: Cooper refers to the avenues of influence Pete Campbell and his connection to the Dyckman name can open, citing admission into the "Century Club." Established in 1847, the Century Association was a club for artists, men of letters, and the patrons who support them. Membership has included Andy Rooney, Mayor Michael Bloomberg, at least one Rockefeller and former JFK aide Arthur Schlesinger Jr. This quintessential "gentleman's club," which was opened to women in 1988, is located in a white Beaux-Arts building on West Forty-third Street, but keeps a low profile for its 24,000 membership population.

Cocktail of Note: While not served in this episode, a concoction named for the best-known old family of the New York aristocracy seems apt. For your snooty drinking pleasure, the Knickerbocker:

> 1/2 teaspoon Italian vermouth
> 1/2 ounce French vermouth
> 1 1/2 ounces gin
> Stir well with ice cubes. Strain into chilled cocktail glass. Add a twist of lemon peel.

Money Part One — Inflation from 1960 to Now

Part of the show's ability to create a seamless verisimilitude is the constant use of dollar amounts that, while sounding slim by today's standards, root the show in its time and place. If you are curious to know how values translate from then to now, may I present a handy list:

Item	Value Then (1960)	Today's Equivalent (USD)
The Campbell's Upper East Side Apartment	$32,000	$230,000
Pack of cigarettes	$0.35	$2.49
Cuban cigar	$1.50	$10.68
Issue of *Playboy*	$0.60	$4.27
Fifth of Jack Daniels	$7	$49.85
Haircut	$5	$35.61
Don Draper's bonus	$2,500	$17,980

1.05 5G

Original air date: August 16, 2007
Written by: Matthew Weiner
Directed by: Lesli Linka Glatter

> "There is in some parts of New England a kind of tree whose juice that weeps out its incision . . . doth congeal into a sweet and saccharin substance."
>
> — Robert Boyle, British chemist, 1663

A photo of Don in Advertising Age *magazine compels a stranger to arrive and claim to be Don's brother. A Draper family portrait is ruined by Don's distraction at the unwanted return of an aspect from his previous life. Account executive Ken Cosgrove has a short story published in* Atlantic Monthly, *a fact poorly received by his envious colleagues at Sterling Cooper.*

The devotion to geographical accuracy and actual companies subsides in "5G" (written by show creator Matthew Weiner, his first script for this season since the second episode). This episode of the show plays fast and loose with Manhattan landmarks and creates a fictional company for Sterling Cooper to work with. However, in an episode where Don Draper's true past threatens to break through his successfully fictional biography, this deviation seems a strategic decision and not a lapse in historic fidelity.

Don is, by all accounts, living a blessed life. The suggestion that his luck is about to run out arrives early on when the horseshoe on his advertising award turns upside down.

War changes a man, but none more that Don it seems. His time in the service is referenced a few times with relation to his identity; the man who first calls him "Dick Whitman" is a crony from basic training; younger brother Adam remembers Don in his uniform and includes a snapshot of the two in a letter with the eldest in his standard issue khakis; and yet in the first episode, Don casually disregards a Purple Heart awarded to "Lt. Don Draper." When did he start life with this new persona?

The room number — 5G — Adam includes in the snapshot and letter he sends to Don echoes neatly the amount Don scrapes together for hush money so his younger brother, and past, can just disappear ($5,000). This poor young man doesn't know what to do with the request, and never intended to blackmail Don. He simply wants a connection to family, to blood. But Don has moved beyond that and while he comforts the poor young man as he dissolves into tears, Don already has an eye on the door and a return to his life as the quintessential self-made American man.

The appearance of the mysterious Adam is not the only ominous harbinger at the Sterling Cooper offices. A rivalry between creative man Paul Kinsey and account executive Ken Cosgrove bubbles up when the latter has a short story published in *Atlantic Monthly*. And while the tedious-sounding "Tapping Maple on a Cold Vermont Morning" drives frustrated writer Kinsey mad with jealousy ("Kenneth Cosgrove . . . I think I'm going to vomit"), it strikes a deeper blow to Pete Campbell ("My father reads the damn *Atlantic*"). While he hasn't shown much in the way of artistic inclination up to now (other than trying to jostle in on the Bethlehem Steel account), Pete is envious of the prestige. So much so that he is willing to offer his wife on the altar of notoriety. Charlie Fiddich, an ex-flame of Trudy's, is a publishing executive and Pete prompts her, as much as encourages her, to

The boys of Sterling Cooper tee up for the AFI/*Mad Men* Golf Classic. (AP Photo/Tammie Arroyo)

"arrange" for his story about a hunter imagining what a bear is thinking to be published in a national magazine. At first, this might seem like a plot point that almost derails the episode, but upon reflection the desperate need for acceptance and stature fits in with the landscape examined in *Mad Men*.

Almost as troubling a change is secretary Peggy learning about Don's wandering eye. She foolishly asks Joan for advice, a moment of weakness instantly leveraged for full gossip disclosure. Joan instructs Peggy to keep the secret for her boss, as that is part of her job. Peggy agrees but has trouble reconciling this with her vision of Don as "different" from the other men in the office.

The Philosophy of *Mad Men* — Don Draper: "I have a life and it only goes in one direction . . . forward."

Period Moment: When Midge calls Don at the office to arrange for a mid-afternoon tryst, she uses the synonym "Mrs. Beiderbecke." During the conversation, she explains that it was in tribute to leading 1920s jazz trumpeter Bix Beiderbecke. At her Village apartment for the hair-pulling and ravishing she desires, they instead listen to Miles Davis's "Blue in Green" from his 1959 landmark album *Kind of Blue*. Recorded in two sessions at Columbia Records' Thirtieth Street Studio in New York, it is considered the bestselling jazz album of all time (certified by the Recording Industry Association of America as quadruple platinum, which is 4 million units domestically). It has been cited as one of the most influential musical recordings of the twentieth century (ranked twelfth on the *Rolling Stone* 500 Greatest Albums of All Time in 2003), and was entered into the Library of Congress National Recording Registry in 2002. Authorship of highly improvised recordings is tough to pin down, but credit for the original melodies on *Kind of Blue*, and "Blue in Green" in particular, have long been a source of controversy. In his autobiography, Miles Davis claims he wrote all tracks on *Kind of Blue*. Pianist Bill Evans recorded the song on his album *Portrait in Jazz* where it was credited as a Davis-Evans composition. Earl Zindars, however, claimed that the tune was "100 percent Evans" because the pianist "wrote it over at my pad in East Harlem . . . and he stayed until three o'clock in the morning playing those six bars over and over."

Manhattan Real Estate: Adam is embarrassed that Don has to see his "temporary" lodgings at the flophouse Hotel Brighton in Times Square. This building is a creation for the show, but there has long been a history of flophouses in New York, and perhaps none more famous than the Bunker in the Bowery.

Long known as a "skid row" area of Manhattan, the Bowery occupies a small swath of the lower east side of the island. The road itself was first known as Bowery Lane and led to Dutch settler Peter Stuyvesant's farm (or, as known in his native tongue, "*bouwerij*"). The flophouses in this area were a step below the room Adam inhabits at Times Square, which were often referred to as "cage hotels" due to the chicken wire that provided a ceiling for the cubicles inhabited by drunks, addicts, and those otherwise down-at-the-heel.

The Bunker (222 Bowery) was so-called as it had no windows; they weren't required in its former incarnation as a YMCA locker room. The Bunker gained notoriety for one of its more famous tenants, legendary Beat writer William Burroughs. He lived in the Bunker from 1974 to his death in 1997. His residence there resulted in oddly notable traffic such as Allen Ginsberg, Mick Jagger, and Andy Warhol who side-stepped through transients to visit the author of *Naked Lunch*.

Not that the Bowery has been a stranger to celebrity: this area was also the home of famous punk club CBGB.

Ad Pitch: The "private executive account" featured in this episode certainly has a foot in reality (as stated by the fictional bank executive, who claims many customers already arrange for such service without extra billing), but the inspiration for the bank Sterling Cooper works for is tougher to nail down. Liberty Savings Bank started as the Lynchburg Savings and Loan Association in 1889, but as the company started corporate life in Ohio, it is unclear whether it would have sought the services of a Manhattan ad firm. A better bet for the basis of this campaign might be Liberty Bank, headquartered in Middletown, Connecticut, which is less of a drive to New York. However, this bank opened as Middletown Savings Bank and did not change their name until 1975.

Cocktail of Note: Poor Adam displays his stolen bottle of gin with pride. Don requests a coffee, but looks like he could use a zinger of a cocktail, perhaps the rightly named Blackout Cocktail:

> 1 1/2 ounces gin
> 1/2 ounce of blackberry brandy
> Juice of 1/2 lime
> Shake with ice and strain into chilled glass.

1.06 BABYLON
• • • • • • • • • • • •

Original air date: August 23, 2007
Written by: André and Maria Jacquemetton
Directed by: Andrew Bernstein

"The caged bird sings
with fearful trill
of the things unknown
but longed for still."
— Maya Angelou, *I Know Why the Caged Bird Sings*

Sterling Cooper tries to land the Israeli Tourism account, which provides Don a pretext with which to contact Rachel Menken. Peggy floors Freddy Rumsen with her abilities while part of a focus group on Belle Jolie lipstick. Roger gives his mistress Joan Holloway a pet for a present.

Birds have always cast a shadow across *Mad Men*. From character names (Harry Crane, Herman "Duck" Phillips, Trudy Vogel, Betty Draper's nickname "Birdie") to various mentions of the Broadway musical *Bye Bye, Birdie* — the allusions are subtle but important to the series as a whole, and integral to this episode in particular.

Circling around Sterling Cooper are representatives of Israel's Department of Tourism. As they become a possible account, there starts much discussion of Jewish emancipation abroad and assimilation at home. A copy of Leon Uris's publishing phenomenon *Exodus*, which details the arduous process of creating the State of Israel through a mixture of fictional and real-life characters (and provides a telling thematic backdrop to a story concerned with imprisonment and freedom), is produced at the meeting to underscore the American fascination with Israel and the tourist boom it might beget.

The hope is to turn Haifa into "the Rome of the Middle East," but early on Don has trouble determining the best way to sell it. A country where "women have guns" and that "is filled with Jews" does not immediately spark a creative firestorm ("oh, and let's not forget there are Arabs"), but Don isn't one to retreat from a challenge. Any opportunity to call Rachel Menken (his "favorite" Jew in New York) is one he will seize, but he claims it is all business as he tries to tap her for understanding of Israel and its importance to Jews around the world. Quite eloquently (for someone who claims to be more American than anything else), Rachel outlines the notion of Israel, a country for people who have spent a long time in exile as something that just "has to be."

Exiles from the Sterling Cooper offices — namely women — are drafted to help sample products for a stilted lipstick line called Belle Jolie. While this results in an essential moment for Peggy, it is preceded by a creepy scene of the Sterling Cooper men watching the women pucker-up through one-way glass. It is a note-perfect display of the voyeuristic "male gaze" theory forwarded by film professor Laura Mulvey (influenced by, among others, Sigmund Freud and Jacques Lacan). The peep show ambience of the ad men watching the office "girls" try on lipsticks lacks only crumpled dollar bills thrown at the women to complete the portrait. The focus group ends with Peggy presenting her "basket of kisses," which starts a career ascent that will chip away at the patriarchal structure of the office. That

John Slattery on the set with director Andrew Bernstein.
(AP Photo/Damian Dovarganes)

this slip through the looking glass from steno pool to creative force is preceded by Mulvey's "gaze" is another display of the deft dramatic irony at work throughout the series.

This is a deceptively important episode for other women of *Mad Men*. Joan Holloway shows that not only can she navigate the treacherous canopy of the office jungle with *élan*, but that she is also more pragmatic than Roger Sterling, whose impetuous desire to leave his wife she skewers with ease. Betty Draper is shown as a fully sexual woman, divulging her encompassing desire for Don in a manner that vaults past earlier impressions of her as a girl in woman's clothing. Rachel Menken shows the full breadth of her education by lecturing wordsmith Don about the origins of the words *Zion* and, with full pathos, *utopia* (which, depending on its pronunciation, means either "the good place" or "the place that cannot be"). She also allows for the full complication of her feelings for Don and all the trouble acting on them might cause. Midge, Don's free-spirited mistress, even introduces a rival for her affections in the grubby Village artist Roy; apparently the fuzzy borders of an illicit affair are too constricting for her.

The most important character development is, of course, Peggy's. The unexpected opportunity to write copy for the Belle Jolie account is nothing short of miraculous and her abilities flabbergast boozy Fred Rumsen ("It was like watching a dog play a piano"). That this career prospect arises from her lack of guile is heartening, but flusters those around her — none more than Joan. Her wordless parting from Roger Sterling at episode's end (part of a haunting montage set to Don MacLean's reworking of an old traditional that provides this episode with a title) is quintessentially bittersweet. They leave the hotel separately, she carrying the cloaked bird cage Roger has given her — a coded suggestion of how he'd like to hold onto her? As they stand on an empty Manhattan sidewalk, the idea of exiles is never more resonant.

While Israel is a country for exiles, Manhattan is a city for them; born elsewhere, its inhabitants travel long distances and tortured trails to reach this Promised Land and often find that the real work starts once they arrive.

The Philosophy of Mad Men — Don Draper: "People want to be told what to do so badly they'll listen to anyone." (Directly or indirectly, this is not the first time Don has alluded to advertising in Third Reich terms.)

Period Moment: Don wrestles with the challenge of turning Haifa into the Rome of the Middle East as much as he grapples to understand the very notion of "Jewishness." While 1960 may seem a delayed response in mulling over the nature of this beleaguered people (with the Second World War ending in 1945 and the State of Israel's declaration of independence in 1948), Rachel Menken mentions the recent capture of a Nazi war criminal in Argentina. This was one development that stoked a renewed interest in all things Israeli.

Adolf Eichmann earned the title "architect of the Holocaust" due to the logistical rigor he brought to forced deportation of Jews into ghettos and concentration camps throughout Nazi-controlled Europe. Once the war tipped over to the Allies, Eichmann hid throughout Germany and Italy before securing an Argentine passport through Alois Hudal, a Franciscan friar who tended the first "ratline" (aptly named escape routes for war criminals fleeing post–Second World War Europe).

A Holocaust survivor spotted Eichmann living in Argentina under the name "Riccardo Klement" and living a quiet life with his family. This information was relayed to Mossad director Isser Harel and a plan was hatched to abduct the war criminal and spirit him to the *Beit Ha'am* (House of the People) to stand trial for his actions.

Psychological evaluations of Eichmann before his trial showed no evidence of anti-Semitism or sociopathic tendencies. While these claims were almost immediately refuted, the notion of a straightlaced bureaucrat enacting horrendous crimes against humanity prompted Hannah Arendt (in her reporting on the trial for the *New Yorker* and her subsequent book *Eichmann in Jerusalem*) to coin the phrase "the banality of evil."

Why would it take the capture of someone like Eichmann to fire interest in "the Jewish Question"? Perhaps the horrors of Dachau and Auschwitz were too difficult for the Western world to immediately comprehend and were submerged by labors toward affluence and success. But if anyone knows that the past doesn't stay buried for long, it's Don Draper.

Manhattan Real Estate: Rachel returns Don's entreaty for drinks with a "lunch . . . Tea Room at the Pierre."

Now known as the Taj Pierre (Fifth Avenue at Sixty-first Street), the five-star hotel's Rotunda offers a full menu along with their famous traditional English tea. The Rotunda features trompe l'oeil murals by American painter Edward Melcarth, but rest assured, that smoking is no longer allowed.

Ad Pitch: There appears to be no Olympic Cruise Lines in existence, but the push for tourism by the Israeli Department of Tourism is valid. Other than the Eichmann arrest, Leon Uris's novel about the creation of the State of Israel hit bookshelves in 1958 and became a bestselling phenomenon. Uris sold film rights in advance of publication and in 1960 Paul Newman starred in the Otto Preminger–directed adaption.

Cocktail of Note: In an effort to set the tone of "a land of exotic luxury," Roger Sterling serves Mai Tai's at the Israel Tourism Board meeting. Many lay claim to inventing this drink, but most concede that Victor "Trader Vic" Bergeron Jr. created it at the Oakland Polynesian-style restaurant that bore his name. According to *Trader Vic's Bartender's Guide* (a bible of sorts for this section of the episode guides), Mr. Bergeron states that "Anybody who says I didn't create this drink is a dirty stinker."

> 1 lime
>
> 1/2 ounce orange curaçao
>
> 1/2 ounce rock candy syrup
>
> 1/2 ounce orgeat syrup (made from almonds, sugar, and rose water or

orange-flower water)

1 ounce dark Jamaican rum

1 ounce Martinique rum

Shake ingredients with ice and strain ito a highball glass with crushed ice. Garnish with mint.

1.07　RED IN THE FACE
. . . .

Original air date: August 23, 2007

Written by: Bridget Bedard

Directed by: Tim Hunter

> "He doesn't even wear a hat!"
>
> — Bertram Cooper, on JFK

The men at Sterling Cooper want to assist Richard Nixon in his bid for the White House, whether the Republican Party wants the help or not. A lonely Roger Sterling invites himself to dinner at the Drapers, and tries to invite himself to something more than a meal. Pete tries to return a duplicated "chip 'n' dip" wedding gift.

Disparities in age and experience are rampant in the Sterling Cooper offices. With a foot still in the 1950s and the student movement a nascent subculture, the balance still tips toward the elders. In a world where those in power resign themselves to the inconsequence of youth, it's hard to imagine anyone truly challenging the old guard.

Throughout "Red in the Face," the notion of proper adult behavior is broached and yet another double standard is revealed. Boys will be boys (as Pete mentions when brandishing his wedding gift exchange at the office) and it is tolerated; similar behavior in women is frowned upon (psychiatrist Dr. Wayne suggests to Don that Betty's anxieties spring from "the emotions of a child"). This is even more ironic given that men of the time worked hard to keep decision-making clout from women and rendered them as powerless as children.

The equation of women as children, and the negative connotation that only applies to that gender, is rife throughout this episode. Don (perhaps emboldened by the psychiatric evaluation) suggests that his marriage is like "living with a little girl," but this only comes out when Betty defuses his rising anger with a knowing taunt ("You want to bounce me off the walls? Will that make you feel better?"). However, Betty is less sanguine when confronted by Helen for giving Glen a lock of her hair. Betty hasn't thought of the gesture as inappropriate, as an adult acting like a child, and is flustered when Helen admonishes her ("What is wrong with you?"). Betty may be confused, but most would agree that Helen is entitled to her outrage.

Roger Sterling's sense of entitlement — because of his company, his war record, his impeccable silver hair — allows him to overreach himself twice in this episode. His wife away for the weekend (and Joan unwilling), Roger casts about for a playmate and lands one in poor Don Draper. Not only does Roger make him late for dinner at home, he tags along, drinks Don's vodka, and makes a sloppy pass at Betty. That Roger manages to keep his head up high while offering Don a half-assed apology ("At some point, we've all tried to park in the wrong garage") is galling enough. He even owns up to the sense of entitlement that a man can have when his name is on the building. But admitting to a flaw is not the same as trying to correct it, and Roger invokes his name's placement when he and Don are late for a meeting with Richard Nixon's people.

Pete Campbell shows little concern for the duplicated wedding gift of a chip 'n' dip, particularly when he exchanges it for a rifle. More shocking than the cavalier manner in which he trains the sights on women in the office (given the rise of workplace shootings over the years) is the frontiersman fantasy he tells Peggy after his wife derides him for bringing home a useless "toy" (another reference to an adult acting like a child). It is not the first time Pete has displayed such outdoorsman inclinations (remember his short story about the hunter and what the hunter *imagines* the bear is thinking?), but perhaps the first time that such a story has resulted in a sexual charge. After hearing it, Peggy wanders around the office in a flushed daze that can only be quelled by a ham sandwich and a cherry Danish.

Roger Sterling, Bertram Cooper, and Don Draper seem to think the idea of a Kennedy presidency is the result of a similar daze. They stomp on Pete's suggestion of Kennedy as a worthy adversary with such disdain ("Now, if the adults can weigh in?") that one almost feels bad for the shamed kid. Before long, however, the old guard will be eating their hats and the opinions of someone like Pete will suddenly take on a great deal of weight.

That is to say that before long, there will be a long line of red faces in and around Sterling Cooper: none more so than Roger, from the embarrassment at his transgression with Betty, to say nothing of his flushed face from climbing all those stairs, and the shame at vomiting on the shoes of visiting Republicans; Peggy's sexual charge from Pete's survivalist fantasy; and Helen Bishop's face slapped warm by Betty's hand.

Perhaps this episode is also about the rush of blood in the cheeks that a child feels when caught in a lie by a parent. Or in the case of the kids at Sterling Cooper, like a kid who misbehaves and waits for punishment that never arrives.

The Philosophy of *Mad Men* — Roger Sterling: "America does not want some greasy kid with his finger on the button."

Period Moment: The Drapers' neighbor Francine Hanson smokes continually throughout her pregnancy. It is a shocking sight, but not that uncommon in an era where medical testimonials in cigarette advertising had *just* come to an end.

Dr. Leila Daughtry-Denmark became one of the first pediatricians to raise the health concerns of childhood exposure to cigarette smoke with the publication of *Every Child Should Have a Chance* in 1971. She denounced the consumption of caffeine and alcohol during pregnancy, and had her doubts about the positive effect of cow's milk. In particular, she thought that tobacco use could seriously damage a child's long-term health in a time when anti-smoking campaigns were unknown. It has since become accepted wisdom that children of smoking mothers are twice as likely to die from Sudden Infant Death Syndrome, and are at a higher risk to develop chronic health concerns such as asthma, learning disabilities, and behavioral problems.

Known almost as well for her adherence to a strict health and diet regiment, Dr. Daughtry-Denmark turned 111 years old on February 1, 2009, and was awarded super-centenarian standing.

Manhattan Real Estate: Paul Kinsey announces a day's-end trip to Chumley's along with Ken Cosgrove, published author.

Opened as a speakeasy in the 1920s, the clandestine nature of the outfit was underlined by a shadowy, unmarked entrance. Word of police sniffing about for Prohibition breakers would often arrive ahead of a planned bust, to which customers were compelled to "eighty-six" the joint. Many believe that this effort to elude arrest through the unmarked entrance of 86 Bedford led to the creation of the term "eighty-six" meaning to get rid of something or to hide.

After Prohibition, Chumley's became famous as a haunt for some of Gotham's literary elite. The Friends of Libraries USA laid a plaque at the bar September 22, 2000, heralding Chumley's as:

> A celebrated haven frequented by poets, novelists, and playwrights, who helped define twentieth-century American literature. These writers include Willa Cather, E. E. Cummings, Theodore Dreiser, William Faulkner, Ring Lardner, Edna St. Vincent Millay, Eugene O'Neill, John Dos Passos, and John Steinbeck.

Framed book jackets of works from authors who frequented Chumley's crowded the walls for years until the structural collapse of the chimney in April 2007 prompted the closure of the bar. Developers razed the building and reconstruction has started along with the promise of a rebuilt Chumley's open for literary barflies for the new century.

Ad Pitch: Political advertising in the broadcast age started with the 1924 contest between Democrat John W. Davis and Republican Calvin Coolidge. Both parties spent money on radio time (for speeches, not ads) with the winning Republicans outspending the losing Democrats three times over. In 1928, Democrats allowed New York Governor Al Smith to announce his ill-fated presidential candidacy on a new fangled contraption called television. The broadcast spanned fifteen miles from Albany to Schenectady but had little impact on a population that had yet to adopt the seductive new technology.

By 1960, television returned the favor of early adoption by the Democratic Party in effectively tipping the scales in the presidential contest between Richard Nixon and John F. Kennedy. The radio audience for the debates knighted Nixon the winner, but his wan performance under the glare of TV studio lights, particularly next to the robust Kennedy (dubbed by one Nixon aide "the Bronze Warrior"), helped to seal the vice president's fate.

The Nixon camp flirts with Sterling Cooper for much of season 1, but in truth Nixon formed his own advertising company called Campaign Associates. Carroll Newton (responsible for the campaign's slogan "They Understand What Peace Demands") and Ted Rogers (Nixon's chief debate negotiator and "Bronze Warrior" phrase-coiner) ran this one-purpose ad firm. Both worked hard to proclaim Nixon's credentials to the American public with proposed ads that would underscore his lengthy public service and foreign policy experience that clearly out-classed the green congressman from the state of Massachusetts.

Nixon declined. He wanted to avoid spending great deals of money on an advertising campaign, and, more important, wanted to avoid *looking* like a spendthrift. According to Newton and Rogers, the attendance of H. R. Haldeman in the campaign resulted in a troubling insularity. Efforts by Newton and Rogers to convince Nixon how integral their multi-pronged approach (including a documentary about Nixon and his family, another spot highlighting his dealings with Soviet leader Nikita Khrushchev, and another attacking Kennedy's spotty voting record in Congress) went unheeded.

Instead, Nixon opted for direct camera appeals that were unscripted and squeezed into his hectic campaign schedule. Given the hurried nature of their production, Nixon spoke with great insight and coherence regarding foreign and domestic policy. Given the kinetic nature of television, the ads were a dull, boring disaster.

Cocktail of Note: Don keeps pace with Roger at their oyster lunch, and even abandons his "beloved rye" for his boss's favored martinis:

> 1 1/2 ounces gin
> 1/2 ounce French vermouth
> 1 dash orange bitters
> Stir with ice and strain into a chilled cocktail glass. Float a stuffed olive on top.
> For a dry martini, substitute Italian for French vermouth, shave off a 1/2 ounce of gin and serve with a pearl onion. Do NOT consume with large quantities of oysters or before an unexpected aerobic workout.

What Are They Smoking?

The amount of cigarette smoke blown throughout the entire series was one of the first things that shocked viewers of the show, reminding people that there was a time when smoking wasn't banned from every public space. Another question that followed quickly on the heels of that was: Are the cast members *really* smoking? The answer is yes — just not tobacco.

The clouds of atmospheric smoke that thickens the air at Sterling Cooper are provided by herbal cigarettes, which do not contain any nicotine. The upside? Everyone in the cast can look suave without worrying about lung cancer (although many believe that inhaling smoke of *any* kind is inadvisable). The downside? The taste, which Jon Hamm likens to "a mixture between pot and soap."

1.08 THE HOBO CODE

Original air date: September 6, 2007
Written by: Chris Provenzano
Directed by: Phil Abraham

> "1. Decide your own life, don't let another person run or rule you."
> — Congress of the Hoboes of America, August 8, 1894

Pete and Peggy collide once again, despite his best efforts to be a respectable married man. Peggy's copy is pitched to the Belle Jolie people. Memories of Don's unhappy childhood break through the wall he has erected around his adult life.

Codes of conduct, codes of language, and codes of behavior . . . they're all dissected in "The Hobo Code."

An early morning office tryst between Pete and Peggy continues what began on the night of his bachelor party. While Pete can only prattle on about his wife (perhaps not the most charming pillow talk available), Peggy seems the more mature of the two (chalk up another one for the women). She seems to hold no illusions about what their coupling means, and, for all her naiveté, is adept at smoothing her transition into the awakening office after the impromptu rendezvous. She not only thinks to cradle a file folder as she exits Pete's office so as not to arouse suspicion, but tells a successful lie about her ripped blouse to king of the liars, Don Draper.

Peggy also has a good handle on the codes of language in the office; her copy for Belle Jolie lipstick is also a success. At first, it looks as if she will be exempt from the post-meeting celebrations, but is quickly brought "into the room" with the creative team and offered the highest indicator of acceptance — a belt of rye. The other women in the office are genuinely happy for Peggy's success, but Joan can't help herself and gives the backhanded comment, "I'm glad your other work was suffering for a reason." Status is of primary concern to Joan and the possible meteoric rise of another woman threatens her place, particularly in a realm in which she cannot compete.

Meanwhile, Don tries to decipher the meaning behind Bertram Cooper's left-field bonus of $2,500. The curiously shoeless second half of the agency name says that it is merely an attempt to measure the importance of Don's work with the agency. But he seems almost more intent on discussing Ayn Rand's *Atlas Shrugged*, not only as a swath of common ground between the two ("completely self-interested") but a recommendation on how to spend $1.99 of his bonus.

Suave, debonair, and plainly gay (from a twenty-first-century perspective, at least), Salvatore Romano glides through the office composed and apparently full of Italian brio. From the first episode, however, he fires off a contrasting mix of bullish straight-guy bluster and sly comments that hint at his true nature. Homosexuality in an office of the 1960s would have been an untenable position, so the desperate attempts to hide this important aspect of his life are understandable but tragic.

One of the Belle Jolie executives drops coded hints when he rhapsodizes about the Roosevelt Hotel bar, messages that Salvatore follows for a drink. A dinner follows and as furtive words give way to a blatant pass, the heretofore unflappable Salvatore becomes flustered. He becomes indignant when the executive works the "what's to worry about" angle. Salvatore has worked hard to achieve his success and is desperate to protect the life he's created.

Sound familiar?

Don's attempt to divine Midge's signals also results in frustration.

Despite what is clear to anyone, namely that Midge and Roy are an item, Don cannot see it until captured in a Polaroid. Despite the gates of his past being opened by joining in with the bohemians ("We're going to get high and listen to Miles" — cue flashback) and his understanding of symbols given to him by the hobo from his memory (and perhaps his love of writing?), Don can't help but skewer the contradictions of his Greenwich Village lover. She never wants to make plans, but when he attempts to spend his $2,500 on an impulsive trip to Paris, she balks.

Even the agreed-upon lexicon of an illicit affair can't be trusted, it seems.

The Philosophy of *Mad Men* — Don Draper: "The universe is indifferent."
Period Moment: Bertram Cooper extols the virtues of Ayn Rand's *Atlas Shrugged* when handing Don an unexpected (and pre-emptive?) bonus check. Cooper believes that he and Don are alike, that they are "completely self-interested."

In *Atlas Shrugged*, Dagny Taggart struggles to keep the family railway company running in an economy stagnating due to collectivist government policies that seem to herald the mediocre and punish the true creators. At the same time, she notices that captains of industry and innovation are disappearing from the world, and that the mysterious John Galt is collecting these leaders of the corporate world in a general "strike" against a society that inhibits advancement and protects parasitical "moochers and looters."

Ayn Rand's libertarian manifesto is a bible of sorts for the philosophy known as objectivism. As a novel, *Atlas Shrugged* met with a similar critical indifference. Her previous novel, *The Fountainhead*, also reviewed poorly but sold in excess of 400,000 copies. As a result, *Atlas Shrugged* had a first printing of 100,000 copies, an amazing number in 1957, the year of its publication, and due to the novel's length, which was over 1,100 pages.

Rand espoused "rational self-interest," a flavor of unfettered, hard-hearted capitalism that made many conservatives blanch. Laissez-faire capitalism makes for the ideal society, Rand contended, although a true version has never been attempted. Altruism (or "forced self-sacrifice") is thought of as unnatural and corrosive to the fabric of such a society, one that engenders throngs of "looters and moochers."

The setting of *Atlas Shrugged* is just such a world order, one felled by a widening disappearance of industrialists and inventors. An answer to the question "Who is John Galt?" leads the enigmatic hero to make clear Rand's principal upset at the twentieth century — that unproductive, slack-jawed yahoos can benefit from the fruits of innovators and giants, to say nothing of hiding behind laws that punish the very industrial titans who create while they merely "mooch."

The use of narrative to convey ideology was around long before Rand descended on a typewriter. But to use a medium meant to entertain as a soapbox strikes me as more than a little megalomaniacal, particularly in the ham-handed talents of Rand. To quote an old Hollywood maxim: "If you want to send a message, use Western Union."

In fact, *Atlas Shrugged* exists less as a novel and more as a dogmatic tract with characters representing broad ideas, or expressing them as in the famous "This is John Galt Speaking . . ." section of the book. The mysterious Galt, ostensible hero of the piece and heart of the "men of the mind" strike, speaks for almost sixty pages about the conditions that have led to the need for a philosophical discipline such as objectivism (a speech that, if performed, would take over three hours).

But the correlation between John Galt and Don Draper is a valid one. A man predisposed to "rational self-interest" might likely say "I'm living my life like there's no tomorrow because there isn't." And the mythology that builds up around John Galt through Rand's tract is mirrored by the story that has added to the Don Draper mythos, namely that he once held a timid account out a window by the ankles to persuade him of the merits of a campaign idea.

Yet Don has an altruistic side, such as putting his weight behind Peggy's move to copywriting, that softens more ruthless acts that he commits in the name of business or protecting his secrets. And this is why Don Draper is a compelling character, and not just a mouthpiece.

Manhattan Real Estate: The gang heads to P.J. Clarke's to celebrate Peggy's copywriting success (and mid-afternoon departure of Cooper, Sterling, and Draper from the office).

Occupying the northeast corner of Fifty-fifth Street since the late 1800s, P.J. Clarke's (915 Third Avenue) has been a saloon of enduring presence on the New York landscape. In fact, the brown-brick two-story all but hollers its history to passersby, dwarfed as it is by a gray forty-five-story skyscraper.

Known for the consistent quality of their hamburgers and the celebrity clientele, P.J. Clarke's opened another three locations in Manhattan: Sidecar (in truth, a private dining area on the second floor of the Fifty-fifth Street

Building), P.J. Clarke's on the Hudson, and another in Lincoln Square. Luminaries such as Richard Harris, songwriter Johnny Mercer (who wrote "One More for My Baby" while perched at the bar), Jackie Kennedy Onassis, and Nat "King" Cole frequented the saloon over the years, but their biggest return customer was Frank Sinatra. "Owner" of Table 20 and beloved by the waitstaff (that is to say, a generous tipper), Sinatra may have hit all the top night spots in New York, but he always wound up at P.J. Clarke's.

Ad Pitch: Belle Jolie has many true-life echoes, but almost as interesting in this episode is the artwork produced by Salvatore and the two-man art department at Sterling Cooper.

The graphic that accompanies "Mark Your Man" seems a little out of step with the times of the series. But perhaps we should trust in the show and see it as an indication that this ad firm has more of a foot in the '50s than the '60s, one that is more "traditional" (as Lily Meyer from the Israeli Ministry of Tourism states in "Babylon").

If you recall, the artwork in the Belle Jolie ad is prim and restrained, more at home in a department store catalog than in a national ad campaign. There is much reminiscent of magazine illustrators like Lynn Buckham's work for Pepsi or favored "glamour" artists Joe De Mers and Joe Bowler from the Charles E. Cooper Studio; the kind of work easily at home on the cover of *Collier's Weekly* or *Good Housekeeping*. These were illustrations that were fresh and fun and refracted through a prism of Norman Rockwell–inspired Americana.

The modernist and constructivist trends apparent elsewhere (Paul Rand, Herbert Bayer, and the legendary Saul Bass) seem to have no place on the easels in Salvatore's art department. This is not so much an anachronism than a red flag signaling changing times; and those who toil in Sterling Cooper may not be prepared for the shift.

Cocktail of Note: While dodging coded passes from the Belle Jolie executive in the Roosevelt Hotel, Salvatore keeps it in the family and sips a fine Italian sambuca. Made from star anise and white elder flowers, sambuca is a digestif meant to aide in the digestion of a meal.

The recipe for a Sambuca Con Mosca is straightforward:
> sambuca served neat (as is the case with most digestifs)
> 3 coffee beans
> Place beans in the glass. These beans are often ornamental, but chewing is said to enhance the flavor of the liquor.

Before Sterling Cooper —
Recommended Viewing:
Delbert Mann's *Lover Come Back*

Of all Matthew Weiner's suggested inspirations, Delbert Mann's *Lover Come Back* (1961) bears the most direct connection to the world of *Mad Men*. Both share the environment of early 1960s Madison Avenue, and even some similar dynamics between characters. But *Mad Men* is an elegant drama with a wicked sense of humor, while *Lover Come Back* is a piffling romantic comedy. If they were champagne, one would be the full-bodied alcohol while the other would be the effervescence. A simple open and shut case. Or is it?

There is no doubt that this second pairing of Rock Hudson and Doris Day (after *Pillow Talk*, both with perennial third wheel Tony Randall) is a lighthearted jaunt around the battle of the sexes that no one would confuse for Noël Coward, but there is a surprising sophistication to the story that feels ahead of its time. Whether an effort to reflect the temper of the times or a prurient appeal to the television-stunned masses, the themes touched on in *Lover Come Back* are a little more grown up than the standard romantic comedy fare (veiled jokes at the expense of Rock Hudson's sexual orientation aside). Oh, there's a last minute marriage proposal all right, but instead of on a rain-swept Parisian night it happens while doctors whisk the woman down a hospital hallway to give birth.

Noël Coward never wrote an ending like that.

When ethics-free ad man Jerry Webster (Rock Hudson) successfully plies the president of a big account with booze and girls he raises the ire of Carol Templeton (Doris Day), an account executive at a rival Manhattan agency. When Webster shoots an ad for a fictitious product to cover his tracks with an Advertising Council hearing prompted by Templeton's complaints, these ads mistakenly slip onto the air and create an immediate consumer demand. Now Webster has to create a product to fill this demand, and, while trying to shake Templeton's surveillance of his movements (she wants to land the mysterious "Vips" account and even the score), Webster assumes the identity of reclusive chemist Dr. Linus Tyler (all the better to keep tabs on *her* intentions). Naturally, Templeton tries to woo Dr. Tyler to her agency, spends much time with the doctor, and falls in love.

Assumed identities are revealed, hilarity ensues.

The prevailing view of the advertising industry as haven for crapulent, hedonistic playboys is confirmed in the character of Jerry Webster. A leering embodiment of every loathsome characteristic you'd expect to find in an alpha male executive (vain, manipulative, priapic, boastful), Hudson plays Webster with an offhanded charm that indicates these tics have become cliché for a reason. There is great concern for ethics, however, both as a standard by which to live (in the case of Carol Templeton) or a disciplinary board to be feared (for Webster). While the Advertising Council is no match for the lies concocted by Webster or the introduction of his nebulous "Vips" product (a pastille that tastes like candy but packs the wallop of a triple martini), the concern for professional behavior feels genuine. As played by Doris Day, Carol Templeton is the incarnation of the Protestant work ethic in a sybaritic universe (or, as the film puts it, "worker" bee to Hudson's "drone"), but she doesn't come across as a peevish wet blanket. In fact, she is the audience's entrée to this world and meant to reflect the moral belief in professional due diligence that is admirable and (according to the filmmakers) wholly American. Why else should we join in Templeton's outrage over Webster's indolent yet successful tactics?

Even more interesting is the ambivalence with which the film treats Templeton's role as a female account executive at a Madison Avenue ad firm. Other than Webster's presumption that early spinsterhood is a natural byproduct of career success, Templeton's gender causes little excitement.

However, Mann and screenwriters Stanley Shapiro and Paul Henning reserve their spite for another timely phenomenon, analysis. Along with the mainstream acceptance of therapy was a strong undertow of suspicion, a belief that psychoanalysis was merely another form of parlor game, one sitting room removed from mesmerism. And while this view is prevalent in the world and characters of *Mad Men*, it is treated with a great deal of respect with regard to Betty Draper and her evolving self-awareness. For the team behind this movie, it is little more than a recurring joke. In fact, the only character to indulge in this quackery is Webster's brittle boss Peter Ramsey (Tony Randall). Not only does this morose milquetoast suffer from ridiculous expectations from his father (despite the fact that the "Commodore" has been dead for years), Ramsey is the only sort of rich kid wastrel who could consider burning his inherited money on such a fool's errand.

A spiteful subtext warrants mention, as I think it is more than just eagle-eyed hindsight. The true nature of Rock Hudson's sexuality was one of the worst kept secrets in Hollywood. And while this was a time when gossip magazines worked in concert with the studios to create the image required for their stars, word about Hudson's homosexuality leaked out of the closet and across America. On the surface, attempts were made to reaffirm Hudson's manliness (which, circa 1962, equaled "heterosexual"), from an arranged marriage to on-screen exploits summarized by the celebrated conquests of one Jerry Webster. But many sly jokes appear in *Lover Come Back* that must have made Hudson cringe in his more private moments: the wan "mass of neuroses" that is the Dr. Linus Tyler he creates; Day's sales pitch on a brief stay in her guest room, which has "your own back entrance"; or the sight of him dressed in nothing but a woman's fur coat (as a result of the ensuing hilarity), which prompts a man to remark, "He's the last guy I would've figured." The script attempts adult sophistication that often works, but when it comes to the thought of such "aberrant" behavior, particularly in the life of a hunky leading man, American film-makers (and audiences, one guesses) were ill-prepared to embrace a sophistication so *European*.

For *Mad Men* fans, there are a few echoes in this film but only one true similarity, to my mind. Certainly there is a vivacious redhead in the bur-lesque dancer Rebel Davis (Edie Adams), but her willingness to suffer the manipulations of men in the film would make Joan Holloway wrinkle her nose with disdain. And even though the set decoration by Oliver Emert is a gleaming primary color marvel, the up-to-the-secondness of it (Webster's space-age bachelor pad has a hi-fi . . . *in the couch!*) dates it badly, whereas an attempt by Matthew Weiner and Dan Bishop to mix elements from before their milieu and current styles as well lends the series a reasonable air of verisimilitude and timelessness (people in the '60s didn't *only* have furniture from the '60s, after all).

The dynamic between hotshot Jerry Webster and Peter Ramsey does feel reminiscent of the one between Don Draper and Roger Sterling. The friendship and occasional inversion of roles between a lower ranking exec-utive and the agency owner by way of inheritance offers a rich relationship to explore, although the similarities end there. Draper would elbow Webster in a bar for his view of advertising, in particular the use of sex (Webster's declaration that with a "well-stacked dame in a bathing suit, I'll sell aftershave to beatniks" would make Draper choke on his Old

Fashioned), and war vet Sterling wouldn't waste the breath needed to insult Ramsey's reliance on analysis (other than perhaps offering a cigarette cloud exhalation of "Boo-hoo").

In the end, what is shared is a great sense of environment — advertising in general and Madison Avenue in particular — and that makes for great complementary viewing.

1.09 SHOOT
· · · · · · · · · · ·

Original air date: September 13, 2007
Written by: Chris Provenzano, Matthew Weiner
Directed by: Paul Feig

> "In order to be truly beautiful you must study yourself and decide what kind of woman you are . . . are you the sultry type, the tall, languid type, or the vivid dynamic type? Perhaps yours is the wholesome-American-girl kind of beauty, or the pale, ash-blond, fragile kind. You must decide now, and plan your makeup, your hair, and your wardrobe to enhance this style . . ."
> — "How to Look Halfway Decent," by Elinor Goulding Smith, *McCall's*, February 1959

An executive at a rival advertising house tries to woo Don to the larger, international agency, attempting to seal the deal by reactivating Betty's long dormant modeling career.

The birds are back, hovering overhead *Mad Men* like a cloud of seagulls warning of coming storms.

At first, they appear hopeful as the neighbor's homing pigeons circle around the Draper home on Bullet Park Drive. They are so lovely they make little Sally Draper clutch her heart, but Betty can only crane her neck and appreciate their grace in flight.

Even more hopeful is the potential of a release from the bleak and limiting role as the Happy Housewife that Betty receives in the form of an overture to return to modeling. Sure, it feels like an afterthought of Jim Hobart in his effort to woo Don away from Sterling Cooper to the "big leagues" of McCann Erickson. But Betty could easily miss Hobart's true intent as she is an undeniably fresh-faced beauty, easily a "Grace Kelly" type,

Jon Hamm on Don Draper: "I think he loves Betty. He just doesn't have a clue how to be vulnerable, how to show it." (AP Photo/Chris Pizzello)

and she did model before marriage. The hope for a return to a life outside of laundry and cooking is enough to obscure her vision, even if it only seems to sharpen Don's.

"The problem that has no name," as Betty Friedan tagged the malaise that affected housewives in the '50s and '60s, is the very essence of Betty Draper's struggle. While men were boxed in by the hollow victory of "happiness" as defined by stature and materialism, women found themselves pushed into a different corner. Much is rightly made of the role women played in sustaining a workforce depleted by wartime service, there is much to suggest that women were already reaching toward a more equitable place in society.

As Friedan states in her epochal work *The Feminine Mystique* (see page 94), stories that filled women's magazines in the years leading up to the Second World War featured all manner of women taking flight in their careers and without sacrificing a rich romantic life. There was also a correspondent surge in women who sought and attained high education. But then, things changed. After the war, men returned to their stateside posts in factories and offices and by all accounts, most women simply returned to the home. As Friedan notes, stories in women's magazines shifted to an overwhelmingly domestic angle, blotting out discourse on politics, art, science, or any sort of rarefied thought.

The immediate response today might be to investigate the editorial boards of such magazines, and as you might imagine, at that time they were primarily held by men. Which is why the ennui housewives such as Betty Draper suffered is even more stinging than that which the men endure. While the men find that what they've been taught to believe is success in fact empties instead of fills their hearts, women have not only been told that what they once sought is no longer possible but downright unwomanly. Add to that the hurt that men are responsible for pushing women down, putting them "in their place" so to speak, and it's no wonder that women like Betty Draper would become consumed with anxiety attacks between daytime errands.

When Don decides to stick with Sterling Cooper (not until leveraging it for a steep pay hike, that is), Betty's modeling work with McCann Erickson dries up. And while it is true that Don rejects the offer after looking at photos from Betty's modeling shoot, it's hard to believe that he turned down Hobart's advance simply in an effort to short-circuit her career dreams, although it could be viewed as a desired side effect on Don's part.

Betty may tell Don that she doesn't want to work, running around Manhattan ("making a fool of myself"), and she might even believe it. But the glimpse she's had of a life of value outside the circle of her apron strings is not one to leave her mind easily.

Keeping this in mind, it is understandable and perhaps even worthy of cheers when Betty, cigarette clamped tight between her lips like a gunslinger, takes a pellet gun into the yard and snipes at the neighbor's fluttering pigeons. If she can't fly, why should they?

The Philosophy of Mad Men — Betty Draper: "[My mother] wanted me to be beautiful so I could find a man . . . there's nothing wrong with that."
Period Moment: When Betty drags Don to the theater, she makes him sit through *Fiorello!*, a little-known musical today that nevertheless won four Tony Awards and was the third musical to be awarded the Pulitzer Prize.

The production dramatizes the life of Fiorello H. LaGuardia through the First World War and his subsequent reign as mayor of New York. "Little Flower," as he was called, campaigned as a Republican reformer who became known for wresting control of New York from the Tammany Hall Political Machine and clearing the corruption from the halls of power.

The musical opened on November 23, 1959 at the Broadhurst Theatre (see below) with Tom Bosley in the title role (*Happy Days*; *Murder, She Wrote*) before it moved to the Broadway Theatre on May 9, 1961. The curtain fell on October 28, 1961, after 795 performances.

While highly regarded at the time, *Fiorello!* has fallen off the American musical repertoire, with the exception of a few regional performances and a 1994 concert presentation of the musical with Jerry Zaks as the diminutive political crusader.

Manhattan Real Estate: Designed by Herbert J. Krapp, the Broadhurst Theatre opened on September 27, 1917, at 235 West Forty-forth Street. The theater was built back-to-back with the Plymouth Theatre (since renamed the Gerald Schoenfeld Theatre) and while they shared nearly identical exteriors, the Broadhurst features elegant Doric columns and a lush lobby mural, while the Plymouth exhibited a more ornate sensibility. Otherwise, Krapp was known for minimal ornamentation and excellent sightlines for these and the thirteen other theater designs that currently operate on Broadway.

Named after British émigré George Howells Broadhurst, and built by legendary Broadway impresarios J. J. and Lee Shubert, this Broadway theater provided Broadhurst with a home to ply his trade as a manager and playwright after managing theaters for the Shuberts around the United States. The first play produced at the theater was George Bernard Shaw's *Misalliance*, but the first of Broadhurst's plays to be staged was *He Didn't Want to Do It* in 1918, followed three years later by his adaptation of *Tarzan of the Apes*.

Throughout the years, popular and important productions have trod the boards at the Broadhurst, including *The Petrified Forest*; *Pal Joey*; *Ten Little Indians*; *Cabaret*; *Play It Again, Sam*; *Kiss of the Spider Woman*; and *Amadeus*. More recently, the building has played host to revivals of *Cat on a Hot Tin Roof* (starring Terrence Howard) and *Equus* (starring Daniel Radcliffe).

Ad Pitch: Don is wooed by Jim Hobarth to step into the big leagues and join him at McCann Erickson.

Formed by the merging of two agencies in 1930, the real McCann Erickson had a global reach even at their inception, with offices in Paris, Berlin, and London. McCann Worldgroup continues to be a major international force in the advertising world today with satellite offices throughout Latin America and Asia Pacific. Clients have included American Airlines, Coca-Cola (as featured in this episode), Unilever, Microsoft, General Motors, and Pfizer. They are perhaps best known for their work for MasterCard, in particular the "Priceless" campaign and the slogan "There are some things in life money can't buy. For everything else, there's MasterCard."

Cocktail of Note: To congratulate Pete Campbell on the Secor Laxative ad buy/Kennedy campaign hip check, Fred Rumsen sends him a bottle of Jack Daniel's ("Unopened! Very nice."). The instantly recognizable square bottle and black label is as totemic a pop culture icon as the Coca-Cola bottle, although the whiskey from Tennessee packs a more significant punch.

How Tall Is the Mayor?

At exactly five feet, Fiorello H. LaGuardia was the shortest man to ever hold the office of the mayor of New York. Abraham D. Beame, who served from 1974 to 1977, came in at five feet two inches. The height of Mayor Michael Bloomberg (sworn in on January 1, 2002) has been the subject of some controversy. While his driver's license claims that he stands at five feet ten inches, his height has been recorded in various New York publications as anywhere between two and four inches shorter.

Before Sterling Cooper —
Recommended Reading:
Betty Friedan's *The Feminine Mystique*

It is hard to imagine North America before the publication of Betty Friedan's seismic bestseller. As an eye-opening investigation into the plight of housewives and the limiting role of life in the home, upon publication, *The Feminine Mystique* forced such cracks in the landscape and profound shifts throughout the following decades that it has since been cited as the start of feminism's Second Wave. It also ranks alongside a few written texts that can truly lay claim to altering the world-view of its readers.

The central thesis of Friedan's examination of the "problem that has no name" — specifically that post–Second World War housewives were forced into subservient roles and soul-sapping work through an absurd ideal of hyper-femininity propagated by women's magazine editors and advertisers

— ignited an immediate debate that raged across the continent and pro-pelled the woman's movement into the radicalized politics of the '70s. Friedan's experience as a writer for those very same magazines may have prompted her to investigate the American periodical's editorial tilt away from strong women creating their own identities, but the impetus for exploring this change came from an exhaustive questionnaire she wrote for a fifteen-year reunion of fellow alumni from Smith College. The responses she received from 200 female graduates alerted her to a dire lack of satisfac-tion among American women that could not be easily dismissed by poor education or low social standing. Once Friedan smelled a story, the journal-istic instinct took over and she followed it through like she would any good lead, knowing that it would resonate with American women who couldn't quite define the ennui that plagued them.

However, while the book spoke to a large segment of the population, it was not without its detractors. Those who found their patriarchal world-view assailed within the covers of Friedan's book found fault not only with the message, but the author's tendency to make broad generalizations, her reliance on specious statistics, and a knack for hyperbole that alone could undercut her intentions.

Many housewives did not identify with Friedan's portrait of a shrink-ing bundle of neuroses who is mortified to fill out a census form as "Occupation: Housewife" and felt that her book diminished the hard work of tending a home and raising a family at best, and at worst excluded them from their share of emancipation. American chronicler of dishpan hands' lighter side, Erma Bombeck, once wrote about the immediate attraction to Friedan's work among her retinue of housewives, only to find the book disparaging of household tasks. "These women," Bombeck wrote about Friedan and her followers, "threw a war for themselves and didn't invite any of us. That was very wrong of them." (Although, this sentiment might have arisen from Friedan's suggestion that even the best and funniest work of the "Housewife Writer" is analogous to that of an "Uncle Tom" — ouch.)

It is tempting to attack Friedan's book for the mishandling of finer points, but it is clear that the redefinition of women's roles — at home and in the workplace — could not have begun without the bold work of *The Feminine Mystique*. Before you can lay an exacting foundation, you are first required to do the blunt work of excavation. And as Betty Draper learns throughout the run of the series — and at least one other character as well

— this sort of hard work only leads to harder work.

Futurist Alvin Toffler famously wrote that Friedan's book "pulled the trigger" on history, but what prompted her to load the gun in the first place? A writer, mother, housewife, and seasoned veteran of the magazine trade, she noticed a strange trend in articles that covered the life of the domestic woman. While columns appeared in *Ladies' Home Journal* and *McCall's* that celebrated the contented mother and wife of suburbia ("Cooking to Me is Poetry"), news reports appeared in the *New York Times* and on CBS Television that reflected a darker, more troubling reality ("The Trapped Housewife").

Friedan conducted an informal survey of articles and stories from 1939 that appeared in publications such as *Good Housekeeping* and *Woman's Home Companion* which revealed that the majority of protagonists featured in their stories were career women with a zest for life and adventure that was enhanced by the love of a man and not impeded or defined by it. Friedan then compared that to the contents of a *McCall's* issue from July 1960 and discovered a pronounced decline. Among the pieces were a glamorous four-page spread on how to "reduce [lose weight] the ways the models do" and a short story about a teenager who doesn't go away to college, but pulls a man out from under a bright college girl.

A startling disparity to be sure, but if the non-scientific approach stirred doubt in her critics, Friedan's reliance on anecdotal evidence also caused great concern. Perhaps Friedan sensed this and decided to front-load her opening chapter with statistics that cataloged the lowering median age for marriage among women, the comparative rate of women and men who attended college, and the increasing percentage of women who dropped out of college to marry — all in the same paragraph. Detractors immediately denounced Friedan's numbers as one-sided or misleading, which is a fair critique of *any* statistical statement, but an argument that misses the point of Friedan's thesis altogether.

More damning was the overall sense of disdain for the housewife that arose out of this seminal work. Certainly Friedan courted misunderstanding (suggesting that the work of an educated housewife is beneath *her*, as opposed to beneath her *skills*, for example) but it seems that the resultant disparagement for homemakers within the woman's movement (or the apparent existence of such a feeling) is more a result of what came after her. Feminists that followed Friedan have harbored a greater animosity toward

Betty Friedan, author of *The Feminine Mystique* and founder of the National Organization for Women, addresses a group in New York on November 21, 1966. (AP Photo)

women working at home than anything displayed by Friedan within the covers of the book that triggered that Second Wave.

What some may have dismissed as part of the fallacious grounding of Friedan's work turns out to be the strongest asset, not only in its continued relevance but as counterpoint to the accepted wisdom of the author's scorn for the housewife. The interpolations of anecdotes from women working in the home (personal and revealing in their admissions due, no doubt, to the anonymity extended by the author) add great weight to Friedan's argument. It is hard to claim women don't feel bound by their limited roles as mother and wife when they say as much time and time again. These first-person anecdotes also display a great deal of empathy on Friedan's part. Not only do these interviews provide the core of her book, she often gives great time and space for these sentiments, refusing to chop them into snippets quoted to support a point but allowing these thoughts to develop unimpeded and in multiple paragraphs; if Friedan can't coach them to sing, she can at least give them the room in which to stretch their voices. In the end, the author reserves her ire for the social and capitalist machinery that has confined them in the home, citing her "stint as a reporter, which taught me how to follow clues to the hidden economic underside of reality." And even if one can see the formulation of this suspicion in Friedan's early involvement with Marxist circles and writing for left-leaning periodicals, her contention that a woman's aspirations are stunted by the "mindlessness" of material acquisition, of "two cars, two TV's, two fireplaces" rings true almost fifty years later (except, perhaps, that it is no longer a gender-specific ailment).

The ultimate affirmation of Friedan's case is borne out in time; even though gender-based discrimination is still a lively force, much of what she argues for — education as empowerment, marriage as partnership, celebration and not derision of career women — is widely accepted as fact or a sensible ideal. And for all the ink spilled about fomentation within the women's movement, and about Friedan's place within it, this does not immediately equal weakness in the argument: what else signifies the intellectual health of a movement than spirited debate among the ranks?

That Friedan herself stated that *The Feminine Mystique* was a "problem of identity" indicates the importance it holds for Matthew Weiner in creating *Mad Men*. As much as Don Draper's search for reconciliation between the man he is, wants to be, and once was, the show is just as concerned with Betty Draper's quest for fulfillment in a world that tells her time and again that she has everything.

A college graduate who once worked as a model, Betty Draper married and started a family at a young age. She is gripped by an unnamable anxiety and a belief that her perfect husband, lovely home, and escalating income are shadowed by a twin existence of a secretive mate, cold house, and empty lifestyle. She fills her hours with shopping, cooking, and chauffeuring the children, but even most of that workload is removed when the Drapers acquire a maid; after that, horseback riding and long lunches can only take up so much of the day. She is a woman of desire, but finds the sporadic attention of her husband inadequate and his duplicity inexplicable.

In almost every way, Betty Draper is the summation of Friedan's book about "the housewife problem." But the character of Peggy Olson occupies a spot in the closing chapter, "A New Life Plan for Women." Friedan counsels women in a few points that don't directly apply to the young copywriter (face the problem, admit that housework is not a creative outlet but a chore that must be done away with quickly and efficiently), but in particular the concern with steps required to make the jump from job to career in a world dominated by men. Friedan suggests that because of the Feminine Mystique, the transition from amateur to professional is the hardest part of breaking through. Despite her steady rise through the ranks, Peggy contends early in her career with patronizing remarks, as if her place in the creative team at Sterling Cooper is nothing but an advertising agency's version of stunt casting. Even when she approaches Roger Sterling in search of proper recognition of her hard work, he finds her "aggressive" behavior "cute."

The search for self through creative work is the recurring motif in *The Feminine Mystique* and while Peggy may have an interesting association with the work, she at least has an easier access to this creative outlet (not to say that it hasn't come without sacrifices). Betty Draper faces a longer road out of her "comfortable concentration camp," but it will make for a more interesting ride for the viewer.

1.10   LONG WEEKEND

Original air date: September 27, 2007
Written by: Bridget Bedard, André and Maria Jacquemetton,
        Matthew Weiner
Directed by: Tim Hunter

> "Oh, please. A white elevator operator?
> And a girl at that? I want to work at that place."
> — Roger Sterling critiques *The Apartment*

Don stays in the city over the holiday weekend. He reluctantly accompanies Roger on a trawling expedition at a double-sided aluminum casting call. Roger oversteps his boundaries to his own detriment.

Roger Sterling has always had a mischievous glint in his eye, maddening and likeable in equal turns. He is also the crown prince of vice in the office, and in the heady (some would say hedonist) world of Madison Avenue in the 1960s, that's saying something. Whether it is drink, smoke, or sex, Roger never met a debauchery he didn't like. But there is something in this episode that is desperate about the urge to satiate, and it is no surprise that there is a price he has to pay for his transgressions. And it is enough to take the gleam out of his eye.

Everything glitters on the surface, like the façade of a crisp Billy Wilder comedy. Joan is resistant to Roger's advances for an open Labor Day weekend, due in large part to *The Apartment*. She is alight with righteous indignation at the treatment of Shirley MacLaine's character, passed among

Christina Hendricks on Slattery as Roger Sterling: "He's got such a sense of humor, and charm . . . that while he's saying these horrible things you can't keep your eyes off him." (AP Photo/Damian Dovarganes)

the callous executives like a dirty joke. Despite the snub, Roger finds a casting call for double-sided aluminum (and the sluggish imagination of Freddy Rumsen's twin girl cattle call) enough to cheer him up.

Wilder also resonates in the episode's title, which echoes the versatile director's alcoholic horror film from 1945, *The Lost Weekend*. (Coincidentally Wilder shot several scenes at the aforementioned P.J. Clarke's.) If Roger has his way the three days will be spent in much the same way, just without the debilitating DTs.

A different sort of delirium is affecting the American electorate. Roger, Don, and the rest of the Sterling Cooper boys fret over the tight race in the polls between Kennedy and Nixon. Other than Pete, no one can see the appeal of a privileged Ivy League boy next to the statesman and war hero who has served the previous eight years as vice president. While the scales have always tipped toward those who served (either in the Second World War or in Korea), the veterans find that the immediate respect afforded men in uniform might be dipping the other way.

The great sacrifice of men and women who serve in war cannot be overstated, but men like Roger who treat it as a twenty-year "shore leave" can be seen as doing a disservice to the uniform. The temper of the times also suggests that the designate "war hero" is losing some of its cachet. Perhaps too much time has been spent away from war for people to appreciate the gift given to them by the military. When President Eisenhower (himself a decorated general, lest we forget) can think of nothing positive to say about Nixon, this seems to effectively put a nail in the coffin of the returning soldier mystique, to say nothing of his underling's presidential hopes.

Don has a difficult time with Roger's heart attack and subsequent vulnerability ("Do you believe in energy . . . a soul?" Roger asks him). But he seems to have an even rougher time when he watches footage of President Eisenhower's notorious press conference flub. He flees the hospital and seeks refuge in the arms of Rachel Menken, who seems the only one able to help Don properly assimilate the confirmation of mortality; he tries with Betty, but she can only talk about her late mother and father's embarrassing behavior with his new girlfriend. It's hard to know which is more shocking: Don's vulnerability with Rachel, divulging the biographical details of his youth — particularly that his mother was a prostitute who died giving birth to him and having been raised by his biological father and his wife — or how Don's perfectly styled hair is in a symbolically tangled mess.

As played by John Slattery, Roger Sterling has been an enjoyable, scurrilous rake up until this point. This makes his fright at the prospect of death, and tears in the arms of his wife and daughter, even more heartbreaking. Until this episode, Roger has stood for the unrestrained id of the post–Second World War American male; from here on, he looks as fragile as a wounded bird.

In the end, what starts in this episode as a hymn to giving into vices turns into a cautionary tale about the legacy such weakness can produce. And whether it is Roger's heart attack, or the extra-marital interests of Don (a man born of relenting to a desire), "Long Weekend" is about the cost it can wreak upon those who give in and the people around them.

The Philosophy of *Mad Men* — Roger Sterling: "Being with a client is like being in a marriage: sometimes you get into it for the wrong reasons and eventually they hit you in the face."
Period Moment: Betty urges her diabetic father to doctor his coffee with saccharin pills instead of sugar. This sugar substitute was first discovered in

1879 and used to supplement shortages of the crystalline sweetener during both world wars, but also as an effective preservative.

Saccharin became popular in the 1950s and 1960s not only as a safe sweetener for diabetics but also as a useful weight control device. The Food and Drug Administration amended the Food, Drug and Cosmetic Act in 1958 to demand premarket approval for substances created prior to the year of the act's alteration. Those products "generally recognized as safe" or GRAS were not subject to such scrutiny and, as such, saccharin remained available to consumers.

In the early 1970s, the FDA started testing substances granted the GRAS status to ascertain their true safety. When tests conducted through 1972 and 1973 led to a link between saccharin use and increased bladder cancer in laboratory rats, the FDA raised a red flag. While they sorted through test data, some of which indicated that impurities were to blame for the cancer, a Canadian study conducted in 1977 ruled out the impurities argument and stated that the link between saccharin and bladder cancer was "convincing." Banned in Canada, a similar prohibition suggested that year by the U.S. Congress met with a public outcry, presumably by diabetics and weight watchers who had grown accustomed to the zero calorie sweeteners.

Saccharin is a banned substance in Canada to this day. And yet in 2000, the United States Congress repealed the law requiring a health warning label to accompany all saccharin products.

Ad Pitch: Pete Campbell delights in passing the bad news to Don about losing the Dr. Scholl's account, relaying the client's review of the creative as "dull and humorless." The Exercise Sandal that Don disparages was first introduced in 1959 and quickly became an iconic fixture in the Dr. Scholl's product line. Celebrity devotees such as Twiggy and Jean Shrimpton cemented the sandal's fashion-forward status.

Speaking of dull and humorless, a print ad of the time created excitement in the marketplace with this kind of riveting copy: "Scholl's quiet revolution makes profitable chemist's lines out of leisure footwear." Zing!

Cocktail of Note: Roger Sterling's heart attack may not have been caused by his heroic consumption of alcohol (although it couldn't have helped — along with the recreational sex and all that cream and butter), but upon admission to a hospital in 1960, he might very well have been served an altogether different kind of cocktail.

Glucose-Insulin-Potassium therapy, or GIK (the chemical element for potassium is *K*), is a treatment for myocardial infarction pioneered at the time. Despite falling out of favor shortly thereafter, it was revisited in the late 1990s as an inexpensive method of arresting the damage of a heart attack and reducing the mortality rate by providing "metabolic support to the ischemic myocardium."

Before Sterling Cooper — Recommended Viewing: Billy Wilder's *The Apartment*

The perks at insurance giant Consolidated Life of New York are considerable, provided you are a high-ranking executive. Or, if you are C. C. Baxter (Premium Accounting Division, desk 861, take-home pay $94.70 a week) and are willing to lend out your apartment to upper management for extra-marital trysts, then you might expect to partake of some fringe benefits.

Billy Wilder's *The Apartment* offers many such benefits to viewers. It is a film that chronicles the business world and romantic entanglements of New York in 1960, and while it is very much of its time the film is smart, funny, and human enough to feel timeless.

C. C. Baxter (Jack Lemmon) is a clerk at the huge New York insurance firm Consolidated Life. He toils at his desk by day, nurtures a crush on the sweet elevator operator, Fran (Shirley MacLaine), and generally goes about the quiet business of leading his uninteresting life. But after a hard day's work, he often can't even enjoy the peace of his own home as he has made a habit of lending out his apartment to a number of Consolidated Life's executives so that they may enjoy their extramarital affairs away from prying eyes. Baxter is always promised a promotion in exchange for his inconvenience and discretion, but it never seems to arrive. However, when the company's director Jeff Sheldrake (Fred MacMurray) shows an interest in this arrangement, Baxter happily watches his career prospects improve, only to discover that Sheldrake's mistress is none other than his workplace crush, Fran the elevator operator.

Wilder's film shares many surface correlations with *Mad Men*: the negotiation of ruthless office politics, the function of alcohol in business and leisure, and the difficulty of women determining their own destinies. There is also an aesthetic kinship — in production design that is — both in style, character, and an ability to pivot from deft comedy to stark drama (often in the same scene). Meek C. C. Baxter doesn't resemble cocksure Don Draper (although both share the good manners to remove their hats in an elevator), but they live in the same world. It's enough to make you wish AMC broadcast *Mad Men* in black and white.

While Don is more like Sheldrake than Baxter, he wouldn't draft underlings into the mesh of his complicated personal life unless it was an emergency (see Bobbie Barrett's stay at Peggy Olson's apartment in "The New Girl"). This discretion is not out of professional courtesy so much as an aversion to vulnerability — whenever calculating the possible outcomes of a choice, Don always keeps an eye trained on the fallout and who will walk away with the upper hand.

The only character Don resembles is, oddly enough, Fran. She exists in the movie as the embodiment of women's frustrations in the professional and romantic travails of the time. Joan Holloway may find enough of a connection with her character ("The way those men passed her around like a tray of canapés") that her opinion of the film starts a tiff with then lover Roger Sterling, but the sadness behind her sunny demeanor is of the same existential stripe as Don's. Fran feels as haunted by her past as Don does ("I've been jinxed from the word go — first time I was ever kissed was in a cemetery"). And while Don would never consider suicide, Fran's decision to drop a bottle of sleeping pills into her stomach on Christmas Eve is not that far removed from his penchant for disappearing.

Billy Wilder's films are often remembered for the rapid-fire dialogue and sophisticated humor. But other than being a proven master in many genres (the film noir of *Double Indemnity*, the wartime mystery of *Five Graves to Cairo*, the uplifting biopic of *The Spirit of St. Louis*, the courtroom suspense of *Witness for the Prosecution*), Wilder's best films are always laced with melancholy. In fact, thwarted suicide attempts often play a vital role in his films (*Sunset Boulevard, Buddy Buddy, Double Indemnity, Lost Weekend*). This tragic touch augments instead of overpowers his jaundiced but comic worldview, a complicated outlook attributable in part to the loss of three family members at Auschwitz.

The set design Wilder requested of Edward G. Boyle (with art direction by Alexandre Trauner) accomplishes similar feats but through different means as the work produced by Dan Bishop at Matthew Weiner's request. The fishbowl windows of the executive offices at Consolidated Life indicate a world where no secret is unknown for long, while the low ceilings and baffling array of desks illustrate the anonymity of a corporate setting. (Wilder once made the apocryphal claim that he seated midgets along the vanishing point of the desks to enhance the feeling of recession.) The offices of Sterling Cooper aren't as intimidating or impersonal, which befits a midsized advertising concern. Solid doors and opaque windows cloak the executive offices, also apt for a world where secrecy is commonplace but dearly held.

Both *The Apartment* and *Mad Men* have won their share of prestigious awards for production design, but they are well-matched companion pieces in that the style never asserts itself but serves the needs of the story and characters: human connection is fragile and the cost for failing to appreciate it is high.

1.11   INDIAN SUMMER

Original air date: October 4, 2007
Written by: Tom Palmer, Matthew Weiner
Directed by: Tim Hunter

> "You are your own worst enemy."
> — Chinese restaurant fortune cookie

Don and Rachel fall into each other's arms. Peggy starts her career as a full-fledged copywriter by working on a product with a very particular "payload." Betty invites an air conditioner salesman into the house.

Stifled desire settles over the women like the October heat wave that provides this episode with its title.

Betty is enduring a long dry spell in the oppressive heat; Don isn't around much and when he is, he isn't terribly present. He hasn't given himself enough time to mourn the passing of his long-standing tryst with Midge when he dives headlong into an affair with Rachel Menken, one that robs him of emotional availability along with sexual ardor. Betty opens the door to a pushy air conditioner salesman, and while he seems all business, Betty dismisses her better judgment and allows the man into the home. Halfway up the stairs for bedroom measurements, Betty stops and asks the man to leave. Whether due to her apparent comfort with him or the sheer dressing gown she wears, Betty doesn't want him to get the wrong idea.

Then, when an unbalanced load threatens to send the washing machine out for a stroll across the laundry room floor, Betty does her level best to restrict passage. That she finds the machine more attentive to her needs than her husband is of little surprise, but that she immediately fantasizes about the pushy air conditioner salesman is more revealing. A young housewife of inherited Grace Kelly beauty, she certainly can't have imagined herself as an underappreciated housewife with the inclinations of a Tennessee Williams heroine, frightening any grocery delivery boy in the area.

The role of romantic fantasy in the life of a woman is alluded to a few ways. Having spent some time without the attention of her husband has given Betty time to create a fantasy, one in which the air conditioner salesman comes close to assuming a role, almost helping it step from fantasy to reality. Rachel also contends with fantasy, fretting that what she and Don have is nothing more than a romantic delusion. While Betty worries about the fantasy becoming real, Rachel worries about the real world impact of a enacting a fantasy, no matter how great the sex.

"What happens when a woman bases her whole identity on her sexual role; when sex is necessary to make her 'feel alive'?" Betty Friedan asked in *The Feminine Mystique*. It is a question that would resonate strongly with Betty Draper. Friedan suggested that it was no shock that a housewife who was asked to define herself exclusively through child-rearing and house pride would heap expectations on the "femaleness" of her marital role (along with an increased expectation on her husband's "maleness"). And in the case of Betty, a woman who admits in an earlier episode that she spends her days fantasizing about her husband's return and the lovemaking that will bring her to life ("It's all I think about, every day") would find it even harder to take when her husband is not up to the task. Submerging into the business of family can only fill a void so far.

That business of family is far from Peggy's mind as she works diligently on copy for an oddball device that has flummoxed all the men at Sterling Cooper: the Relaxacisor, an electric muscle stimulator meant to battle weight gain through "passive exercise." While no one can pretend to know if it actually shaves off pounds, one thing all the men can agree on is that Peggy may have a unique perspective on the inventor's claims — partially because she's a woman but mostly due to her sudden weight gain.

An interesting note in this episode is the men's reaction to what they perceive as things in the "womanly" arena. While they have no compunction about issuing the most glaring of sexual come-ons, the notion of mentioning Peggy's weight to her face brings the Sterling Cooper boys' mouths to a stammering halt. And while they are quite happy to regale one another with sexual conquests real or imagined, the thought of being replaced by a machine leaves them stunned and ready to fight (witness Freddy Rumsen and that impolitic Ken Cosgrove). The unique perspective that they hoped Peggy would bring is not one they could have foreseen (and a foreshadowing of electric muscle stimulators as self-satisfaction tools for decades to follow), but her ability to present her take on how to sell the device and the copy to do it impresses the boys, even a begrudging Pete Campbell.

All of this isn't to suggest that the boys of Sterling Cooper don't have much to contend with here: Roger tries to show Lee Garner Sr. from Lucky Strike that, heart attack notwithstanding, he's up to the task of business, which just results in another heart attack; Don benefits from his friend's infirmity with a promotion up to partner; and Pete considers a moral dilemma for all of sixty seconds when he has the chance to take a package of Don's, put in the mail by Don's half brother, Adam Whitman, at the beginning of the episode.

While an end to the heat wave may bring about relief for these boys, the women in this episode find a different reprieve, one that is both "rejuvenating" and "refreshing." Even if the boys aren't involved in the outcome.

The Philosophy of *Mad Men* — Don Draper: "Just think about it deeply and then forget it . . . and an idea will jump up in your face."

Period Moment: When Roger congratulates Lucky Strike head Lee Garner Sr. on the outcome of their recent lawsuit, the notion of "liability without malice" is treated as a victory . . . by Roger, at least. In truth, when the jury ruled on the case of Edwin Green vs. American Tobacco, both sides claimed victory.

Edwin M. Green filed a complaint on December 20, 1957 in the Southern District of Florida Miami Division, claiming that "as a result of smoking Lucky Strikes . . . plaintiff has been injured in that he has been caused to develop cancer of the lung." Green sought $1.5 million in damages as a result of the ensuing "embarrassment, humiliation, and great emotional instability" and because his "life expectancy has been reduced severely."

Green died in 1958 before the suit proceeded to trial, but the case was carried on by his widow Mary. Lawyer for the plaintiff, Larry Hastings, claimed that Lucky Strikes "caused or contributed" to the lung cancer that proved fatal. He asserted that despite being aware of the harmful effects prior to 1954 American Tobacco failed to warn Green about the dangers of cigarette smoking.

Counsel for the defense, David W. Dyer, stated that no doctor could claim to understand the nature of cancer, the "great mystery of the century." Any number of external factors could have contributed to the illness that took Edwin Green's life, he argued, from radiation, heredity, and air pollution among others. The only link in controlled laboratory tests between cigarette use and cancer rates occurred in animals, which could not easily be attributed to humans.

The jury ultimately faced four questions:
1. Did the decedent Green have primary cancer in his left lung?
2. If so, was this cancer the cause or one of the causes of his death?
3. If yes, then was the smoking of Lucky Strikes responsible for the cancer in his left lung?
4. If yes, then could the defendant have known that smoking its product could have resulted in the cancer that killed him?

On August 2, 1960, under foreman Henry J. Ayres, the jury said "yes" to the first three questions and "no" to the fourth. While a landmark case in the attribution of cigarette smoking to cancer, this final answer barred the Edwin Green estate from any damages in this case. Opponents of big tobacco found enough in the moral victory to claim the winning side, and while cigarette manufacturers staked out the home team advantage in public, many saw it as a hint of things to come.

Manhattan Real Estate: When Adam sends the incriminating package to Don's office, the address of Sterling Cooper is visible on the plain brown wrapper: *405 Madison Ave., New York, 17 NY.*

Interested tourists arriving in Manhattan to see the bustling skyscraper and swank marble-lined lobby glimpsed in the pilot episode will be disappointed (or, for those with a facility for Google Maps, disappointment can be achieved at home). The closest one could come to that address in New York is a Chase Manhattan ATM located on the southeast corner of Madison Avenue and Forty-eighth Street. On the upside, Manhattan Transit Authority buses BM1 through BM5 frequent the bus stop at that intersection, but offer drop-off service only from the outskirts (Mill Basin to Spring Creek).

Ad Pitch: The Relaxacisor causes some awkward moments and flushed cheeks (particularly with Peggy), but the device is not a flight of fancy.

Introduced as a "passive exercise" device, this electric muscle stimulator (EMS) was introduced to the marketplace in the 1960s, with the promise of a toned athlete's muscles without any of the effort. While it received the *Good Housekeeping* Seal of Approval, by 1972 the Food and Drug Administration banned the devices as dangerous. This decision stemmed from a court case in California the previous year, wherein Judge William P. Gray stated the device "could cause miscarriages" and aggravate existing conditions such as "hernia, ulcers, varicose veins and epilepsy."

The creative use Peggy discovers for this device was not an isolated case. EMS units were euphemistically purchased throughout the decade until the FDA ruling in 1971. But once that unit was declared unsafe, a new version arrived in the form of the Transcutaneous Electric Nerve Stimulation (TENS). While still used by physical therapists in the treatment of chronic pain, those in search of "rejuvenation" managed to bend TENS to their own requirements.

Following within the decade by a negative FDA ruling, new versions of the "passive exercise" machine continually cropped up. Whether for medical quackery (the size of electrical current required to benefit the muscle would be "agonizing") or sexual pioneering, the idea of a portable electrical current generator doesn't look ready to disappear.

At least it's less cumbersome than a washing machine with an unbalanced load.

Cocktail of Note: While on a date with an earnest bumpkin, Peggy tries to look every bit the cosmopolitan New Yorker by sniffing at the preparation of her Brandy Alexander.

> 1 ounce brandy
> 1/2 ounce crème de cacao
> 1 ounce fresh cream
> Shake with ice cubes, strain into chilled glass, and dust with nutmeg.

1.12   NIXON VS. KENNEDY

Original air date: October 11, 2007
Written by: Lisa Albert, André and Maria Jacquemetton
Directed by: Alan Taylor

> "Kennedy appeared vigorous and athletic . . . As much as he
> loved sports, Nixon had no athletic grace or ability."
> — Michael O'Brien, "John F. Kennedy"

Pete wants to be knighted the head of account services and tries blackmailing Don to get it. We see how Don became Lieutenant Don Draper in Korea. The boys and girls at Sterling Cooper gather round to watch the election results come in.

An eerie green glow emanates from "Nixon vs. Kennedy," and revels in all the symbolic contradictions associated with that color.

Pete Campbell becomes a full-fledged green-eyed monster, coveting the head of account services position that has opened due to Don's promotion to partner. Pete pores over the incriminating package that he intercepted at the office, and considers his next move. Desperate for affirmation of his worth, Pete is enraged that Don won't even take him seriously for the position. When he drops the bomb of knowing Don's secret, Pete pretends to have distaste for his own actions, but the greed for stature blinds him. And when Don stalks across his office to confront Pete the senior man's potential for violence is never clearer, along with how much the younger man is in over his head. He cringes at Don's advance, even brings his hands up defensively, but is intent on seeing his blackmail scheme through to his desired end, even if he fears for his safety.

The contest between Nixon and Kennedy provides an interesting thematic backdrop for the conflicts at play here. On the surface, a similar battle between older seasoned pro and young ambitious upstart is reflected in the Draper and Campbell dynamic. But the outcome bears a greater likeness to what most thought *should* have happened in the presidential race; Don's experience and seasoning in the business world serve him well in the office contretemps, and Pete's inexperience cuts his reach well short of his grasp.

Speaking of grasps, Paul Kinsey faces down his past clutching with Joan,

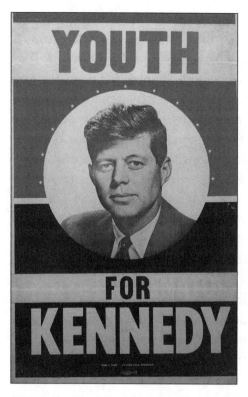

and is displeased with himself when the nature and end of his affair with Joan is revealed. Paul's "big mouth" about his conquest is surprising at first, and while he is "not proud" of it, the Paul we see near the end of this season is different from when we first met him. His artistic inclinations and sensitivity (best displayed around "new girl" Peggy) have crumbled; if a hack like Ken Cosgrove can be published in the *Atlantic* then he holds little hope for his own aspirations. By season's end, Paul is the first to engage in coarse talk and blatant ass-kissing.

A glimpse of his literary yearnings is seen in the impromptu production of a one-act play found in his office on election night. It is stilted and didactic (certainly not helped by Sal's stentorian delivery and the wooden kiss he plants on Joan, who suddenly seems to know *all* about him as a result), but gives us a look into Paul's worldview ("Galt is a thug").

The quiet scene Paul and Joan share, the office asleep from an election all-nighter fueled by Joan's supply of crème de menthe, reveals much about their affair, but also about Joan. While she carries herself as a calculating man-eater, her attraction to Paul (and hurt at his betrayal of trust) indicates that she can make decisions from her heart as well as her hips. Paul certainly has none of the power, influence, or means that Joan avers an attraction to, so she must give in to foolish emotion once in a while. Perhaps the character of office vamp is more about protection than desire.

Shelter is hard for Don to find, from Pete's snide office politics and the deeply harbored secret that initiates it. The truth of his sudden appearance as "Lt. Don Draper" is revealed, and in the flashback to Korea we are surprised at the youthful demeanor of Dick Whitman, such a stark contrast to the confident and swaggering Don Draper. The pitch of his voice as he hops off the back of a transport truck is high and unsure. Whitman's innocence is well matched by his new khaki uniform. Perhaps the stronger correlation between old and young guards is within Don himself. Dick Whitman, as he appears in Korea, is just a kid, a hapless oaf whose actions (however accidental) result in the death of a more experienced senior officer. But when Whitman assumes the identity of Draper, he becomes a better version of both — more than the original Draper who wanted to be an engineer ("I'm supposed to be building swimming pools, not latrines") and the disadvantaged Whitman who aches for more in his life with a hunger that outstrips his innocence. The innocence of young Whitman finds a complement in Peggy, whose disgust over the juvenile behavior at the office during election night comes across as fusty and spinsterish. The state of the office, and a theft from her locker, prompts her to contact building security but instead of the guilty receiving punishment, two African-American employees are fired instead. She sobs at the injustice of it, how some are wrongly prosecuted while the guilty walk about with impunity. It's not fair, she says. And a flustered Don can agree.

Unknowingly, she inspires Don to take the fight to Campbell ("You haven't thought this through"). The attempt by this callow whelp to embarrass Don into compliance backfires beautifully; the confrontation in Bertram Cooper's office ends in a manner which Pete does not possess the imagination to predict. Only a devotee of Ayn Rand could find no harm in a self-created man ("This country was built and run by men with worse stories") and could find more to admire about such a man.

The Philosophy of *Mad Men* — Don Draper: "If your information is powerful enough to make [someone] do what you want, what else can it make them do?"

Period Moment: When Don introduces Herman "Duck" Phillips to Cooper, he mentions that he had been in London with Young & Rubicam. "Isn't this a step down?" Cooper asks.

Maybe not but you can see the old man's point. Young & Rubicam started, as these things often do, from the combined efforts of two disgruntled colleagues. Raymond Rubicam wrote copy for N. W. Ayer Company, gaining notoriety for two campaigns that made him a strong candidate for the position of head copywriter (Steinway Pianos' "Instrument of the Immortals" and "Priceless Ingredient" for Squibb's over-the-counter medications). When the position went to an older man, Rubicam left to strike out on his own. Along for the ride was account executive John Orr Young and in 1923 Y&R Agency opened up shop.

Known for a lax corporate atmosphere and unfettered creativity, the nascent agency soon landed General Foods as a client, and their work for several different brands (including Grape-Nuts, Jell-O, and Sanka) led to boundless growth that resisted the economic slide of the Great Depression. By 1937, Y&R had secured prestigious clients such as Gulf Oil, Bristol-Meyers, and Packard cars, and billings upward of $22 million.

A period of consistent expansion followed. Acquisitions of many smaller advertising houses worldwide resulted in a truly global presence for Y&R and in 1975 it reached the top of the American advertising pyramid with $477 million in billings.

In the 1990s, Y&R became embroiled in legal troubles with charges of bribery relating to a Jamaican tourism account. A partnership with Japan's Dentsu and the United Kingdom's Eurocom fell apart as a result, but Y&R affirmed its resiliency through a merger with Dentsu and subsequent buy-outs of agencies and PR firms throughout Asia, Africa, and Latin America. In 2000, Y&R was acquired by London's WPP Group at a value of $4 billion; it has been called the biggest deal in advertising history.

Interesting crossovers between Y&R and the world of *Mad Men* include a stint advertising for the Eisenhower presidential campaigns and other Republican senatorial campaigns from 1949 to 1961, and counting American Tobacco (makers of Lucky Strikes) as a client, although the firm resigned the Pall Mall account over the incessant meddling of company owner George Washington Hill.

Manhattan Real Estate: Cooper recounts attending a smoker at the Waldorf on election night that hosted "every Republican luminary, save McCarthy and Jesus."

The Waldorf=Astoria (301 Park Avenue) is the gold standard for white-glove hotel service. First established on Fifth Avenue, two hotels joined forces and at the time of its opening, November 1, 1897, became the largest hotel in the world. Up to that time, hotels were mainly for traveling sales-men or transients (much like the Hotel Brighton where Adam Whitman spends his last days). Instead of providing a utilitarian service, this new kind of cosmopolitan lodging was a social and cultural hub. In a 1900 edi-tion of *Harper's Bazaar*, the hotel was called "the fashion of New York and the Mecca of visitors . . . the gathering place of New York society, which comes here to see and to be observed."

In 1929, the building was demolished to clear way for the Empire State Building. Architects Leonard Schultze and S. Fullerton Weaver designed and built the current Park Avenue address in the grand art deco style. The elite of New York and the world happily followed this hop across Madison Avenue.

The double hyphen in Waldorf=Astoria became local shorthand, as in "Meet you at the hyphen." This was a typographical representation of a corridor that joined the original Waldorf and Astoria hotels into one and is officially written not as a single, but double hyphen.

Ad Pitch: Duck Phillips may have landed American Airlines for Y&R while in London, but are they responsible for the 1960s slogan "America's leading airline"? Young & Rubicam *may* have crafted the campaign for American Airlines, but other possibilities include longtime advertising firm TM Advertising (created in 1934 as Glenn Advertising) or McCann Erickson (current hands-off owner of TM). But by 1961, Doyle Dane & Bernbach had taken over the American Airlines account, a big enough step up that it took the quirky boutique agency to a new level of acceptability in the advertising world.

Cocktail of Note: Crème de menthe is a liqueur made from fresh mint, sugar, water, and grain alcohol (although older recipes call for brandy). This drinkable confection actually comes in three colors — green, red, and white — but is best known for the emerald variant.

Crème de menthe appears in a number of cocktails, but in keeping with this episode I thought it prudent to keep it color-coded. The Grasshopper:

> 1/2 ounce fresh cream
> 1/2 ounce white crème de cacao
> 1 ounce green crème de menthe
> Shake with ice cubes and strain into a chilled glass.

Nixon, Kennedy, and the
Changing Face of American Politics

Context is all, particularly when discussing numbers.

119,450.

If the above figure represented footsteps between your house and the nearest well or the amount of dollars in your bank account, it would seem a large enough number indeed. But in the context of a national political win it is slim, and when placed alongside a final tally of 68,836,385 votes cast, it is almost transparent. In terms of the popular vote in the presidential election of 1960, it represented a less than 0.1 percent margin between John F. Kennedy and Richard M. Nixon. And while the Electoral College count won by the Democratic candidate (303 to the Republican's 219) suggests a more emphatic win, the slender popular vote triumph remains one of the most remembered aspects of this election, and stood as the closest in recent American political history until Bush faced Gore in 2000.

An oft forgotten statistic of the 1960 presidential election is the record turnout of eligible voters that shot past 63 percent, a ratio unreached since William Howard Taft won in 1908 and not matched since. The historic percentage of Americans who took part in the democratic process, along with the razor-edge margin of Kennedy's victory, is enough to suggest that the country was at a turning point and struggled with the dilemma of what course the country should take. Kennedy may have stood for the idealism and hope of a new direction, but early on pundits placed even money on the ideological right-hand turn Nixon would chart if he stepped out from behind President Eisenhower and got his hands on the wheel.

A fair suggestion — on paper, then–Vice President Nixon looked an obvious candidate for the highest office in the land. A lieutenant commander in the United States Navy during the Second World War, Nixon returned to the United States with two service stars and a citation of commendation. After leaving the service, Nixon ran and won against a five-time incumbent Democrat to represent California's Twelfth Congressional District. During his tenure as congressman, he gained national notoriety as a patriot and ardent anti-communist for his involvement in breaking the Alger Hiss spy case. In 1950, Nixon sought a seat in the Senate and earned a reputation as a bare-knuckle political operator in his campaign against incumbent Helen Gahagan Douglas, whom he painted as a

Kennedy's age and inexperience could have handicapped his presidential bid, but he managed to look vital where Nixon looked haggard. (Art Selby/NBC Newswire/AP Images)

left-wing sympathizer in the notorious Pink Lady scandal (circulated on sheets of pink paper Nixon claimed that Douglas was "pink right down to her underwear"). Nixon won the seat and continued his anti-communist saber-rattling, which gained the attention of General Dwight D. Eisenhower who selected Nixon as his running mate for the 1952 presidential race. During two terms as vice president, Nixon cultivated an image as an international statesman with official trips throughout the world. He solidified his foreign policy credentials during a face-off with Nikita Khrushchev. While at the opening of the American National Exhibition in Moscow Nixon entered an impromptu debate with the Soviet premiere and handled himself admirably, extolling the virtues of capitalism over communism during the widely reported "Kitchen Debate."

Richard Nixon: war hero, seasoned politician, diplomat, patriot. Who wouldn't think that a sitting vice president with those bona fides would make a natural choice to assume the duties of the most powerful office in the world?

By comparison, John F. Kennedy looked like the dark horse with an outside chance. Privileged, erudite, inexperienced, handsome, politically green, and Catholic — many Americans felt justified in their dismissal and contempt of the Democratic candidate.

But Kennedy won, and Nixon didn't.

There are many factors that contribute to the outcome of even the dullest electoral battle, and this one was anything but dull. What made the election so exciting was not a clash of widely diverging agendas — to a great extent both candidates held similar hopes, namely to safeguard the country from the encroaching threat of communism, and to move the country into a positive direction — but the pivotal times in which it was held. A presidential candidate at the start of the 1960s would have to convince the public that he could protect the country in the lengthening atomic shadow of the Cold War, but that he could also adapt to the changes certain to develop in the coming decade. The victor would also have to prove equally adroit at turning a perceived weakness into an advantage.

Kennedy did and Nixon didn't.

John F. Kennedy confronted many challenges in his presidential bid, but how he faced three in particular helped define him not only as a true leader in the eyes of many Americans, but as a true leader for the times.

1. Media

The importance of the televised debates between candidates is clear, but out of the four debates it was the first that had the greatest impact, the largest audience, and showed one man as savvy about the importance of this young medium while the other failed to recognize it and let an all-important first impression tilt away from him.

There is the unavoidable fact of luck, both good and bad, that broke each way for the candidates. Kennedy broadcast the robust vigor of a man ten years his junior but, at his best, Nixon looked like a meek and frail man ten years older than he actually was. In truth, there was only a four year difference between them; Kennedy was forty-three and Nixon was forty-seven.

Nixon also had the bad luck of circumstance leading into the debate. An innocuous knee injury later flared into a full infection that required an array of antibiotics and a two-week stay at Walter Reed Hospital. Not only did this leave him in a poor position with regard to the debate, but it also meant time off the campaign trail, a fact that Kennedy and his people capitalized on and used to gain further momentum.

A poor showing in the televised debate cannot be blamed on chance alone. CBS executives invited Nixon to review the debate venue along with camera and lighting placement. He refused. Nixon likewise refused the offer of professional makeup application, opting instead to use an untrained adviser to apply a thick pancake to hide a shallow growth of beard. And without an experienced communications adviser, there was no one on staff to dissuade Nixon from wearing a grey suit that folded him into the monochrome background.

Executives extended the same courtesies to Kennedy. He accepted.

Not only did Kennedy review the debate set along with long-time Democratic communications adviser J. Leonard Reinsch, he chose a dark blue suit for better contrast and accepted the application of makeup from a professional (although he appeared on set looking tan and rested, so little cosmetic work was required).

However, there was more to the story than just flimsy optics. Kennedy rested and prepared for the debate, whereas Nixon did not, or could not, due to his illness. And preparedness is the best foil against nerves. Ready for battle, Kennedy remained at ease but consistent in his comments and critique of Nixon's answers. By contrast Nixon, whose face appeared tight and grim, did little to further his case and betrayed his academic background on the debate team; at one point he rebutted a Kennedy answer with a terse "No comment."

Seventy-five million people watched the first debate and while the content was not memorable, Kennedy's star-making turn was immediate. A number of Southern governors who balked at supporting Kennedy threw the full weight of their recommendations behind him following the debate. Crowds at Kennedy rallies grew exponentially befitting, as journalist Theodore White wrote, a "television or movie idol."

Nixon wasn't a fool. He prepared for the next three debates in greater detail and never made the same mistake again. But it was too late. Despite successive claims that each debate was too close to call, it was generally held that Kennedy won them as a whole.

2. Religion

The thought of a politician's faith playing such a naked role in considering his viability for office may surprise us today, but it shouldn't. A recent election had its share of such concerns (with no shortage of "Is America Ready for a Mormon President?" headlines), and the American people have not even had the choice of a Jewish commander-in-chief. The voting public's wariness at having a Catholic president in the Oval Office can be ascribed to the usual characteristics of bigotry: tradition and ignorance.

The United States never claimed an official faith, and of course provided religious freedom in the constitutional bones of the country, but unofficially the establishment religion was Protestant. From the cold strictures of Calvinists and Presbyterians through the North to the fiery theatrics of Baptists and the Pentecostals through the South, different temperatures of Protestantism ran through the country and were judged part of the American culture. Perhaps that has as much to do with tradition as the rebellious spirit of Martin Luther nailing his theses to the door, and signaling the start of a split from an oppressive and corrupt governing body — a country born of separation from British imperialism could well relate to such a pioneering spirit.

As important is the view of Catholicism as a "foreigner's" religion. Well established as a Protestant country after the revolution, an influx of Catholic immigrants to America (from Ireland and Italy in particular) designated that faith as belonging to the "other," deserving of scorn and contempt from "established" Americans. They could easily cloak their intolerance in patriotic concern over new citizens who took their lead from the infallible papal figure who lived in a far-off country.

Al Smith was the first Catholic to attempt the steep climb to the White House as the Democratic nominee in 1928. A product of Tammany Hall who managed to emerge unmarked by the corruption associated with that political machine, Smith graduated from a term as the forty-second governor of New York with eyes on the presidency. And while his Republican opponent Herbert Hoover benefitted from the roaring economic climate inherited from fellow GOP member and outgoing President Calvin Coolidge, Smith could not overcome the prejudicial sentiments toward Catholics. How else would a seasoned politician like Smith lose to a man like Hoover, who served the country in an appointed position but had never run for election in his life?

The specter of Smith's failed 1928 run loomed large for Senator John F. Kennedy and the "problem" of his religion dominated strategic conversations early on in his campaign. His very candidacy reignited anti-Catholic sentiment in the country, stoked further by the propaganda campaign waged by the National Council of Citizens for Religious Freedom. A benign enough organization by name, the group was comprised of mostly evangelical Protestants who warned that as a Catholic, Kennedy was unfit to serve as president because "his church insists that he is duty-bound to submit to its direction."

So pervasive was the anti-Catholic sentiment throughout the country that it came from unexpected sources. Dr. Norman Vincent Peale, author of *The Power of Positive Thinking*, was a member of the aforementioned council who suffered a great backlash from the anti-Catholic cage-rattling and later

119

resigned from the organization and apologized for the sentiments. Even Martin Luther King Sr. claimed that he thought he could never vote for a Catholic.

"Imagine Martin Luther King having a bigot for a father," Kennedy remarked. "Well, we all have fathers, don't we?"

The turning point in this debate occurred in Texas when Kennedy addressed the Greater Houston Ministerial Association on September 12, 1960. Many advisers to Kennedy's campaign worried about their candidate fielding unscreened questions from an unfriendly crowd about religion on television. They need not have worried. Kennedy did answer questions, but his opening remarks to the congregation were measured and passionate.

"I believe in an America where the separation of church and state is absolute — where no Catholic prelate would tell the president (should he be Catholic) how to act, and no Protestant minister would tell his parishioners for whom to vote . . . where no man is denied public office merely because his religion differs from the president who might appoint him or the people who might elect him."

Kennedy went on to gently admonish those who might use the luck of religion as a factor for deciding who should run the country, which was not surprising. The deft work of a consummate gamesman occurred when he turned the Catholic "impairment" to his advantage. He managed to redefine a vote for him not as a vote for the "Catholic candidate" but as a vote *against* intolerance. He also managed to reach out to Catholics who might otherwise vote Republican and offer Protestants with more liberal views to shrug off a constraining tradition.

The advisers concerned about a hostile crowd sandbagging Kennedy in front of cameras also switched opinions. Footage from the speech appeared on television over the following seven weeks in forty states.

3. Race

The "black vote" was one of many demographics that were critical to Kennedy winning the election. Once again recent history obscures the past — African-Americans may overwhelmingly vote Democratic in recent years, but that was not always the case. In fact, Kennedy's work through the 1960 campaign, along with the Civil Rights legislation passed through his and Lyndon Johnson's administrations, started the association between African-Americans and the Democratic Party.

Fidelity with the Republican Party may have started with Lincoln and admiration and respect for his work to end slavery, but a deeper root might again have sprouted from religion. The more conservative strains of Protestantism found an ideological bunkmate in Republicans, and the thought of political affiliations aligning with religious ones does not require a huge leap of logic. This political and religious team spirit made Kennedy an unlikely candidate for African-Americans. Not only would his candidacy as a Democrat count him out among large numbers of churchgoing blacks, but his membership in the Catholic church would put him out of the running completely.

Richard Nixon also had the advantage in courting the black vote. Not only did he have a long-standing history of support on civil rights, he developed a good relationship with Martin Luther King Jr. (much better than Kennedy's), and even received endorsement in 1960 from King's father.

The opportunity to adapt came late in October 1960, when Martin Luther King Jr. was arrested for demonstrating at a "whites only" section of the Magnolia Room at Rich's department store in Atlanta. He was taken into custody along with a number of black students, but was not released along with them. Already a leading face and voice of the Civil Rights movement, King was kept in jail on the grounds that his arrest violated the terms of a twelve-month suspended sentence he had received for driving with an invalid license. Authorities moved him to a remote prison in Georgia to face four months hard labor and all manner of threats to his safety in a racist prison system.

Nixon dithered. Despite his relationship with King and the Department of Justice at his disposal as vice president, Nixon feared alienating white voters in the South and did nothing.

Kennedy acted. When he received word of King's imprisonment from civil rights advisor Sargent Shriver (by way of Harris Wofford, who took a call from a tearful — and pregnant — Coretta Scott King), Kennedy placed a call. He spoke to Mrs. King, expressed his concern, and extended any help he could offer in the safe return of her husband.

Expecting resistance from Kennedy's inner-circle, Shriver appealed directly to Kennedy when he was alone. Kennedy responded in a manner that was beyond simple political gamesmanship. As Dr. King himself later said, Kennedy reacted out of "moral concern" that happened to also be "politically sound."

Shriver must have also known that the fallout from circumventing Kennedy's closest advisers would be great. The move made Robert Kennedy angry, and worried him that it would tip the tight race into an advantage for Nixon. At one point he even referred to Shriver and Wofford as "bomb-throwers." But upon reflection, the injustice of Dr. King's treatment irked Robert Kennedy and offended his sense of legal fair play.

"You can't deny bail on a misdemeanor," he said, and called the presiding judge. Shortly after, the judge agreed to release Dr. King.

The Kennedy camp was careful not to solicit the story to mainstream press for fear of estranging Southern white voters. But black newspapers and editors in the North picked up on the story and lauded Kennedy for his efforts, and, just as important, lambasted Nixon for his silence. Two million copies of a pamphlet entitled *The Case of Martin Luther King Jr.* were distributed among black churches in the northern states, wherein "No Comment" Nixon suffered greatly in comparison to Kennedy, "a candidate with a heart."

It was enough to tip the balance in the election. Kennedy provided African-American voters with a reason to vote for a Catholic Democrat, and they did so in large numbers.

The ultimate success of Kennedy's campaign may have rested on luck as much as his charisma. Both Kennedy and Nixon spoke about foreign or domestic policy in similar terms and it is interesting to note that a closer look at their platforms reveals more similarities than differences (certainly more than has been seen between the two parties since). This is not just a factor of passing time leading to greater insight; many thought much the same at the time. Journalist Eric Sevareid wrote in the *Boston Globe* that he found little of substance to distinguish between both candidates, that they were examples of the "managerial revolution" coming to politics, and that "Nixon and Kennedy are its first completely packaged products."

Perhaps the greatest advantage Kennedy had over Nixon was not a better hold on policy or legislative acumen. In words and actions, Kennedy showed during the campaign that he had an idea not only for what America could become but a new idea for the presidency itself, one that acknowledged the change in attitude of the 1960s, and a desire to change along with them. Whether domestic (in his handling of civil rights issues), international (his idea of sending youth around the world as ambassadors in the Peace Corps), or interstellar (the drive to land on the moon), President Kennedy celebrated the greatness of his country and hinted at the heights it could reach.

1.13 THE WHEEL

Original air date: October 18, 2007
Written by: Matthew Weiner, Robin Veith
Directed by: Matthew Weiner

> "... a continuous vibration of animal spirits
> through those fibers in the middle brain in which the
> impressed traces of ideas of the Fatherland cling."
>
> — Johannes Hofer, "Medical Dissertation on Nostalgia," 1688

Don picks Duck Phillips as the new head of account services. Kodak wants an exciting campaign for their new add-on to the slide projector. Don starts to regret taking his family for granted while Peggy suffers through an unexpected family development.

Families are not just a club you enter without asking admittance. Most people have an opportunity to create their own family, but so many forget the preciousness of the bond. Don Draper should know this — he's created every aspect of his life — but it is a wisdom that eludes him.

In a tender moment of nostalgia, Don tries to contact his brother Adam through the Hotel Brighton, only to find out that he hanged himself in that seedy flophouse. And yet, despite his anguish, Don can't see that he is in danger of losing his created family. He's already used his new position as partner to evade Thanksgiving dinner with Betty's family. She can't fathom why he won't make her family his family as well.

Betty first has to worry about neighbor Francine ("she's like a sister to me"), who has learned of her husband's cheating ways. The instrument of knowledge is all the more poignant for its banality — a strange number on the phone bill. Betty can't help but look under her own rock and finds evidence not of a mistress but another kind of betrayal, that of her therapist Dr. Wayne. In an effort to communicate with her husband, she begins divulging her suspicions about Don's fidelity to the doctor, knowing full well they'll make their way back to him. If the stolid Dr. Wayne had any idea of the dysfunction on display, it would surely make him sit up and actually ask a question for once.

The sessions with Dr. Wayne may have questionable results, but when Betty bumps into Glen Bishop in a parking lot where he waits patiently for his mother, Betty makes more emotional progress in a few minutes than she has in hours on the psychiatrist's couch. While many viewers found the scene creepy and inappropriate, there is no doubting the genuine sadness on display when Betty admits that she has no one to talk to, in essence nobody who "knows" her. A grown woman (often accused of acting like a child) reaching out to a child for affirmation ("Please tell me I'll be okay") is almost tragic, a fact underscored by the earnest response from the boy ("I wish I was older").

Back at Sterling Cooper, Harry Crane has apparently confessed to his wife that he's had an impulsive affair on election night. Living out of his office and shuffling between the desks in his underwear, he doesn't exactly cut the figure of a dashing William Holden–type.

Harry's emotional reaction to Don's moving monologue to the Kodak people ("It's not called 'The Wheel'. . . . it's called 'The Carousel'") is genuine and understandable. Early in the speech, Don sounds like he's talking about advertising the way he should talk about his family. But it becomes clear that he is talking about his family, having loaded slides of Betty and the kids to show during his presentation. Like all the best sales pitches, this one has the ring of conviction.

Peggy has her own problem with family, in that she has one thrust upon her. Many fans had difficulty with this development. While the 1960s were a more innocent time, that explanation only carries so much weight. Is it possible that she could be so naive as to be unaware of her pregnancy until giving birth? While this is a phenomenon that occurs right up to modern times, the majority of women who unwittingly reach full term have the pregnancy masked by obesity; with Peggy, the weight gain occurs in tandem with the gestation period. The likely answer for Peggy's mysterious childbirth is a talent for denial, as if she subconsciously puts on the extra pounds in an effort to hide the pregnancy from her co-workers and herself.

Whether blinded by biological camouflage, work stress, or denial, Peggy is unable to accept her new family at episode's end. Almost as heartbreaking is Don's final scene in an empty house. His moving "Carousel" pitch betrays a longing for a simpler time, perhaps that brief moment when he had the family he always wanted, before he started using work as an excuse to stay away, or as an alibi for a clandestine fling. As he walks into his empty home (even more heartsick after the fantasy of a triumphant homecoming), Don seems to realize that guilt can create a pain deeper and more profound than nostalgia.

Sitting alone on the steps, he has realized that family bonds are fragile, whether given or created. But is it too late?

The Philosophy of *Mad Men* — Don Draper: "[The Carousel] lets us travel the way a child travels. Around and around and home again . . . to a place where we know we are loved."

Period Moment: Pete's father-in-law, Tom Vogel, suggests that Nixon never had a chance in the election, not citing campaign commercials or alleged voter fraud but a football game. The fate of the Washington Redskins in their final home game has correctly predicted the outcome "of the last six elections." The story goes that if the Redskins lose this game, then the president or party last in the White House will lose; if they win, then the most recent leader or affiliation will continue to rule.

True? While one can argue whether it is the cause of the outcome or merely a harbinger, the fact is that Mr. Vogel is right. Even more astonishing is that the result of this game continued being right through to 2004. Factoring in the most recent election, the Redskins hold a record of 18 out of 19 predictions.

Manhattan Real Estate: Duck Phillips chairs a blunt inaugural meeting as new head of account services, making clear the need for everyone on staff to drum up business. By way of illustration, Duck tells the boys that he spent ninety minutes in a steam bath at the Athletic Club, lost four pounds, and discovered that the Kodak slide projector account was ripe for plucking.

The New York Athletic Club (or NYAC, 180 Central Park South) is housed in an Italian Renaissance–style twenty-one floor building designed by the firm of York and Sawyer, the team also responsible for the Brooklyn Trust Company and the Federal Reserve Bank of New York.

NYAC was founded in 1868 by Henry Buermeyer, John Babcock, and William Curtis as a hub for the development of amateur sport in the United States, and the club's lodging and dining facilities served to make it a networking dream (the kind of place where you can, as Duck says, "run into people"). Luminaries on the membership list have included John F. Kennedy Jr., Jack Dempsey, George Steinbrenner, and Peter Jennings. The commitment to amateur sports has resulted in NYAC members winning a multitude of Olympic medals (123 gold, 39 silver, and 52 bronze).

Redskins Presidential Prediction Record

Year	Against	Won/Lost Correct?	Prediction Winner	Loser
2008	Lost to Steelers	Yes	Obama (D)	Sen. John McCain
2004	Lost to Green Bay	No	G. W. Bush (R)	Sen. John Kerry
2000	Lost to Titans	Yes	G. W. Bush (R)	V-Pres. Al Gore
1996	Beat Colts	Yes	Clinton (D)	Sen. Bob Dole
1992	Lost to Giants	Yes	Clinton (D)	Pres. George H.W. Bush
1988	Beat Saints	Yes	G. H.W. Bush (R)	Gov. Michael Dukakis
1984	Beat Falcons	Yes	Reagan (R)	Sen. Walter Mondale
1980	Lost to Vikings	Yes	Reagan (R)	Pres. Jimmy Carter
1976	Lost to Cowboys	Yes	Carter (D)	Pres. Gerald Ford
1972	Beat Cowboys	Yes	Nixon (R)	Sen. George McGovern
1968	Lost to Giants	Yes	Nixon (R)	V-Pres.Hubert Humphrey
1964	Beat Bears	Yes	Johnson (D)	Sen. Barry Goldwater
1960	Lost to Browns	Yes	Kennedy (D)	V-Pres. Richard Nixon
1956	Beat Browns	Yes	Eisenhower (R)	Gov. Adlai Stevenson
1952	Lost to Steelers	Yes	Eisenhower (R)	Gov. Adlai Stevenson
1948	Beat Yanks	Yes	Truman (D)	Gov. Thomas Dewey
1944	Beat Rams	Yes	Roosevelt (D)	Gov. Thomas Dewey
1940	Beat Pirates	Yes	Roosevelt (D)	William Willkie
1936	Beat Cardinals (as Boston Redskins)	Yes	Roosevelt (D)	Gov. Alf Landon

In the first year of existence, the NYAC introduced the first bicycle race, or "velocipede" race, to America.

Ad Pitch: Pete lobbies hard to land his father-in-law's business, after Richardson-Vicks buys Clearasil.

Invented by Ivan Combe (also responsible in later years for Odor-Eaters, Vagisil, and Just for Men hair coloring), Clearasil was specifically designed to fight acne on young skin and was the first of its kind. While still piloted by Combe Incorporated, Clearasil became the second product to sponsor *American Bandstand*. As a preferred sponsor, the product was endorsed on-air by host Dick Clark. Teenagers in search of musical inspiration and clear skin found both on one TV show and sales soared.

Interestingly, Ivan Combe worked as a merchandising account executive for Raymond Rubicam at Y&R (see "Nixon vs. Kennedy") in 1940.

Cocktail of Note: Upon learning of Carlton's long-standing infidelity, Francine considers poisoning him a reasonable response. "He's so stupid, he'd drink anything."

Maybe so. There has been a long line of women who have dispatched with their husbands in such a manner, and a number of notorious cases around that era. In Oklahoma in 1954, Nanny Doss, or "The Giggling Granny," confessed to poisoning four husbands along with her mother, her sister, her grandson, and one mother-in-law. In Romania, Vera Renczi, through the 1920s and 1930s, killed thirty-five men, including two husbands, one son, and twenty-nine gentlemen callers; newspapers around the world covered the story. The prodigious body count and preferred method may have provided the inspiration for Joseph Kesselring's play *Arsenic and Old Lace*.

While these scorned women seem to prefer lacing alcohol with a devastating reagent (presumably to cover any telltale smells or tastes, although Kool-Aid will apparently do the trick), some have been known to infuse it in prepared meals.

The difficulty of married life is not to be discounted, and the desperation of a dysfunctional arrangement can take its toll. However, the author cannot in good conscience provide a recipe for such an endeavor. He would also like to say that he loves his wife very, very much.

EPISODE GUIDE SEASON TWO

Notable guest cast in season 2: Mark Moses (Herman "Duck" Phillips), Joel Murray (Fred Rumsen), Gabriel Mann (Arthur Case), Missy Yager (Sarah Beth Carson), Channing Chase (Dorothy Campbell), Melinda McGraw (Bobbie Barrett), Patrick Fischler (Jimmy Barrett), Colin Hanks (Father John Gill), John Getz (Dr. Eric Stone), Peyton List (Jane Siegel), Melinda Page Hamilton (Anna Draper), Sarah Drew (Kitty Romano), Ryan Cutrona (Gene Hofstadt), Darby Stanchfield (Helen Bishop), Marten Holden Weiner (Glen Bishop), Laura Ramsey (Joy), Philippe Brenninkmeyer (Willy), Sam Page (Greg Harris), Ryan McPartlin (Gentleman in bar)

2.01 FOR THOSE WHO THINK YOUNG

Original air date: July 27, 2008
Written by: Matthew Weiner
Directed by: Tim Hunter

> "Now I am quietly waiting for
> the catastrophe of my personality
> to seem beautiful again,
> and interesting, and modern."
> — Frank O'Hara, "Mayakovsky"

Despite his instincts, Don submits to Duck Phillips's demand for a stronger youth presence on the creative staff at Sterling Cooper. Peggy settles into her job as copywriter but contends with the placement of the new Xerox machine in her office. Betty reconnects with an old girlfriend as she takes up horse riding.

While the first season was about the onset of change — the need, desire, and willingness for it — the second season is about the practical application of change. As we pick up eighteen months after the end of the first season, we see the beginning of shifts on almost every level, from the national perspective of JFK's presidency to the burgeoning Civil Rights movement. The Sterling Cooper office seems a quiet place at the outset of season 2, but it is certainly the lull before the storm.

The placid nature of the office seems a gift not only to the audience but to the characters of *Mad Men*. After the dramatic wallop the first season built toward, a little breathing room is required. And while there is much on the viewer's mind that requires recap, show-runner Matthew Weiner is in no rush to divulge the news.

The bulk of this episode is concerned with the allure of youth, summed up in the Pepsi ad campaign that gives this episode its title; for the first time, young people were starting to make themselves heard as powerful political, social, and economic voices. And while the usually prescient Don Draper dismisses it as a "fad," he is unaware of the catastrophe he flirts with in underestimating the youth market, and it is the first true sign of his unpreparedness for the rest of the coming decade.

Caught in these doldrums is our man Don Draper himself. He is striving to be a better husband and father but looks more disconnected than ever. He tries to wake himself up with a shot of romance at Valentine's Day. When he takes Betty for a romantic dinner she runs into an old roommate from her modeling days, Juanita Carson (Jennifer Siebel Newson). Don points to her elderly male companion as evidence that she is a working girl, a prostitute out on a "date" with a client. Betty is shocked but also intrigued.

The romantic night winds up with a room at the Savoy, all seems perfect; Betty even dresses in saucy piece of negligee (the sort of clothing preferred by Juanita perhaps?). But Don can't perform and the night whimpers to a close with the muffling of desires and expectations that is commonplace in a marriage.

Don's work also starts to suffer, or would if he wasn't the master manipulator. While he can almost always shrug off an office absence due to a trip "to the printers," he starts to test the limits of his powers when staff are gathered for a morning meeting and wait a few hours while he attends a matinee or lunches at a bar.

Don spots a man at the bar reading Frank O'Hara's *Meditations in an Emergency*, which neatly sets up one half of a bookend for this season. The intellectual at the bar reading O'Hara's truly modern poetry collection tells Don that he probably wouldn't like it (a snap judgment that bothers Don more than it offends). But he reads it later with a determination, as if he hopes the book will act as a prism and filter his life down to easily identifiable elements.

Youth is catching in other ways as well. Harry Crane's forgiving wife is pregnant, a development that pushes Pete Campbell's wife Trudy (or "Tweety," continuing the avian theme) to tears. Fruitless attempts at conception may bother his wife, but Pete is less concerned. He even asks Peggy if she wants kids, and agrees with her when she says "eventually."

Peggy's new career as a copywriter garners a great deal of attention; not only her place on the creative team, but her work refining the pitch for Mohawk Airlines. Don continues her education in the art of persuasion, and uses a macaroni-trimmed Valentine's Day card from his daughter to define the difference between "sentiment" and "sentimental." He seems to suggest that children are everything to a man, but it's hard to tell whether this is a truism for Don or an ideal he hopes to attain.

But the burning question about last year's weight gain and subsequent slimming (dismissed as either a child springing from an affair with Don or a stay at a "fat farm") remains achingly untouched. More important is Peggy's development as a writer, and the de facto respect Don offers her by not coddling or couching his criticisms in bromides (his response to her statement that "sex sells" is brutal in its frankness: "Just so you know, the people who talk that way think monkeys can do this"). There is a developing mentor/protégé relationship that many in the office can only grapple with by thinking the worst. There is a connection between the two, a commonality that Don knows, but one that is, again, not rushed to the fore.

For all his accumulated wisdom in the advertising world, Don is still at loose ends. At the behest of Duck Phillips Don interviews a young writer/artist team (for marquee value more than any respect for their work) and seems resigned to letting a few of the kids slip into his kingdom. The wisdom he has is of a world that is quickly changing, and while he might be the first to say that youth is wasted on the young, he might prove a prime example of wisdom being wasted on the old.

Oh, and by the way . . . Sal is *married?*

The Philosophy of *Mad Men* — Don Draper: "*You* are the product. You, feeling something — that's what sells."

Period Moment: The office's first Xerox machine, a mammoth chunk of machinery that looks bigger than a child's playhouse, arrives on a straining skid. The ladies of the steno pool cluck over the versatility of the machine, but Joan can't find a suitable spot to house the beast.

The Xerox 914 was available commercially in 1959 and the culmination of inventor Chester Carlson's desire to create a machine that would provide "dry" copies on plain paper. However, he created the process first known as electrophotography much earlier, in 1938, and didn't receive a patent until 1942.

The gap between invention and commercial viability was due to a simple fact: Carlson had invented a process (now dubbed "xerography") that no one wanted. He traveled great lengths to convince the business world that it would benefit from a machine dedicated to the rapid duplication of multiple copies, but encountered indifference with each stop. In 1944, Carlson caught his first break when he entered into a royalty-sharing agreement with a nonprofit research group called the Battelle Institute. Three years later, Battelle joined forces with a photo-paper company called Haloid (later rechristened Xerox), which gave that paper concern the rights to develop the copying machine.

The Smithsonian Institute's National Museum of American History currently holds a Xerox 914 at the Kenneth E. Behring Center in Washington, D.C. Number 517 off the assembly line, the machine weighs 648 pounds, and measures 42" high x 46" wide x 45" deep. At the peak of its powers, the Xerox 914 could produce 100,000 copies per month.

Ad Pitch: The drinking public long knew Pepsi as an inexpensive soda, running behind Coca-Cola in the soft drink market. During the Great Depression, Pepsi introduced a twelve-ounce bottle that dwarfed Coca-Cola's six-ounce staple. When the upstart decided to charge the same price (5 cents) for twice the drink, Pepsi positioned itself as the usurper of Coca-Cola's throne. But even when sales topped 500 million bottles in 1936, they still placed second behind the long-standing giant.

Searching for a foothold with their new account, ad agency BBDO developed a daring strategy. In 1960, the youth of America were still regarded as second-class citizens, but Philip Dusenberry at BBDO saw the potential for massive market identification. Framing Coca-Cola as a stodgy, old-folks beverage, Pepsi became the brand for the young, fresh, and vivacious. "Now it's Pepsi for those who think young!" ads proclaimed.

BBDO also created the Pepsi Challenge campaign, which went even further to establish Pepsi as a leader in the business and seared itself on the collective unconscious of the popular culture.

After forty-eight years together, Pepsi Co. moved their domestic marketing business to TBWA (lead communications for Pepsi and Diet Pepsi) and the Arnell Group (for branding and packaging).

Manhattan Real Estate: Don's first encounter with O'Hara's *Meditations in an Emergency* is in a restaurant while he eats lunch. "He wrote some of it here," the bespectacled reader tells Don.

Most think the bar is Larre's (50 West Fifty-sixth Street), which was around the corner from the Museum of Modern Art where Frank O'Hara worked as a curator. O'Hara often lunched and wrote in the restaurant in hurried bursts of creativity, in stark contrast to the meditative nature of the poems.

Many avant-garde artists ate at Larre's, including surrealist titans Max Ernst, Salvador Dali, Yves Tanguy, Arshile Gorky, Marcel Duchamp, and sculptor Alexander Calder. The restaurant disappeared in the late '70s and the building now hosts a collection of private medical practices.

Cocktail of Note: After a fumbled night of Valentine's Day passion at a hotel in the city, Don calls room service and orders two Shrimp Cocktails at Betty's behest — the least he could do, it seems.

> 10–12 tiger shrimp, poached and deveined
> 2 tablespoons horseradish
> 1/2 cup crushed tomatoes
> pinch of salt
> freshly ground peppercorns
> dash of Worcestershire and Tabasco
> juice of half a lemon
> 2 lemon wedges
> springs of fresh rosemary
> Combine horseradish, tomatoes, salt, pepper, Worcestershire and Tabasco sauce, and lemon juice in a bowl. Spoon into a serving bowl. Fill martini glasses 1/2 with crushed ice, then arrange shrimp on the rim, add lemon wedges and sprig of rosemary.

2.02 FLIGHT 1

Original air date: August 3, 2008
Written by: Lisa Albert, Matthew Weiner
Directed by: Andrew Bernstein

> "No one can serve two masters. Either he will hate
> the one and love the other, or he will be devoted
> to one and despise the other."
> — Matthew 6:24

An airline disaster strikes close to home for Pete Campbell. Duck Phillips tries to turn the plane crash into a business opportunity, despite Don's moral protest and fidelity to a regional airline client. Peggy's mother wants her to accompany her to church.

As is often the case with *Mad Men*, words from a previous episode resonate with a current one, and "Flight 1" is no exception. When Bertram Cooper suggests that Don keep Pete Campbell around the office because "one never knows how loyalties are born," this cryptic homily rings clear as Don and Duck Phillips unknowingly battle for the young man's soul.

Strong words? Yes, but it seems apt for an episode where the triumphant lower Manhattan parade to celebrate John Glenn's three-time trip around the Earth is overshadowed by an American Airlines jet going down in Jamaica Bay, killing all ninety-five people onboard and ranking as commercial aviation's worst disaster to that date. Office concern soon devolves into gallows humor and Pete can't help but jump in, which makes the appearance of his father's name on the passenger list all the more shocking.

Don acts quickly to remove all advertising for regional Mohawk Airlines, but Duck Phillips smells an opportunity. He calls an old friend at American and the resultant news that the airline might be shopping for a new agency revs his engine. The only hindrance to the opportunity is the conflict with Mohawk. The pitched discussion between Don and Duck is the first sign of the apparently natural tension between account services and creative. And while Don fights the good fight to keep the regional airline, the demands of business (and Roger's hope for a summer house) appear ready to win.

Kartheiser and Hamm, drinking like Mad Men.
(AP Photo/Chris Pizzello)

Pete stumbles into Don's office in search of help with the news and finds an understanding if not consoling ear. Pete has always sought Don's approval (even before, during, and after his attempt to "kill" him in the Freudian sense) and in the absence of an actual father, his need for such a figure is even more acute.

Don tries to counsel Pete on a course of action, as the news has left the young man in a fog. At first glance, shock is the root of Pete's confusion at how to act (and equal concern with how his behavior qualifies with the accepted standard for grief). But it is just as likely that he can't locate his sorrow because, by his own admission, he hardly knew the man ("I don't even think I know how old he was. Someone's going to ask that.")

Once again, however, Duck sees an opportunity to use Pete's recent tragedy for leverage in the bid for American Airlines. Pete's discomfort with the idea is gratifying and a seemingly definite brush of that devil off his shoulder. But he makes the mistake of approaching Don for further guidance regarding Duck's American Airlines request. It is an elegant mirror of scenes — Pete talking to a sympathetic Duck in his darkened office followed by a cold rebuff from Don — and sets into motion the turn Pete makes to Duck in the final moments of the episode.

Other elements touched on in "Flight 1" include Bobby Draper's growing disobedience and Joan Holloway's true age — but the other strong thread developed is the continued alignment of Don and Peggy. Director Andrew Bernstein achieves this in another mirror of scenes: Don watches his children sleep after an argument with Betty, following a scene of Peggy peering through the crib bars at a sleeping child. The information on her pregnancy isn't spelled out, and leaves the audience with many questions.

Has Anita adopted her sister Peggy's discarded child? Is Peggy dropping the child off with her sister and mother, contributing to the raising on weekends? It's hard to know, and, as usual, Weiner is in no rush to divulge.

Peggy also has to deal with her mother and the concern she has for her soul. There are concerns raised about Peggy's state of mind during her hospital stay, a fact that Anita is not above mentioning over the dinner table in an effort to bring her sister down a peg. Also, Peggy hasn't been attending church and that, along with the out-of-wedlock pregnancy, fuel her mother's worry. While the battle for human souls may seem a heavy-handed approach for appraising a serialized drama, it's hard to make that argument when the episode closes on Peggy guilted into a pew appearance while the priest recites the *Domine non sum dignus* liturgy ("Oh Lord, I am not worthy"). And if further evidence of the show's cinematic elegance were required, this scene is the third mirror with Don leaving his own temple (a bar) after cutting loose a loyal client in favor of the chance at a more prestigious one.

Loyalty remains the vibrant theme, and the trouble of maintaining this high ideal. Pete loses a little of himself by stooping to profit from his tragedy, and Don is anguished over the cessation of business with Mohawk Airlines. No one said being good was easy.

A personal observation: I don't know if it is more pronounced in this episode or I'm slow to absorb (I'm thinking the latter), but there is something about the cast's enunciation that struck me while viewing. Actors speak the dialogue with crisp clarity, without any shaved T's or dropped G's; a mode of speech that is not theatrical (in a pejorative sense) but certainly trained. The sharp elocution reminds me of the oddly proper language of Damon Runyon's fairy-tale New York (big-hearted gangsters who speak without vulgarity or contractions), although with a different effect.

The quality of the dialogue demands it (and I'm certain Matthew Weiner does too). But the clear enunciation also adds to the alien formality of the series and setting, underlining the allure of a world where men doffed their hats and women wore elbow-length gloves — charming despite the roiling anxiety and injustice that bubbled beneath the glassy surface.

The Philosophy of Mad Men — Don Draper: "I can't believe I look like an idiot for wanting to be loyal to these people."

Period Moment: Literary references are wide and deep within this show, but one throwaway in this episode is a particular highlight. Peggy asks her mother if she can pick anything up at the library for her, but Momma Olson demurs as she is still knee-deep in another book about Michelangelo's tempestuous relationship with patron Pope Julius II and the commission to build the pope's tomb that stretched into a forty-year job: "I have to renew *The Agony and the Ecstasy*. It's taking *forever*."

Ad Pitch: The craven attempt to profit from the Flight 1 crash is a source of much consternation in the episode but this kind of duplicitous navigation of choppy waters is not unusual in the business world; cutting loose a smaller account for a larger one is not uncommon. Roger Sterling's contention that even vying for the account will elevate their status is also sound.

When the Doyle Dane & Bernbach Agency acquired the American Airlines account in 1961, it was a huge boost to their image. Advertising insider Tom Messner mentioned in an interview with Barbara Lippert that it represented a huge leap for the boutique agency, one that put them into the "establishment of America."

In the same interview, Messner mentions that after the Jamaica Bay crash, American was *not* looking for new representation. In fact, John Dillon — DDB copywriter and author of the 1972 novel *The Advertising Man* — wrote the copy for a small space ad for American proclaiming, "We are not looking for a new advertising agency. We have enough trouble with the one we have."

Manhattan Real Estate: Duck meets his American Airlines contact at the University Club and asks Pete to "take the lead." We can only assume Duck has glued his forked tongue together before asking.

The University Club (West Fifty-forth Street at Fifth Avenue) was created in 1861 by a group of Yale alumni to foster their collegiate friendships after graduation and to celebrate the meeting of civic duty and intellectual rigor. An exclusive club of the highest rank, most of the public must content themselves with enjoying the exterior architectural splendors of the building, which are many. Designed by architect and club member Charles McKim, the Italian Renaissance–style palazzo is constructed not of limestone as many might assume, but pink Milford granite from Maine. The six-floor building appears to be only three levels through the use of high, arched openings. Even more impressive are the bronze balconies (now weathered an historic oxidized green), and an intricately molded cornice.

Cocktail of Note: While hosting a card night with Francine and Carlton, Don instructs the making of a perfect Tom Collins — that he's directing his young daughter Sally in the making is unsettling, but it does sound delicious.

1 ounce lemon juice
1/2 ounce sugar syrup
1 ounce gin
1/2 lime
club soda

Mix lemon juice, syrup, and gin into glass with ice cubs. Squeeze in lime juice and fill with soda. Often decorated with squeezed lime rind, or, in the Draper house, with a cherry kept "near the top of the glass."

Before Sterling Cooper — Recommended Viewing: David Swift's *How to Succeed in Business Without Really Trying*

By the time 1967 dawned and Hollywood mounted an adaptation of this Tony Award–winning musical, the genre was about to take its last bow. The poor returns from a lackluster adaptation of 1966's *A Funny Thing Happened on the Way to the Forum* (made, by the way, minus most of the music from the original stage production) did little to dissuade studios from making beach party movies and Elvis vehicles by the dozens. And even though two years earlier *The Sound of Music* opened to rave reviews and stellar box-office sales, the faith in musicals as surefire money-makers started to falter, confirmed before the end of the decade by expensive and bloated box-office duds like *Paint Your Wagon*, *Finian's Rainbow*, and *Doctor Dolittle*.

Between the 1961 Broadway debut of *How to Succeed in Business Without Really Trying* and the Hollywood premiere in 1967, the movie business and America itself underwent tumultuous changes far greater than six trips through the calendar might suggest. The intervening six years were full of change and tumult, the likes of which America hadn't seen since the Second World War; one of the casualties in the world of entertainment (other than the erosion of movie audience due to the bat-

Rudy Vallee, Virginia Martin, and Robert Morse in the Broadway production of *How to Succeed in Business Without Really Trying.* (AP Photo)

tering forces of television) was the musical. Chipper, aw-shucks characters that break out into choreographed song did not play well to a public increasingly jaded by civil unrest and war footage played at the dinner hour.

How would a musical about the rapid rise of a window washer through the corporate ranks thrive alongside a burgeoning appetite for bristling realism (*In the Heat of the Night*) or frank violence and sex (*Bonnie and Clyde*), to say nothing of the rising anti-consumerist sentiment?

The recipe might look like this: a lively story of an ambitious young man who plots a rapid ascent from window washer to vice president in charge of advertising at the World Wide Wicket Company, music and lyrics by Frank Loesser (*Guys and Dolls*), based on a Pulitzer Prize–winning book by Abe Burrows (with Jack Weinstock and Willie Gilbert) and the inimitable Robert Morse. Mix well, let loose, and stay out of the way. The result is a musical that is deft, timeless, a pleasure to watch.

The success of the film in a hostile climate is a perfect reflection of J. Pierrepont Finch's unlikely corporate ascent. Director David Swift (*The Parent Trap, Pollyanna, Under the Yum Yum Tree*) makes the bold choice to acknowledge the changing times but doesn't allow it to interfere with the fun.

The classic movie musicals of the 1950s — which this clearly emulates — were often written and performed in a bright and cavalier fashion but were pinned down by cavernous studio sets built to contain the frivolity. This was no doubt an economic choice (location photography deemed prohibitively expensive), but more important it was technological. The amount of artificial light required to deliver a serviceable image on film (in the classic three-point Hollywood key-fill-back-light equation) demanded almost limitless vertical space. The result is an often static mise-en-scène that imitates the rigid proscenium-arch presentation of live theatrical productions with none of the immediacy.

The best directors of 1950s musicals used this artificiality to their advantage (Vincente Minnelli, Stanley Donen, Gene Kelly, and the lesser-known Charles Walters), but by the 1960s, younger audiences came to associate the soundstage with stodgy films that were out of touch with the times. This happened concurrently with technological breakthroughs in smaller cameras and faster film stock that required less light. From-the-hip location photography became synonymous with sharper, edgier films.

Director Swift opens *How to Succeed . . .* with great Manhattan location work that solidly roots the film in a time and place that would have been instantly recognizable to audiences. But unlike an obligatory opening credit shot of New York minus the lead actors (see *Lover Come Back*), Swift places Robert Morse's Finch right on Fifth Avenue. And instead of limiting the exploration of New York just to a first act opener, Swift moves the action outdoors as often as the story will allow.

That Swift doesn't lose the momentum when the film moves indoors to a more traditional soundstage presentation is a testament to the peerless quality of the actors and composers. Morse, Rudy Vallée (both reprising their Broadway roles), and a fresh-faced Michele Lee in her screen debut, all fill the wide Panavision canvas with charm and skill. Most of all is Robert Morse, who manages to appear hopeless and conniving at once, in particular when he sings "I Believe in You" to his own reflection. His performance, big but never broad, may be the true reason the interior soundstage sets seem apt; the abundance of air space doesn't feel like an accommodation for spotlights but for Finch's boundless ambition.

The work of art director Robert F. Boyle (*Cape Fear, The Thomas Crown Affair*) and set decorator Edward G. Boyle (*Sex and the Single Girl, The Apartment*) doesn't overwhelm, which would be an understandable mistake if less seasoned hands set about framing such a raucous, fun-loving show. Instead of compressing the characters in a vice of regimented desk rows and banks of low-flung fluorescent lights, the sets are comprised of clean and modern lines (although the preponderance of broadloom dates badly). The color palette is muted and never threatens to distract from the show (but here again carpet is the lone offender, in particular the blood-red wall-to-wall in the office of Vallée's company president).

The iconic weight of casting Robert Morse in what he called the "Rudy Vallée CEO part" isn't the only obvious connection between *How to Succeed . . .* and *Mad Men*. The meteoric rise of copywriter Peggy Olson travels a similar trajectory of J. Pierrepont Finch. However, Finch furthers his career through adroit placement, whether to hear a useful piece of inside information or appear like a hard-working employee. Peggy is an actual asset to Sterling Cooper and even though her talent does get her noticed initially, it is only when she insists on further recognition of her efforts that she continues her rise.

But I think the more natural relation is between Finch and Pete Campbell, despite birth into completely different circumstances. Both are young men aching for success and believe that the mere fact of wanting advancement is enough to merit it. The fact that Finch progresses more swiftly than Pete is largely a matter of tact, in that one has it while the other doesn't, even if both can drop themselves into a potentially advantageous situation. Within the timeline of *Mad Men*, Robert Morse would appear on Broadway as Finch into the second season. One can only think what kind of havoc Pete Campbell might wreak if he saw the stage show. If he waits until 1967 to see the movie, however, it might be wisdom gained too late.

2.03 THE BENEFACTOR

Original air date: August 10, 2008
Written by: Matthew Weiner, Rick Cleveland
Directed by: Lesli Linka Glatter

> "The old days were the old days.
> And they were great days. But now is now."
> — Don Rickles

Don spends an afternoon at the movies while trouble brews on the set of a commercial shoot. He tries to set insult comic star Jimmy Barrett straight but comes up against his formidable business manager and wife, Bobbie Barrett. At the stables, Betty flirts with a young man who expresses doubt regarding his upcoming nuptials.

Some of the criticism aimed at this episode after the initial airing was that it was aimless, even more pronounced in a show known for a casual pace. Many thought it played like a standalone, a diverting short story in the middle of a novel. A short-sighted response, I think, but understandable if viewed in a week-to-week context. If seen in the larger view of the whole season, it is a pivotal chapter that introduces important characters and revisits vital themes.

Perhaps after the dramatic punch of "Flight 1," anything other than a dramatic torrent would feel underwhelming. There is also the surprising amount of time given to Harry Crane, who struggles not only with impending fatherhood but his own value and worth within the company. He mistakenly receives Ken Cosgrove's paycheck, and, despite his better instincts, opens it. And while the shock that a "mannequin like Cosgrove" (his wife's words) makes significantly more almost sinks him, it does lead to a burst of initiative around an upcoming episode of *The Defenders*. This doesn't bear any direct fruit, but does allow him to pitch a television department with him as the head, which Roger Sterling approves with a three-point benediction and a small pay bump.

In the first season, Don may have equated success at business as "the key to your salary, your status, your self-worth," but now he continues his disengagement with work. A car wreck occurs on the set of the Utz Chips commercial shoot as he sits in a near-empty theater watching a black-and-white French film. When he vows to take care of the situation, he receives a withering "Where were you?" from Roger (long overdue perhaps, but still strange considering the source) and must wonder how his self-worth will suffer if he can't salvage the operation.

Cosgrove and Freddy Rumsen both take a hit on the self-worth front as they are blamed for allowing the nice Schilling couple from Utz Chips to visit the set of their commercial, only for the rotund Mrs. Schilling to suffer the slings and arrows of a new addition to the colorful cast.

Jimmy Barrett is often compared to insult comedy godfather Don Rickles, and while there are many surface similarities, Barrett remains a full-blooded fictional creation apart from Rickles and the comic styling Rickles helped define. "Insult comedy" should not to be confused with the earlier incarnation known critically by some as "sick comedy." "Sick" comedians such as Tom Lehrer, Nichols and May, Don Adams, and the king, Lenny Bruce, were often derided for their "tasteless" takes on red-button issues like religion and politics, material not touched by the comic giants of the time, Bob Hope and Jack Benny. This style of comedy arose from the anxiety of a post-atomic Cold War world. In explaining the need for this style of comedy, novelist Nelson Algren said, "This is the age of genocide. Falling on a banana peel used to be funny, but now it takes more to shock us."

Insult comedy is a surface replication of this cutting approach, all the outrage with none of the weight. Without Bruce there's no Rickles, but the transition to mainstream acceptance of the style flattens it out (reminiscent of an old Woody Allen joke about his mother's chicken soup, and how she wouldn't serve it until she ran it through the deflavorizing machine). Don Rickles always occupied a strange place in the insult comedy pantheon. While his work bears none of the satirical heft of a Lenny Bruce or Mort Sahl, he isn't a simple character assassin either. The racial attacks he could level at his audience members felt more like a peg-lowering for humanity, punctuated by his genuine end of routine epilogues that depicted the erosion of cross-racial divides in the heat of battle.

Jimmy Barrett may have the fidgety energy of Rickles and even a whiff of appropriated cool from the Rat Pack. He mentions Sinatra's fondness for his drink of choice, and Sinatra was one of Rickles's biggest fans and paved the way for his success in Las Vegas. But Barrett is out for blood, the guy who suffered a punishing regimen of abuse as a kid and is rebuilding himself through the abuse of others. He's a sniper who picks off targets for revenge. Rickles had a better view of himself, to say nothing of keener insight; he insulted Sinatra onstage but made him a friend once in the wings.

The whole idea of value and worth is appraised this episode, one that is memorable not for its own events so much as what it builds into the over-arching narrative of the season.

There are two exceptions: Betty's equestrian hobby with friend Sarah Beth continues, and while Betty may find momentary escape in running her horse around the track (and similarly shackled once she returns it to the stable), she does have an opportunity to talk alone with Sarah Beth's horse-track crush, Arthur Case. Even though Betty is guilty of some low-level flirtation, she does not expect the full overture Arthur makes toward her, especially after meeting his fiancée earlier. He is drawn to Betty by her profound sadness, but she refuses both his pass and his assessment of her character ("No," she replies. "It's just my people are Nordic").

The other important plot point is the dinner at Lutèce that Don sets up to smooth things out between Jimmy Barrett and the Schillings. While Don is a complicated character who is as easy to dislike as like, the casual brutality of his scene with Bobbie Barrett is shocking, more so than any insult, as he attempts to wrestle an apology from Jimmy.

The Philosophy of _Mad Men_ — Don Draper: "We all work for someone."
Period Moment: The episode of _The Defenders_ that gives Harry Crane an opportunity clearly did exist, but more important is the correlation between that golden-age drama and _Mad Men_. Both came out of a character-driven tradition more at home in the theater or in literature than on television, and both made a name for themselves in the midst of a sea of mediocre programming that included formulaic genres and vapid game shows.

Another interesting point: the title of that controversial episode? "The Benefactor."
Ad Pitch: Utz is a genuine company, a family-run business for its eighty-plus years history. Known for high quality and freshness in their snacks, the company refuses to deliver products made in their Hanover, Pennsylvania, facilities anywhere outside of the Eastern Seaboard.

Shoe factory worker William Utz decided to leave his job in 1921 and start a business selling homemade potato chips cooked by his wife Sallie, well-versed in "Pennsylvania Dutch" style cuisine. She cooked and he sold, to farmer's markets and stores in Hanover and Baltimore. By 1936, they moved production out of a room in their house to a cement plant erected in their backyard. By 1949, business grew so rapidly that Utz built a plant over a ten-acre spread of land. As sales continued to grow, Utz increased its product line but never strayed from their narrowly defined market area.

This led to a notorious campaign created by long-time agency Gray Kirk-Vasant dubbed "No Utz in Paris," which depicted an outraged Frenchman in black beret throwing a tantrum because Utz Chips were not available in France. Further editions of the ad included Los Angeles and North Dakota.

In 1998, Utz dropped this agency and hired another Baltimore firm called MGH Advertising to oversee their account. The family-run nature of the business is not the only thing that hasn't changed; the packing of the chips remains much the same (as seen in this episode), and still features the "Utz Girl" logo, also known from billboards throughout the Northeast. Rumor has it that Sallie Utz herself was the model for this regionally renowned logo.

Manhattan Real Estate: The French restaurant Lutèce is mentioned from the first episode of this season (Roger mentions to Joan that he's taking his wife Mona — "Let me know what the living are up to"), but the détente meeting between the Schillings and Jimmy Barrett marks the first visit to this American landmark of French cuisine.

Opened in 1961 by André Soltner, Lutèce (249 East Fiftieth Street) quickly gained notoriety for the pastoral fare such as the puffy onion tart from the chef's native Alsace. Along with La Côte Basque, Lutèce helped make this old-world elegance synonymous with high dining in Manhattan. In fact, at one point celebrated chef Julia Child once pronounced Lutèce "the best restaurant in the United States."

Unfortunately, the expensive-account lunches that kept this milestone profitable in later years all but disappeared in the aftermath of 9/11 and forced the closure of the restaurant in 2004.

Cocktail of Note: Before "Monsieur Le Pew" can take their order, Jimmy needs to order because he's "down a quart." He takes two Johnnie Walkers on the rocks but Bobbie opts for a classier aperitif. While there are many cocktail recipes for Dubonnet, most aficionados would balk at anything other than how Bobbie orders it: on the rocks with a twist of lemon.

Money Part Two —
What They Made Then and What They Make Now

Inflation aside, it is interesting to think about how much the characters on *Mad Men* earn and to compare them, not only to what the
others in the Sterling Cooper office make (why is Cosgrove making
so much more than Pete?), but also to what those same positions
earn in the marketplace today.

Employee & Position	Weekly Salary Then	Weekly Salary Now
Peggy Olson Secretary	$35	$732
Peggy Olson Copywriter	$40	$931
Pete Campbell Account Executive	$75	$765
Harry Crane Head of Television Department	$225 (plus drinks)	$883
Ken Cosgrove Account Executive (and mannequin)	$300	$765
Don Draper Creative Director & Partner	$865 (plus 12%)	$918 (Don really knew how to negotiate a raise!)

2.04 THREE SUNDAYS

Original air date: August 17, 2008
Written by: André and Maria Jacquemetton
Directed by: Tim Hunter

> "Your glorying is not good. Know ye not that a little leaven leav-
> eneth the whole lump? Purge out therefore the old leaven that
> ye may be a new lump, as ye are unleavened . . . therefore let us
> keep the feast, not with the old leaven of malice and wickedness;
> but with the unleavened bread of sincerity and truth."
>
> — First Corinthians 5:6-8

Peggy dutifully follows her mother to church, where she meets the hip young priest recently assigned to the parish. Everyone at the Sterling Cooper office works over the weekend to prepare for the big American Airlines pitch. Don helps Bobbie implement her idea for a network television show starring Jimmy.

The pain of birth is one thing, but the burden of rebirth is quite another. Metaphysical soul mates Don and Peggy deal with their respective pasts and the effort required to move beyond them to a different future.

Betty can't fathom Don's reluctance to take their son's recent disobedient streak in hand and punish some sense into him. The stress of the impending American Airlines pitch (which, due to the untimely departure of Duck Phillips's liaison Shel Keneally, is a non-starter or "still-born" as Don says) and his own turmoil at succumbing to an extra-marital affair with Bobbie notwithstanding, Don is unwilling to raise his voice let alone a hand to his son. By the same token, Betty appears extra harsh on the boy and it is difficult to tell if it is masked animosity toward Don or simple frustration with life on the home front. Tensions boil over between Don and Betty (ostensibly over the raising of the children) and while he is unwilling to spank his son, in the heat of argument he still manages to shove Betty hard, with little concern for her wellbeing.

But it is a major step for Don when he finally confesses that he suffered an abusive upbringing at his father's fists that made him "fantasize about the day I could murder him." Don's vulnerability quickly defuses Betty's anger but does not lead her to ask further questions, as if she is so startled by the sight of her husband defenseless that she doesn't know what to do, worried that to probe further may cause him to curl up like a pill bug.

A more formal confession between Peggy's older sister, Anita, and the fresh new pastor, Father Gill, further broadens the scope of knowledge about her giving birth. Peggy continues to attend church with mother and sister, and this can't be simply a function of guilt. She finds the brimstone talk of "evildoers and evil deeds" a little tough to handle and tries to leave the service but stumbles across the fresh-faced Father Gill. He is the kind of priest who flirts with "hipness" — he sneaks a smoke during a service, plays the guitar — but there is a genuine aspect to him that Peggy finds charming. She may not see herself as a believer, but doesn't fight Father Gill when he says that their meeting is providential ("This is the way God works").

Anita is tired, and angry at Peggy, but it is unclear why. Is it her ability to get whatever she wants? Or is she actually caring after Peggy's child? Anita is also a little jealous of Father Gill's interest in Peggy and, despite her true love for "Pegs," she can't help but try to sully her in the pastor's eyes in confessional. He doesn't seem to judge, but makes it known to Peggy that he is aware of her situation, one that she struggles to push back so she can go on with her fabulous life as Manhattan copywriter.

American Airlines is looking for a rebirth following the Jamaica Bay disaster. They push up the pitch date for Sterling Cooper, and the creative and account services teams put in long hours on a Palm Sunday to prepare. Bobby Draper has burned himself on the griddle Don makes pancakes on and while Betty takes him to the hospital, Sally must join her dad at the office. Her comfort with handling liquor leads to a first drink and passing out, a startling occurrence for a girl in grade school.

Suffer the little children, this episode seems to say, for the sins of their parents. Not that the parents have it any easier; Peggy thinks herself unworthy of a child and withdraws from his life while Don tries all he can to limit the pain his children might face. Both actions only lead to further damage, most immediately to the parents.

It is worth noting how the show's writers continue to reward those who pay attention. As preface to his clumsy attempt at a pass, Arthur Case mentioned F. Scott Fitzgerald's novella *The Diamond as Big as the Ritz* in "The Benefactor." Betty may feign ambivalence, but she reads Fitzgerald's *Babylon Revisited* (itself an echo of an episode title from the first season), a collection that contains the very story Case mentioned.

The Philosophy of *Mad Men* — Don Draper: "There is no such thing as American history . . . only a frontier."

Period Moment: Bobbie Barrett's idea for Jimmy's TV show is precisely what Don thinks the networks look for — "derivative with a twist." The idea of a hidden-camera show with Jimmy as the host but Jimmy "being Jimmy . . . you know, not nice" is a sly twist on a premise that by that time was already a classic.

Candid Camera began life on the radio — as, one might imagine, *Candid Microphone*. Host Allen Funt wanted to capture the reactions of regular people thrown into unusual circumstances, and described the switch to television in a *Psychology Today* interview as wanting to "record what they did — their gestures, facial expressions, confusions, and delights."

The genesis of the idea came from Funt's work as a research assistant at Cornell University, where he helped psychologist Kurt Lewin record the results of experiments on mothers and their children. Funt also found inspiration during his time in the Army Signal Corps, where he taped soldiers reading their letters home to family and friends.

Candid Camera bounced around many networks with varying degrees of success but finally found a permanent home on CBS in 1960, where it enjoyed a successful run for the next seven years. Often referred to as the longest running show in television history, iterations of the concept aired at some point during each consecutive decade from the '40s to the '90s.

Ad Pitch: Although the American Airlines pitch is "still-born," we get a tantalizing look at the artwork and copy that Sterling Cooper has prepared. The quick peak adheres to Don's desire to "know what 1963 looks like." The art Sal lovingly props on the easel is forward-thinking without being futuristic: a bold illustration of a jetliner and the line "This is American Airlines" — copy that is brash in its simplicity.

The slogan American used from the early '50s into the '60s was "America's leading airline," followed in 1964 by the somewhat muddled and pedestrian "American built an airline for professional travelers." Too bad Shel Keneally was fired.

Manhattan Brooklyn Real Estate: Through much of the Easter Season Peggy wrestles with her mother's expectations and her own guilt while at church.

The Church of the Holy Innocents (279 East Seventeenth Street) was founded in 1909 near Beverly Street and named after a December 28th Feast (once called "Childermass"), which commemorates the boys of Bethlehem two years and younger who were murdered by King Herod in an ill-fated attempt to avoid the trouble of the birth of Christ. In 1922, the church received approval for construction of a larger church (seating for 1,100) and rectory on the existing plot of land. It was a late Gothic revival design by Helme & Corbett, also responsible for St. Gregory's Church, another Brooklyn worship site.

A Skinner Organ would have provided the grand East Sunday music that plays throughout this episode. Upon installation in 1922, the organ had 30 stops, 27 ranks of pipes, and a total of 1,176 pipes. Two 35-foot tall oak cases in the gallery house all the pipes and mechanisms.

Cocktail of Note: Sally Draper continues her perilous career as a bartender (after tending drink orders in "Flight 1") when she makes an eye-watering Bloody Mary that is heavy on the vodka and light on the blood (and spices).

> 1 ounce vodka in a highball glass filled with ice (and not a tumbler, as per Sally Draper)
> Tomato juice (pour in around vodka to top of glass (and not the other way around, as per Sally Draper)
> 1 dash celery salt
> 1 dash pepper
> 1 dash Tabasco
> 2 dashes Worcestershire sauce
> 1 dash lemon or lime juice
> Shake or stir, then serve.

2.05 THE NEW GIRL

Original air date: August 24, 2008
Written by: Robin Veith
Directed by: Jennifer Getzinger

> "Be a woman. It's powerful business when done correctly."
> — Bobbie Barrett

After a network picks up Jimmy's television show, Don and Bobbie take their celebration on the road and suffer the consequences. Joan announces her engagement to her doctor boyfriend. She also finds Don the perfect secretary. Freddy Rumsen plays Mozart on his zipper.

New York is the Mecca of reinvention. As de facto capital of the United States, this is fitting. People the world over are drawn to the cosmopolitan sprawl, the bustle of commerce, as perfect camouflage to rewrite their biography. A city of such tumult — where no story is too outlandish, no personality too extreme — is the perfect place from which to devise a new identity, clutching at all the colors in the rainbow that the city provides.

Bobbie Barrett knows a thing or two about reinvention. Whether as "just" Jimmy Barrett's wife, his "sister," or outright manager, she has done whatever is necessary to get the job finished. It's all negotiation, she says, whether it's for a traffic ticket or a TV pilot for *Grin and Barrett*. Her philosophy on career is one with which Don can easily align, but when it comes to negotiation, he's of a different opinion; he thinks it's a bore.

He can disagree with Bobbie so easily because he knows that, to a great extent, they are alike. He is at ease with her in a way he isn't with the other women in his life (although, as one who is a different man to every woman, this is not hard to imagine), but there is a commonality in their world view that comforts. He may not have found a soul mate so much as a kindred spirit.

On the other hand, Don leaps to his feet when he sees someone crossing the dining floor at Sardi's. He has his first look at Rachel Menken in a long while, and she looks no worse for wear. She's gained a little weight — but not around the waist, around her ring finger. She is now Mrs. Katz and he can't mask his disappointment. This is one of those passing moments

"Negotiation is a bore." (AP Photo/Matt Sayles)

that makes this show resonate for me; people from the past pop up unexpectedly, not even at an inopportune time, but at just the right time to exact a blithe whiplash with thoughts from the past and what might have been. It is a kind of irregularity around the margins of life that gives this show richness and complexity that eludes other television series.

Also unexpected is the car crash that sidelines Don's call to the ocean (he'll get there, just not yet). Yet, for those who are fans of another Matthew Weiner–produced show, the wreck may not come as much of a surprise. In an episode of *The Sopranos* called "Irregular Around the Margins," Tony Soprano is driving his nephew's girlfriend out to New Jersey in search of some cocaine, and, it is implied, a trip to bed together. A car wreck scuttles those plans, but does not stop the questions this compromising position raises.

This is a point many fans have brought up on blogs and discussion boards, less to cry foul than to suggest a connection. Weiner has stated that Don is different than Tony in that he doesn't kill anyone . . . with his hands. I think they are both governed by an outsized sense of entitlement that is either childlike or sociopathic, I'm not sure which.

Unlike season 1, Don pays the price for his transgressions this year. He may think negotiation is a bore, but talent at it would come in handy as he faces a county police officer over his accident. Bobbie thoughtfully claims the open bottle of booze as her own, but Don has blown the sobriety test and the officer is in no mood to let this slick cat from the big city slide by on his charm. He is quite happy to make Don suffer an embarrassment to writhe out of this pickle.

At first glance, there are a number of people Don could call on for aid;

Roger Sterling would take care of things without a word to the wise, but then Don might slip a few notches in his friend's eyes and he enjoys Roger's approval as much as Pete craves Don's; even a number of underlings at the office could be glowered into silence.

Peggy's arrival at the police station is surprising but it leads to further shading on her labor and hospital stay. And what was held out like a carrot on a stick turns out to serve only as underline for the similarities between Don and Peggy.

The details of her convalescence and recovery are the stuff of soap opera and too easy a dramatic stop for a show as elegant as *Mad Men*. Instead of a scene showing the difficulty of her slow build back to health, we see Don visiting Peggy's bedside — not to offer flowers or platitudes but cold words of survival ("Get out of here and move forward. This never happened. It will shock you how much it never happened"). One could argue that Peggy's willingness to follow his advice is more a facet of her fragile state than anything else, but the determination that she follows through on it shows they were kindred spirits all along.

Bobbie can only think of Peggy and Don's connection as romantic, but senses Peggy is sincere when she says they "work together." Even though the young copywriter is disdainful of the seasoned professional, she follows the spirit of her advice if not to the letter. When she asks Don for repayment of the bail money, it's not for leverage. But she does call him "Don" for the first time, and it is another shade of maturity that is no less powerful for its subtlety.

As for the "new girl," Joan may have found a terrific match for Don in slinky Jane Siegel (Peyton List). Perhaps Joan has selected her because of her college education or their similarities in the sultry department (after the more mousy Peggy and Lois don't last long on Draper's desk), but she may have chosen someone similarly adept at using feminine wiles in the workplace without realizing she might not appreciate the competition. Even though Joan is dizzy from her recent engagement, she isn't so stratospheric that she will let Jane's revealed décolletage pass without comment, although her pronouncement that the office is run on "professional decorum" is memorably countered by Freddy Rumsen's impromptu pants-fly Mozart recital.

In the end, the rainbow they all grasp for is always there for New Yorkers. Like the multicolored Afghan we see throughout the episode — first at

Peggy's, then with her at the hospital, and in the final shot slung over the back of a chair at the Drapers' — the colors are there for the picking.

The Philosophy of Mad Men — Bobbie Barrett: "This is America. Pick a job and then become the person who does it."

Period Moment: Pete flips through magazines to help provide a sample for a fertility test. After passing *Nudi-Fax, International Nudistour Guide*, and, perhaps sexiest of all, *U.S. News & World Report*, he settles on *Jaybird USA*.

The launch of *Playboy* in 1953 helped usher in a new era of frank sexual freedoms (for better or for ill), but the publication could not show genitalia or pubic hair without breaking the country's obscenity laws. The state and federal regulations known as the Comstock laws forbade the production and distribution of any "obscene, lewd, or lascivious book," or for such a publication to be "carried in the mail." The definition of obscene at the time of the law's creation in 1873 included not only visual depictions, but literary erotica as well, along with letters containing "indecent or scurrilous epithets" or those "intended for the prevention of conception or procuring an abortion." That definition has changed over time and courtroom battles over the Comstock laws have underscored those changes over the years.

In 1958, the Supreme Court ruled that magazines depicting nudity in a nonsexual manner were not obscene. As a result, publishers of periodicals that covered the nudist subculture (*Sunshine & Health* the best known of the time) were the first to legally present unflinching pictures of female and male genitalia. While photographers took great pains to arrange their nude models in non-erotic settings (volleyball, sunbathing, and, least wise of all, barbecuing), the desired use among the bulk of the audience contradicted the Supreme Court's findings.

Jaybird USA was one of a number published under that moniker, a ploy by the publishers to generate interest in "new" magazines. *Jaybird Safari, Jaybird Happening*, and *Jaybird Nude/Image* were all variations on the newsstands. The first issue — entitled *Jaybird Journal* — arrived in 1965, which would make its inclusion in this episode anachronistic by at least two years.

Ad Pitch: Don reaches for a foothold when he meets Mrs. Katz and can only think to slide an inside jab to the firm that took over the Menken account. "How are things at Grey? They still taking credit for everything we did?"

Now known as Grey Global and one of the largest advertising firms in the world with offices in eighty-three countries, Larry Valenstein's Grey

Advertising was, even in 1962, a long-standing player in the advertising game. Named after the color of the walls at the agency's first offices on Fifth Avenue, Valenstein and partner Arthur Fatt built on early experience in the direct-mail business and the garment industry (furriers in particular) to secure a strong position as advertisers for soft-goods merchants whose products were sold in department stores.

In 1956, Grey Advertising began a long and profitable relationship with Procter & Gamble, and, by 1959, they began their global expansion with their first international office in Montreal.

Manhattan Real Estate: Bobbie calls Don from Sardi's where she is "surrounded by clowns."

Perhaps, but she was also surrounded by the renowned celebrity caricatures. Luminaries of the stage were drawn to the restaurant due to Arthur Sardi's habit of keeping the doors open very late to cater to the schedule of Broadway performers.

Alex Gard first drew the caricatures that cover the walls, in exchange for one meal a day at the restaurant. His first official drawing was of Ted Healey, a vaudevillian star. Before his death in 1948, Gard drew over 700 caricatures. John Mackey, Don Bevan, and Richard Baratz have successively taken over the pad and pencil for the restaurant, which has resulted in over 1300 drawings currently on display.

On the day James Cagney died, a craven-hearted thief stole his portrait from Sardi's wall. Since then, once a drawing is completed the Sardi's staff immediately makes a copy, with the original sent to the subject and the duplicate affixed to the wall.

2.06 MAIDENFORM
• • • • • • • • • • • • • • • •

Original air date: August 31, 2008
Written by: Matthew Weiner
Directed by: Phil Abraham

> "Women right now already have a fantasy and it's not going up
> the Nile . . . it's right here in America. Jackie Kennedy and
> Marilyn Monroe. Every single woman is one of them."
>
> — Paul Kinsey

Sterling Cooper devises a new campaign for Playtex that suggests there are two kind of women in the world. Peggy is frustrated when she is not included in late-night revelries with clients. Don is distressed to learn how women around town talk about him.

The roles men squeeze women into are as constricting and uncomfortable as the undergarments in vogue during the time of "Maidenform." The advertising challenge Don faces is a new direction for the Playtex campaign ("Nothing fits both sides of a woman better than Playtex") and is a neat underscore to the Madonna/whore complex women grapple with. Meanwhile the creative bull session that leads to the Jackie O. by day/Marilyn by night idea hollers the absurdity of a male-dominated industry trying to sell such a product ("Bras are for men," Paul Kinsey asserts).

The series is critical of this limited view and is not afraid to spell it out. As in other episodes, the comment or result is offered before the problem is fully revealed (as we see in the previous episode when Don calls Peggy to bail him out of jail before the flashback of the hospital bed visit). In this case, the opening montage puts forward the argument. Three women wriggle into their underthings, and while Betty and Joan fit nicely into the Jackie/Marilyn dichotomy, Peggy is a lone dissenter. It is also telling that, in an episode where mirrors play such a major thematic role, Peggy is the only one of the three who doesn't dress in front of one.

The music played over the montage is jarring, not only in sound but in context. A series known for scrupulous attention to historical detail, *Mad Men* has employed music in a similar manner. However, the use of the song "The Infanta" by the Decemberists raised the ire of some fans who had grown accustomed to musical selections that did not contradict the

I dreamed I was cut out for fun in my *maidenform* bra

First Star*. . . new Maidenform teenage rage (shown on model) . . . scalloped frame around horizontally stitched cups defines the most *divine* curves! First Star Regular, 1.50. Or First Star Contour (secret foam lining to fill the needs of the junior figure) in white AA or A cups, cotton broadcloth with petite bow trim, 2.00.

Billboard charts of the day. A choice so flagrant does make a viewer pause, but if RJD2's electronically contrived snare whips and high-hat taps don't establish an ironic view of the times covered, then the sly humorous comments that are woven through each episode should. Also, it is not the first time music from another era is used within the context of the actual drama; in particular the Cardigans track "The Great Divide" that closes "Ladies Room" from the first season is also out of time.

The use of "The Infanta" falls into the category of strategic anachronism (and was used once before in the episode "Shoot," as circulated in review copies for the press but removed for broadcast). The Decemberists' song accomplishes the task of relating the concerns of 1960s women with the women of today, much like the contemporary opening of Jane Campion's film *Portrait of a Lady*.

Peggy does not conform to either of the archetypes dreamed of by men (she's more "Gertrude Stein," according to Cosgrove) and also has a difficult time fitting in with the boys in the office. The Playtex brainstorm happened during an after-hours sojourn, and Peggy bristles at her exclusion ("Believe me," Freddy says, "You didn't want to be at *that* bar"). She is a pioneer of the office, but they don't make handbooks for that kind of travel. And while she will show herself eager to succeed and willing to act contrary to her character, as a result she might struggle with her own identity.

Joan is never surer of her place in the world, one solidified with her recent engagement. The advice she gives to Peggy in her pursuit of work-place respect is tart and possibly motivated by suspicion of her copywriting career ("Stop dressing like a little girl").

Sartorial advice of another type hits Betty across the head. She buys a bikini from the recent country club rib and fashion show and wears it later. Don's reaction to the mother of his children looking sexy is bad enough, but his cruel definition of it ("desperate") is enough to make her feel dirty. There is jealousy in his remarks, but he is almost as concerned with the leering of "fifteen-year-old lifeguards" and "loafing millionaires." Many have suggested that men want a lady in the living room and a harlot in the bedroom, provided, it seems, that no one else see that wanton side of her.

This brings up an interesting point regarding the Jackie/Marilyn Playtex campaign. Like many men, Don has difficulty reconciling the attraction to both types of women in the same package, and perhaps this foretells the failure of the campaign. The dual nature of the Playtex creative goes against how men view women, in that they generally want one or the other, not Madonna and whore in the same lingerie. (Remember Don's inability to perform on Valentine's Day when Betty wore the racy corset?)

Another interesting theme in this episode is the presence of JFK. While a recurring name throughout the first season, once elected president there is rarely a mention of him within the second. But the mere fact of Kennedy's presidency seems to give credence to the Playtex campaign, as he was a man who *had* both women (Jackie his Madonna, Marilyn his whore). And perhaps the Playtex executives are wise not to get behind the campaign; near the end of 1963 and Kennedy's assassination, the fictional Jackie/ Marilyn campaign certainly would cause Don and the gang to scramble faster to pull artwork than they did when American Airlines Flight 1 went down in Jamaica Bay.

But for all his concern over how Betty's bikini will affect her "reputation," Don is the one with a notoriety that precedes him, and the only male in the series to deal with the usual female quandary of double standards. Don's is a self-imposed double life, but he starts to feel crushed by it, to the point that he can't even bear to be looked at lovingly by his daughter (to say nothing of the respect afforded him as a veteran at the country club). The revelation from Bobbie Barrett that other women have spoken about him as a "connoisseur" makes him consider his actions for the first time in a while. Many fans weren't sure what to think when Don responds to one of his fan's remarks with a horrified "I don't know who you're talking about." A woman at Random House has appropriated a friend's encounter with him? He's erased it from his memory, as he does with many foul deeds. Or is it the work of the *other* Don Draper catching up with him?

Whatever the answer, it is the last one that intrigued the audience and is the first hint of the flipside of Don's dilemma. In the final shot as he sits on the toilet flanked by his reflection, it is the first time that his major concern isn't someone discovering his true identity. What if part of that life has lapped back up into his? He is also confronted with his reflection as an extension of how other people view him. And he doesn't like it.

The Philosophy of Mad Men — Don Draper: "Jacqueline Kennedy, Marilyn Monroe . . . women have feelings about these women because men do. Because we want both, they want to be both."

Period Moment: At the country club, Don gets the inside scoop from a former employee on the recent shakeup at the public relations firm Lem Jones and Associates — and why he left it "burning behind" him.

In 1960, Lem Jones, New York public relations mainstay and one-time press secretary to 1940 Republican presidential hopeful Wendell Willkie, entered into an agreement with the CIA to represent Cuban exiles in an effort to counter Fidel Castro's political and media campaign against the American way of life. From hotel rooms to a crowded Grand Central Terminal, clandestine meetings with CIA agents ensued with the intention of mounting a successful propaganda campaign against the charismatic Cuban leader.

This offensive did not start well. Castro led a delegation to the United

Nations in September of 1960. The CIA launched a "Caravan of Sorrow" to rebut the Communist Party leader's volcanic oratory — two busloads of exiled Cuban mothers were dispatched from Miami, with the intention of making many emotional and telegenic pleas to show the dark side of Communism and Castro's political showmanship. Unfortunately, the CIA failed to place an agent aboard either bus and, as a result, lost contact with the caravan for two days. Frantic CIA agents contacted Jones for assistance. He suggested they stop the buses when they reached Philadelphia, for fear that the caravan would arrive in Manhattan in the dead of night without any press coverage. The buses finally rolled into Manhattan the next morning and a picture of one of the mothers praying at St. Patrick's made the New York papers.

The formation of the CIA-backed Cuban Revolutionary Council was announced at a March 22 press conference arranged by Lem Jones. On April 16, 1960, the Bay of Pigs invasion began, and Jones started to release communiqués under the CRC banner dictated to him by CIA operatives, in particular one E. Howard Hunt who would later come to light as a key co-conspirator in the Watergate burglary and coverup. While Lem Jones and Associates could not take the blame for the failure of the Bay of Pigs invasion, the firm did weather intense scrutiny in the post-invasion criticism of the CIA's shadowy involvement in the propaganda campaign and for issuing the CRC press releases from their Madison Avenue office.

Ad Pitch: Maidenform's "I dreamt . . ." campaign catapulted the company into the number two slot for intimate apparel in America, and garnered a great deal of both acclaim and denigration along the way. The firm of Norman, Craig & Kunnell was responsible for the creative that launched in 1949, and ran, in various forms, for nearly twenty years, establishing it as one of the longest running campaigns in advertising history. In the '70s, Maidenform dropped the fantasy theme in favor of depicting women as professionals such as doctors, lawyers, and basketball referees.

Unfortunately, the desire to feature their products in the advertising resulted in spreads with fully dressed men surrounding women wearing nothing but underwear. A great many women were outraged, and in the early '80s a New York–based group called Women Against Pornography chastised Maidenform for sexism in advertising.

Cocktail of Note: Due to Duck Phillips's struggle with sobriety this episode, this section is appropriately dry. Try a club soda with lime.

2.07 THE GOLD VIOLIN

Original air date: September 7, 2008
Written by: Jane Anderson, André and Maria Jacquemetton
Directed by: Andrew Bernstein

> **Ken Cosgrove:** You're not like everyone else around here.
>
> **Salvatore Romano:** I don't know if that's true.

Don considers buying a Coupe de Ville, remembering his time as a car sales-man. Sal reads Ken's new short story and invites him over for dinner. The youthful outlook of creative duo Smitty and Kurt helps set the mood for a new Martinson's Coffee campaign. Jimmy Barrett forces Betty to face her worst fears.

Fathoming the depths of expression (and expressions, for that matter) is the prime motivation in "The Gold Violin."

Don struggles with buying a car that will properly show that he's "arrived." He looks over the 1962 Coupe de Ville but balks at committing himself to such a grand display of affluence (while he spies a man looking over a more modest, gold car in the showroom). Roger flirts with getting "too deep before the cocktail hour" (see "Philosophy" below) before urging Don to take the leap.

Don also has to grapple with the Martinson's Coffee people, who are having difficulty with market share because the kids don't drink much coffee. Smith and Smith, Sterling Cooper's resident young anti-establishment fixtures, who eschew standard office wear for tieless shirts and one-piece jumpsuits, prepare a pitch that sells a product to a generation that doesn't want to be sold. Smitty (sans tie) produces a sixty-page manifesto from the Students for a Democratic Society that a friend still in school "back in Michigan" sent him. Don appears to appreciate the idealism but is only interested in the document as a focus group prospectus. He can't (or won't) stare too long into a concept that Smitty marvels at as "deep."

The depth required to understand the new Mark Rothko painting in Cooper's office comes from an unexpected place. Harry Crane is worried that Cooper uses it as a skill-testing question to weed out philistines who don't "get" it. The apparently devious Jane Siegel convinces Crane, Cosgrove, and Romano to sneak into Cooper's office for a look. The development of

In "The Gold Violin" Cosgrove, Kinsey, Sal, and Crane try to understand Rothko's multiform expression of his "not-self." (AP Photo/Chris Pizzello)

Cosgrove as an oddly sensitive soul continues (jock/poet?) when he has the most insight into the painting, suggesting that the painting isn't supposed to *mean* anything, but has been created to provoke an emotional response. "Like you're staring into something very deep . . . you could fall in."

Equally deep is Ken Cosgrove's short story, which provides this episode with a title. He senses that Sal is sensitive enough to provide a critical appraisal of his latest work (or, more likely, fawning praise). Sal, still impressed with Ken's last work (pegging it as "beautiful and sad"), is thrilled to give an early insight and jumps at the chance to invite him over for dinner. We finally get a good look at Sal the married man and the terrible cost incurred by living a false life. Sal can't stop himself from bathing in Ken's presence at his table — or from shushing his poor wife, Kitty, when she tries to become involved in the conversation. Unlike some deceitfulness, Sal's lavender marriage is not intended to exact pain but to provide cover; that does little to mitigate Kitty's own beautiful and sad existence.

Joan doesn't have to spend much energy discerning the new girl's intentions in the office. She may already fear that Jane is out to replace her (even their names are similar), but when Joan tries to exert her power by firing Jane for the Rothko adventure, she finds herself overmatched. Jane outflanks the office manager by appealing to Roger Sterling's vanity and saving her job, a maneuver that sinks lower than her plummeting décolletage from "The New Girl."

Many viewers were thrown by the lows Jimmy Barrett will plumb to exact revenge. When he blindsides Betty with the news that his wife and her husband have coupled, many fans felt a strange anger toward him for making such a mess of things. Don is hardly an innocent and in no way deserving of clemency, but Jimmy's sniping at the man who embodies everything he despises ("I've stood behind guys like him my whole life") is galling. Even more so when one considers that Jimmy owes much of his recent success to Don. Some viewers weren't sure whether their upset sprang from the thought of the damage the aftershocks would wreak on the Draper household: others felt it was overdue and simply a matter of time before Don's secrets unraveled in such a destructive manner.

A single flashback to Don's early days as a used car salesman hint at the depth of his desire to keep his identity safe, and the lengths to which he will go to safeguard it. The appearance of a fragile blond woman with a limp is all we see, but foreshadows the revelation of one of the more bittersweet aspects of the enigma that is Don Draper.

The Philosophy of _Mad Men_ — Roger Sterling: "Do I need to remind you of the finite nature of life?"

Period Moment: Harry, Ken, and Sal creep into Cooper's office behind ringleader Jane Siegel to take in the mysterious abstract expressionist painting that cost $10,000. "It's a Rothko," Sal says.

Born in Latvia in 1903 as Marcus Rothkowitz, the self-taught Mark Rothko first gained notoriety with a series of "mythomorphic abstractionist" works that rode the wave of surrealist art popularity begun in New York with shows by Joan Miró, Max Ernst, and Salvador Dali.

Rothko shifted away from the mythic surrealism in the late '40s, composing a manifesto with fellow artist Adolph Gottlieb that appeared in the _New York Times_. "We favor the simple expression of the complex thought. . . . We are for flat forms because they destroy illusion and reveal truth." Rothko's movement toward explorations of color and shape (inspired by the American painter Clyfford Still) resulted in the "multiform" works of which Bertram Cooper's acquisition was a part.

Although knighted a leader of a second wave of abstract expressionism, Rothko resisted the application of labels to his work. "I don't express myself in my paintings," he once said. "I express my not-self."

Cooper is vague on his feelings for the painting (no more so than on any other topic) but is happy to note that he expects the painting to double in value by the following Christmas. If he holds onto it to the beginning of the next decade, that number will spike. Rothko committed suicide on February 25, 1970, and a year later the Marlborough Fine Art gallery sold a total of 100 paintings for an estimated $1.8 million, double the value of those works before he took his life

Period Moment #2: Smitty reads a lengthy screed from a friend at school preaching a "power and uniqueness rooted in love, reflectiveness, reason, and creativity." The suggestion here is that one half of the Smith and Smith team knows Tom Hayden, primary author of *The Port Huron Statement*, an idealistic manifesto for the student activist movement that looked "uncomfortably to the world" they were about to inherit. Concerns about racial bigotry and civil rights for African-Americans along with concerns about nuclear weapons and the slim prospects for peace are the main thrust of the document. The manifesto also examined the role students have in shaping a world more in line with the idealistic tenets that the country was built upon ("all men are created equal").

Perhaps Mr. Hayden should have also worried about spirited demonstrations he would face from conservatives while serving in the California State Senate, or his impending marriage to and divorce from Jane Fonda.

Ad Pitch: Don mentions the lame attempts made by Martinson's (or Martinson, as the coffee has alternatively been known) Coffee to reach the youth market, in particular commercials with puppets.

True, although they weren't puppets, but Muppets. In 1957, a young Jim Henson created 179 commercials for Washington-area Wilkins Coffee. The spots were only ten seconds long (eight seconds of talking Muppets, with a two-second product shot) and highly effective. Henson eventually revamped the idea and sold it to other regional coffee producers, including Martinson.

The ads feature two characters, the cheery Wilkins and the grumpy Wontkins. The former, an early Kermit the Frog, extols the virtues of Wilkins Coffee, while the latter resists. Wilkins makes the point for trying his coffee in bizarre, violent ways, including a club to the head, a cannon-ball, a gunshot, a guillotine, and throwing Wontkins beneath the wheels of the Wilkins Coffee Bandwagon (clips all available on YouTube). Despite the gruesome executions meted out, there is an undeniably chipper flight-iness surrounding the spots and indicative of a deft touch that would mark Henson's work in later years.

Manhattan Real Estate: The Stork Club is the setting for Jimmy Barrett's cel-ebration of his new show (*Grin and Barrett*) and his devious plan to upend the Drapers' marriage.

The story of the Stork Club, and the proprietor Sherman Billingsley, is a uniquely New York one. Billingsley started his bootlegging career as a young boy along with his brothers in Anadarko, Oklahoma. The Billingsley boys sold their whiskey cloaked in medicine bottles through pharmacies in Oklahoma City before expanding to neighboring states as the government spread the net of Prohibition wider. By 1926, Billingsley leased a nightclub space at 132 West Fifty-second Street and opened the jazz-era speakeasy called the Stork Club.

Billingsley managed the club successfully throughout the run of Prohibition, despite numerous tangles with the police, one address change, and a standoff with a union controlled by ruthless mob boss Dutch Schultz.

After Prohibition, the Stork became *the* spot for New York's elite, boast-ing celebrity clientele such as Bing Crosby, Ernest Hemingway, Damon Runyon, and writer-in-residence Walter Winchell, who famously christened the club "New York's New Yorkiest place on West Fifty-eighth." Hollywood stars weren't the only habitués; tennis star Fred Perry once handed head waiter Victor Crotta a $10,000 tip, which wasn't the biggest he'd received by half (tendered by a lesser-known but exceedingly generous millionaire guest). The Stork Club's star power was so legendary that Billingsley hosted an eponymous live television show from 1950 to 1955, where he circulated among the tables and interviewed luminaries of the day.

Only in New York could a one-time bootlegger from Oklahoma grad-uate to ringmaster of the upper class. But Billingsley was not without detractors, in particular staff members who bristled over his dictatorial management style. He papered common areas with dictated litanies of expectations and threats, which he initialed "S.B." with enough room for an employee to squeeze an *O* in the middle; he had continued battles with unions, who picketed his club frequently through the '50s and '60s; and he weathered accusations of racism, in particular from Lena Horne and Josephine Baker.

In the '60s the New York restaurant landscape changed, along with the rest of America, and the appetite for that golden-age flavor of luxury waned. Billingsley tried to save the business by offering a $1.99 hamburger and French fries in 1963 but this was nothing more than the warning bell. He had no choice but to shutter the operation on October 4, 1965, and died a year to the day of the closing at the age of sixty-six. The building was demolished that year and is now the site of Paley Park.

Cocktail of Note: Jimmy is kind enough to flag down a glass of champagne for Betty at the Stork Club before dropping the infidelity bomb.

The "wine of kings" is a sparkling variety, one that captures a secondary in-bottle fermentation to create the bubbly carbonation, brought about by the addition of yeast and rock sugar before corking. The name is restricted to wine created in the long-standing tradition and region of Champagne, France — a designation protected first through the Treaty of Madrid in 1891, and again in the Treaty of Versailles following the First World War.

2.08 A NIGHT TO REMEMBER

Original air date: September 14, 2008
Written by: Robin Veith, Matthew Weiner
Directed by: Lesli Linka Glatter

> "Gentlemen, we are in a precarious position.
> We must be prepared to abandon ship."
> — Captain Edward John Smith, *A Night to Remember* (1958)

Betty throws a dinner party that goes well but ends with an argument. Joan performs double duty as a script reader in the new television department at Sterling Cooper. At Father Gill's insistence, Peggy does some pro bono copywriting work for the church.

The title of this episode refers to the dinner party Betty throws and the

Catholic Youth Organization dance Peggy volunteers her copywriting skill for, but it reminds us of another night to remember that is even more emblematic of this installment — the 1958 movie of the same name, which charted another disaster: the sinking of the *Titanic*.

As Betty wrestles with the news Jimmy sideswiped her with at the Stork Club in "The Gold Violin," a green swath is cast once again across this episode. The green-domed paperweight on Don's desk is placed in the frame as he and Duck Phillips discuss the shortsightedness of the Heineken account, who fail to see the effect their green bottles have on housewives and the untapped market they represent ("Housewives love green," Pete says).

This time around, the presence of green doesn't seem to just represent jealousy or greed, a natural association with the color. In an episode that passes the easy road, it is apt that green evokes a different emotion — one that is by turns exotic, foreign, and disruptive.

The view affluent housewives take on Heineken (see "Philosophy" below) is one that Don easily pegs, and the fact that his intuition is borne out at the dinner party where Betty buys the beer as part of her "trip around the world" menu only exacerbates the anger she feels. The argument starts as an accusation of humiliation, but soon turns from the standard oblique Matthew Weiner–mandated discussion to a full-on assault. Betty appears almost more appalled at the nature of Don's fling ("She's so old") than the fact that he's had one.

Betty sinks into a wine-soaked haze the following day while she rummages through Don's clothes and desk. Here again, Weiner and crew refuse to take an easy dramatic route; Betty doesn't find a smoking gun, a lipstick-marked collar, or a phone number on a matchbook. Don is too good a liar for that, but Betty is unshakably certain of his infidelity — not because of any hard evidence but due to her perception of how Don and Bobbie interact, a subtle psychological shading that resonates more with the sort of daily divination we all experience but don't see in television dramas.

Betty claims that she doesn't "want it to be like this," and even seems like she might gloss over the whole thing and stick her head back in the sand; after all, she's had her suspicions about Don's infidelity, telling her psychiatrist that when he makes love to her "sometimes it's what I want . . . sometimes it's obviously what someone else wants" ("The Wheel"). Instead, after she has time to think about it, she makes a stand that is quite different from the Betty we saw throughout the first season. She is no longer happy to sit idly by and watch other people make decisions about her. She tells Don not to come home. Now all she has to worry about is if she's going to become like Helen Bishop, a pariah in her perfect suburban neighborhood.

Joan also has to contend with her role and how she's perceived. She is all too happy to help Harry Crane read television scripts without extra compensation, and knocks it out of the park when she meets with a client and mentions the unmissable "summer storyline" that Crane would never have noticed. Even her fiancé is nonplussed about her extracurricular work activities when she reads the scripts at home ("Joanie, you should be watching those shows, not reading them").

Her success is made all the more heartbreaking when (due in large part to her contributions) the television department is thought profitable enough to afford a second employee, a man that Crane hires it seems because he knows him and he is, well, a man. Joan may put a fine face on her response, but secretly she seethes at the dismissal of her worth.

Peggy's secrets intrude on her own carefully structured life. Father Gill volunteers her (in that patient way of his) to donate her time and talent to create a snappy flyer for an upcoming CYO dance. The two characters haven't shared a scene since Easter Sunday where Father Gill gave her an egg for "the little one" ("Three Sundays"). Peggy conducts herself at work and even with Father Gill and the meddling members of the CYO Committee with strength and poise (worthy of Don Draper himself), but when the pastor presses her on any sins she may have to confess, a brief flutter appears. While Father Gill claims "there is no sin too great to bring to God," Peggy seems to have her doubts. Before she can say anything, Peggy rises to fetch copies of the flyer made on the Sterling Cooper Xerox 914 and hands them to Father Gill in a green box as tidy as the one she uses to order her thoughts.

Men use women throughout the episode to get what they want — Don uses Betty as a test market, Father Gill uses Peggy for her copywriting, Harry uses Joan for script reading — and once the men have what they want, the women are pushed back into their confining roles. Some (like Betty) fight back however they can; a few (like Peggy) actually break free and thrive; but most (like Joan) feel they have no choice but to return to their previous places and lead their lives of quiet desperation.

The Philosophy of *Mad Men* — Don Draper: "For women entertaining in the home, Holland is Paris."

Period Moment: During her all-too-brief stint as head of broadcast operations, Joan reads scripts in search of potential conflicts with Sterling Cooper clients acting as sponsors. She claims that *As the World Turns* is about to become "unmissable," but asks her doctor-in-training fiancé, "Is it possible for someone to come out of a coma and have no recollection of who they are?"

Irna Phillips broke into the soap-opera business through radio, creating and starring in *Painted Dreams* in 1930. Following a dispute with the WGN radio network, Phillips moved to rival WMAQ and created other successful radio serials: *The Guiding Light, The Road of Life*, and *The Right to Happiness*. Phillips created what became a standard soap opera technique in bridging scenes with melodramatic organ music. She also brought her own quirks to bear in her work; a notorious hypochondriac who consulted doctors daily, Phillips was the first to make medicine a central force in daily dramas.

Phillips moved to television with *The Guiding Light* in 1952. During this time, Phillips entered into a long-term relationship with Procter & Gamble, who sponsored all of her subsequent serial creations. This included her longest lasting work, *As the World Turns*, the most successful soap opera until *General Hospital* ascended in the mid '80s. About the familial troubles in the fictional town of Oakdale, Illinois, *As the World Turns* bucked the fifteen-minute episode length of all soap operas of the day, becoming the first to run half an hour.

As for the coma patient that Joan asks her fiancé about (the one who awakens speaking with a different accent than before she had the accident), this incident appeared in a storyline that ran from August to November of 1962. The character Penny Hughes (later known as Penny Hughes Baker Wade McGuire Cunningham, showing a great resiliency) was pregnant with Jeff Hughes's baby (after their initial elopement was annulled by Penny's parents because she was underage, followed a year later by a lovely church wedding) but when Jeff couldn't make a run of the family business and left town to make his way as singer Jack Bailey, Penny caught pneumonia and miscarried. When Jeff returned to Oakdale a successful musician and reconciled with Penny, they had a car accident that took his life and her memory.

The less said about her amnesiac romance with Neil Wade, the better.

Ad Pitch: The need for a head of broadcast operations arises when there is a conflict between Maytag's "Amazing Agitator" spot and the ABC Sunday

Night Movie, which features repeated references to a "communist agitator."

As it happens, the Leo Burnett Agency tended to Maytag's advertising needs, and any concerns the account may have had regarding their public image in 1962 would disappear five years later. In 1967, Vincent Vassolo created their signature campaign in the underused Maytag repairman known as Ol' Lonely. First played by Jesse White, the Maytag repairman's redundancy in the face of durable washers and dryers became an advertising icon that has proven as resilient as the product itself, existing in various incarnations for over forty years. Once White retired, Gordon Jump (best known for *WKRP in Cincinnati*) took up the role in 1988. In 2003, Hardy Rawls assumed the role, limited to print and personal appearances.

A nationwide search for a new Maytag repairman began in 2007 and out of 1,500 entrants Clay Earl Jackson won the coveted role.

Manhattan Real Estate: Duck Phillips arrives late for the Draper's dinner party, but at least he had a chance to enjoy the "beautiful drive" along the Saw Mill.

The Saw Mill River Parkway (New York State Reference Route 987D) is named for the river it runs parallel to and begins at the border of Westchester and the Bronx, carrying through to New York as the Henry Hudson Parkway. In 1955, Westchester County initiated plans to modernize the parkway, which included widening it to eight lanes with an eye toward a ten-lane expansion in the future. Community groups in Yonkers, Dobbs Ferry, and Hastings-on-Hudson mounted a vigorous and effective campaign against the modernization. One positive change that arose from these ashes was the construction of a three-level "half-stack" interchange with the Taconic State Parkway. This replaced Hawthorne Circle, a notoriously dangerous roundabout fed by the Saw Mill, Taconic, and Bronx River Parkways.

Construction on this improvement did not occur until 1969, so Duck Phillips may have negotiated this treacherous junction. He would have also had to pay a twenty-five cent toll, instituted by Westchester County in 1936. The New York Department of Transportation assumed control of the parkway in 1980 and in 1994 removed the toll.

Cocktail of Note: Heineken is a pilsner, a pale lager flavored with hops and named after the city of its creation, Pilsen in the Czech Republic. This is a drink best served cold and in a clear stein, all the better to appreciate the clear golden hue and creamy head.

Before Sterling Cooper —
Recommended Reading: Richard Yates's
Revolutionary Road and *Disturbing the Peace*

The writer's writer. A backhanded compliment? Code for "relentlessly bleak" or "slim book sales"? Lamentation for a visionary unappreciated in his own time?

Many authors can lay claim to one or two of those designations, but of the truly American twentieth-century novelists, Richard Yates holds the dubious honor of checkmarks across all columns. The publication of his first novel *Revolutionary Road* (1961) heralded Yates as an unparalleled chronicler of post–Second World War malaise and earned him consideration for the National Book Award alongside Joseph Heller's *Catch-22*. In *Revolutionary Road*, and the six novels that followed, Yates proved himself an unblinking witness of the American Dream and its sometimes rotten core. He investigated the crashing decline of hope and innocence not only in the men who rode trains in from the suburbs to mind-numbing office jobs, but also the wives they left behind each day. This mapping of the human heart — whether New York's cold grid work of streets or New Rochelle's plastic latticework communities — caused many to call Richard Yates the foremost novelist of the Age of Anxiety.

For such a particularly American writer of the American landscape, perhaps it is of little surprise that Yates succumbed to a uniquely colonial phenomenon: Young Literary Lion Fails to Follow Through on Expectations, or the Sophomore Curse. *Revolutionary Road* generated a great deal of critical excitement but sold no more than 12,000 copies in hardcover, a number that none of his novels would surpass in his lifetime. And while his work always inspired staunch defenders, subsequent novels such as *A Special Providence* and *Disturbing the Peace* produced no small amount of negative response, prompting the attachment of the dreaded "one book writer" epithet to his name (a stigma finally removed with the publication of *The Easter Parade* in 1976). After Yates's death in 1992, his novels slowly disappeared from print, despite glowing notices from writers ranging from Tennessee Williams to Kurt Vonnegut to Richard Ford. These same positive blurbs adorn the covers of Yates's novels re-released to coincide with the debut of a film adaptation of *Revolutionary Road* starring Leonardo DiCaprio and Kate Winslet. No doubt these editions have outperformed the sales numbers Yates saw in his lifetime.

Mad Men creator Matthew Weiner and Richard Yates travel the same roads in search of answers to an all-American question: What happens when you've got everything you want but it still isn't enough? It is even more interesting that, while many have connected the nebulous anxiety of *Mad Men* and the fiction of Richard Yates (and January Jones was given a copy of *Revolutionary Road* to prepare for portraying Betty Draper), Matthew Weiner hadn't read any of his work prior to writing the pilot.

"It was given to me by the people at AMC," Weiner said in a *Variety* interview. "So I read it in between writing the pilot and starting the series. My reaction to it was, 'If I had read this book before I wrote the show, I never would have written the show. I would not compete with that. I don't have the balls.'"

In *Revolutionary Road*, the marriage of Frank and April Wheeler is eroding. The existential troubles of Frank, who occupies "the dullest job you could possibly imagine" at Knox Business Machines in Manhattan, and his vague sense of potential greatness take up the majority of the novel. However, the real beauty and heartbreak is April Wheeler's yearning for a life more fulfilling than the one of crust-cut sandwiches and dreary community theater. Her desire for a nobler existence — not just for herself, but her husband as well — and her efforts to make it possible not only echo truthfully for women of the time but also with the young housewife Betty Draper. April and Betty share struggles, but complex characterization as well; by turns sweet, hopeful, cruel, and manipulative, they never fail to stir empathy in the audience for the sheer humanness of their virtues and shortcomings.

There are hallmarks of Yates's Age of Anxiety fiction that are reflected in *Mad Men*. The unrelenting internal nature of his investigations in *Revolutionary Road* are the most identifiable facet of Yates's fictional voice — not a trope that transfers well to a visual medium. Yates provides an effective but enervating undertow for this fishbowl point of view by the constant self-doubt in the internal monologues of the protagonists, permanent states of second-guessing that approximate an unease in the reader that also exists in each of the characters.

However, there is a languorous tempo to *Mad Men* that attempts to chart a similar internal cartography. Often Don Draper or Peggy Olson will gaze out a window or reflect in an empty office with as much time and space afforded any scene filled with dialogue or action. This evokes a kindred emotion to the nervous internal chatter of Frank or April Wheeler, not only by suggesting similar moments of doubt in the characters, but also in the break from the fast pace of most television dramas resulting in an unease in the viewer's equilibrium.

One of the Age of Anxiety hallmarks is the unsettling nature of home ownership, from the real world financial burdens of maintenance and the conspicuous consumption of suburban house-pride competition, to the metaphorical role in defining the Nuclear Family. This hallmark is notably absent in *Mad Men*. The Drapers have a well-appointed home but do not struggle to maintain their level of comfort, due to Don's swiftly rising income level through the first two seasons. They do not suffer through any home-related catastrophes, and do not engage in garish displays of wealth, other than Don's purchase of a Coupe de Ville, which he can easily afford.

The Wheelers are another matter. Not only does Frank struggle to remove an entrenched tree root, he does so only to place a crooked stone path appreciated by no one. There is no escape for the Wheelers, doomed by a house whose defects a neighbor lists as "warped window frames, wet cellar, crayon marks on the walls, filthy smudges around all the doorknobs and fixtures." Even the life they've built is on soil so acidic as to prohibit the growth of anything but the heartiest ground cover.

The famous opening scene of *Revolutionary Road* — which describes in excruciating detail April's appearance in a production of *The Petrified Forest* that starts badly and ends worse — sets the tone for the novel and an era. While Betty Draper may not appear in a play that is plagued by a "virus of calamity," she does suffer through a similar infection of doubt that spreads through her marriage and threatens to erode it from the inside.

A similar destructive force is at work in *Disturbing the Peace* (1975), but instead of it gnawing through a marriage, it exacts a toll on one man and slowly lays waste to those around him. John Wilder from *Disturbing the Peace* is a man of the moment in the New York of 1960. He has a burgeoning career in advertising, a beautiful family, a great Manhattan apartment and a place in the country. But something is wrong beneath the skin, an unnamable pressure that no amount of alcohol or meaningless sex can dull. And while John Wilder heads down a path that Don Draper avoids, the reader wonders whether there is more than just a surface resemblance between the two men.

The novel opens with a distracted and upset Wilder calling his wife at their Manhattan apartment. Just returning from a week-long business trip, he hasn't slept for a week and is drinking too much, all of which combines to put him into a psychiatric ward for treatment of exhaustion. He spends more time in the ward than he would like, but the treatment seems to do him well. Once out, he puts things back on track with his family and begins an unexpected surge in his work, selling advertising space for the *American Scientist*. But before long, that ineffable hollow feeling returns and he embarks on an affair with a younger woman, attempts an ill-fated career in film production, and finds himself further down a crooked road that leads to madness from which he might never return.

As you might expect from the storyline, *Disturbing the Peace* is a grim novel, unrelenting in its depiction of the circuitous route of degenerating mental health. But it does not wallow in John Wilder's crumbling spiral. From the outset, there is no doubt that the stakes are high for Wilder. And while the picture that is sketched of him is not flattering — he can be, in equal measures, nasty and cruel, short-tempered and dismissive — there is something in him that is instantly identifiable. A good deal of his character flaws could be attributed to his illness, but more telling is his bone-deep insecurity, a feeling that he is "some turd under everybody's feet." The strength in Yates's characterization is that when things start to go well for Wilder, the foreboding is unavoidable and invokes a feeling of helplessness in the reader. As Wilder's life and mind slowly unravel, it is much like watching a character in a slasher film who makes a sandwich, blissfully unaware of a hooded killer stalking behind him.

The correlation of this book by the elder statesman of the Age of Anxiety to a more visceral genre is fitting. *Disturbing the Peace* reads like a chilling horror novel dressed in a gray flannel suit, a story with John Cheever characters dropped onto a bleak psychological landscape designed by Jack Ketchum. The body count is low but the price, particularly for John Wilder, is high.

The picture sketched of the *Mad Men*–era Manhattan is evocative. As Weiner put it, "The guy was there," and *Disturbing the Peace* has an effortless verisimilitude the show achieves through excruciating attention to detail. Wilder bounces from the Commodore, a Manhattan bar where his nervous breakdown hits full stride and the reader can hear the tinkle of ice cubes in the glass and smell the sulfur of freshly struck matches in the air, to a Varick Street apartment. Located in downtown SoHo, back when it was just South of Houston Street, Wilder rents the place with a friend to conduct clandestine affairs away from prying eyes. Sounds like the kind of shabby hideaway many men of the era might maintain (and in fact, the kind neighbor Carlton Hanson surrenders when wife Francine discovers his penchant for infidelity).

There are passing similarities between the protagonists; John looks every inch the dashing executive, with a "well-cut business suit, fresh shirt, and dark tie" and a head of slick hair that he manages with a fastidiousness that skirts "the point of vanity" — all words that might well describe Don Draper.

But while John Wilder builds his life on shifting sand and struggles with his identity and place in the world, he crumbles under the pressure and is committed to Bellevue. Don embraces the ever-changing spirit of his life and can create and recreate himself at will. John is hobbled by paranoid delusions and lacks the creativity to think himself out of his problems or envision a likely solution and put it into action. It is as if both men represent different outcomes of the particular anxiety of the age; Don thinks about it deeply and when an idea presents itself, he pushes it forward, while John puts the worry on a treadmill and runs it through until he drops from exhaustion.

In the end, Yates's work has a greater impact on the female characters of *Mad Men*. The men of *Revolutionary Road* and *Disturbing the Peace* exhibit either a naiveté or timidity not seen in Don Draper. Frank Wheeler senses greatness in himself but cannot pinpoint the outlet, whereas Don has no illusions about his talent and where it is best spent. John Wilder faces an identity crisis and falls into the abyss, whereas Don dives into it. On the other hand, April Wheeler and Betty Draper are two of a kind; sensitive and intelligent mothers at a young age, both stare down a long road of parenting that will end before they exit their forties.

In the end, it can best be described in these terms — if Betty Draper and April Wheeler bumped into each other while horseback riding, they would inevitably share a drink, a pack of cigarettes, and commiseration over their lot in life. If Draper ran into Frank Wheeler and John Wilder in a bar, he'd sidestep the pie-eyed dreamer and tetchy lunatic to catch a matinee of *La Notte*.

2.09 SIX MONTH LEAVE

Original air date: September 28, 2008
Written by: André and Maria Jacquemetton, Matthew Weiner
Directed by: Michael Uppendahl

> "Three wise men of Gotham
> Went to sea in a bowl;
> If the bowl had been stronger,
> My tale would have been longer."
> — *The Merrie Tales of the Mad Men of Gotham*

Freddy Rumsen's drinking puts his job in jeopardy. Peggy steps in and saves the Samsonite account. Roger comes to a decision about his marriage. Betty distracts herself by playing puppet master to old friend Sara Beth.

Once upon a time, a collection called *The Merrie Tales of the Mad Men of Gotham* detailed the misadventures of the "simple" villagers found in a parish of Nottinghamshire. There are competing versions of the source of their foolish ways; some claim they feigned idiocy in an effort to elude the king's anger, while others suggest their feebleness was genuine and attributable to geography (like the Newfoundlanders of Canada, or the residents of Chelm in Jewish folklore, groups of people also known as the butt of jokes).

Although long credited to quack traveling doctor and writer Andrew Boorde, scholars widely agree today that his connection with these tales is apocryphal. Another writer better remembered along with the name "Gotham" is Washington Irving, who applied the name of that sleepy parish for his adoptive village filled with its own brand of fools — New York.

Either way, the wise men's trip to sea in a bowl is part of a long line of allegorical tales. Stories concerning a "ship of fools" contain a broad selection of panicked characters adrift at sea in a boat without a captain. In such a tale, there are many opportunities for satirical swipes at archetypal figures, and their blustering follies are underlined by a voyage that is destined to end in shipwreck.

This assessment is wisely applied to "Six Month Leave," and while fashioning a template from a nursery rhyme might sound simplistic, nothing is quite as it seems (just like the Wise Men of Gotham who climb into a bowl); there are no happy endings, and in this regard "Six Month Leave" is less like Hans Christian Andersen and more like the Brothers Grimm.

Once upon a time the Drapers gave every impression of a perfectly happy married couple. Now Don stays at a hotel but tries to keep the nature of his new address a secret (big surprise). When Jane Siegal detects something wrong and provides the sensitive foresight that one would expect from Joan (namely, buying him shirts from Menken's for his office drawer stash), it doesn't put him at ease but makes him uncomfortable. He may want that level of attention and discretion from a secretary, and might have found it less unnerving if supplied by Joan, but when provided Jane, the new addition to the office, it rattles him, as if the very notion of letting another person into his world (no matter how peripherally) is overwhelming. No surprise then when Don demands that Jane be taken off his desk (although for reasons that have more to do with Roger's indiscretion with Jane and the subsequent separation from his wife, Mona).

Meanwhile, Betty rambles around their house smoking, drinking, fuming, and reading (Katherine Anne Porter's 1962 bestseller *Ship of Fools*). Betty is so angry about the betrayal she has faced, and the implied betrayal of their perfect marriage, that she tries to find solace in manipulating Sarah Beth into a romantic clinch with the groom-to-be Arthur Case.

Once upon a time, African-Americans did not have a visible or respectful role in white society. The burgeoning Civil Rights movement and the tectonic shift about to occur in America is telegraphed by featuring black characters with more dialogue in this episode than in the entire series to date. Whether it is Hollis the elevator operator sympathizing over Marilyn Monroe's recent death ("Some people just hide in plain sight") or Carla, the Drapers' maid ("I've been married almost twenty years, you know"), the ghostly presence of African-Americans in *Mad Men* changes in this episode. While out on the town with Freddy and Don, even Roger can't help but notice, mentioning that BBDO has hired a "colored kid."

Once upon a time, Freddy Rumsen was a legend for the right reasons. Now a famous lush, he pisses himself at the office and is sent away on the euphemistic six-month leave of the episode's title. But not before our three merrie mad men go for one last trip around Gotham. And the importance of a man's name is paramount. Consider the pseudonyms used to gain entrance into the floating craps game. Don picks "Tilden Katz," the name of Rachel Menken's husband and Don pulls a "real Archibald Whitman maneuver" when he clobbers Jimmy Barrett. A man's name is everything, along with what he does ("If I don't go in that office every day, who am I?"). The only thing more heartbreaking than Freddy's back-alley farewell is Don's earlier defense of Rumsen's reputation ("It's just a man's name, right?").

If only Freddy could have kept it together, then his tale might have been longer.

The Philosophy of *Mad Men* — Don Draper: "It's your life. You don't know how long it's going to be, but you know it's got a bad ending."

Period Moment: In lieu of a sentimental farewell with Freddy, Roger departs by claiming he has to "give a Chinaman a music lesson." This saying is old British slang which refers to urination — the porcelain of the bowl results in the China aspect, whereas the tinkling of urine hitting the toilet explains the music lesson. Thankfully, the time has passed when use of casual racism to mask a natural function seemed like a good idea.

Ad Pitch: Before Freddy wets himself and goes down for the count, he recites the ad created for the Samsonite Silhouette. "I just got a brand new Samsonite Silhouette . . . and I hate it." The ad copy created by Peggy saves things (and her presentation saves the day), but the thrust of the ad is not so much envisioning the travels the suitcase will see, so much as the things that will be put in it.

Ads of the time for Samsonite did focus on the exotic thrill of travel. A 1960 magazine spread suggested the Silhouette was the perfect accessory to a ski vacation ("From Sun Valley to sunny Sorrento") while a 1964 piece made a correlation between the sleek lines of the luggage and the chic traveler who uses it ("Silhouette is you . . . slender, fast-paced, daringly elegant").

The interesting thing about all three campaigns is the focus on women. At the time, men were considered the breadwinners and financial stewards, but it seems accepted as fact that women were in charge of the luggage decisions, and, by implication, travel plans as well.

Manhattan Real Estate: Don spends his marital banishment at the Roosevelt Hotel, where deliveries to the room include shined shoes and a newspaper reporting Marilyn Monroe's death.

The Roosevelt Hotel (45 East Forty-fifth Street) opened in 1924 and was designed by the esteemed architectural firm George B. Post & Sons (also responsible for the New York Stock Exchange, the New York Cotton Exchange, and the Wisconsin State Capital). Known for a white-gloved service that once included an underground passageway to Grand Central Station, the Roosevelt has also had a foot in the history of New York: Guy Lombardo started the New Year's Eve tradition of broadcasting "Auld Lang Syne" over the airwaves at the Roosevelt Grill; and presidential hopeful Thomas Dewey located his election headquarters at the hotel. He also mistakenly announced his triumph from here, losing to incumbent Harry Truman in 1948.

Cocktail of Note: While on their last whirl around town, Roger orders drinks for the three wise men, in particular for Freddy a "Grand-Dad on the rocks."

Old Grand-Dad Kentucky Straight Bourbon Whiskey is a reliable if unremarkable drink with a high rye content in the mash that fuels its old-fashioned kick. First made in a Boston, Kentucky, plant in 1840 by Raymond B. Hayden, and named after his grandfather Basil Hayden Sr. (a well-known distiller in his own right), this bourbon has never ceased production through to present time, despite Prohibition (when sold as a "medicinal" elixir) or changes in ownership.

2.10 THE INHERITANCE
• • • • • • • • • • • • • • • • • • • •

Original air date: October 5, 2008
Written by: Lisa Albert, Marti Noxon, Matthew Weiner
Directed by: Andrew Bernstein

> "All we have to do is go over there, get her signature,
> mourn over the loss of our birthright, and move on . . .
> [raising a glass] to the end of the line!"
> — Bud Campbell

Betty and Don reunite when they visit her father as he recovers from a stroke. Betty and Glen reunite after she finds him living in the playhouse in the backyard. Pete tries to comprehend what his father did with the family estate while he prepares to attend an aerospace convention in California.

We inherit many things from our parents — some we hope for and others we fear. The starkest question asked in this episode is if we profit from our lineage or if we are doomed by it.

January Jones and her Screen Actors Guild Award for Outstanding Performance by an Ensemble in a Drama Series. (AP Photo/Matt Sayles)

The benefits of a strong family name are nearly incalculable. Although Pete Campbell can list a swank Park Avenue apartment in the plus column (see "New Amsterdam"), the expectations of such a name — success, social standing — weigh heavily on Pete, who never seems younger than when dealing with his family. This is clearest when he and his brother Bud encounter the penultimate step in maturity, becoming parents to their parents. The prospect of "mourning" the loss of their birthright (thanks to father's profligate ways) and withstanding the brittle recriminations of their widowed mother makes the brothers dream of that ultimate step in maturation, becoming an orphan. "Do you remember *Rope?*" Pete asks. It is odd to watch the brothers laugh so heartily over the connection to a movie about a pair of privileged snobs who plan and execute a murder for a cold, intellectual thrill.

The expectation to carry on the family name is chief among Mrs. Campbell's concerns. Her abhorrent view of adoption (Pete's only opportunity to give wife Trudy a child) is specific to the time and her social standing. And even though many still view adoption as a weaker form of the family unit, the notion that taking in an abandoned infant is "pulling from the discards" only makes Pete's later admission that he "hates" his mother all the more understandable.

In an episode devoted to the rocky nature of heredity, Don is naturally at the sidelines, and for once maybe he counts himself lucky. As Gene Hofstadt says, his daughter's husband "has no people" and even though the lack of family history may feel like a burden to Don, it also means that he doesn't have to deal with the more difficult aspects of inheritance. He normally avoids family strife, but perhaps he is willing to get involved in Betty's developing family drama following patriarch Gene's recent stroke in an effort to at least act like a married man again, even if it is a charade. As odd as the efforts toward the appearance of normalcy are at the Hofstadt household, the setting is reminiscent of the happiness that once perfumed the Draper home, but that has turned sour and toxic.

Betty may dislike Gene's second wife Gloria for purely Freudian reasons (her Electra complex — although Freud preferred the term "feminine Oedipal attitude" — is not all that complicated), but she is right to harbor anger over how long it took to receive the news of her father's stroke. And if a three-day wait wasn't enough, Betty learns that this is not Gene's first cerebrovascular incident.

"Just a couple little strokes," Gene says blithely. "Runs in the family."

Betty also can't bear the disappearance of family heirlooms, whether the jardinière or the ottoman "with the birds on it." She also has to contend with that other icky step of the adult child, wondering if you have to "go around and write my name on all the things" you want. But the underlying fear of change to the childhood home and the parents you once thought invincible is the true anguish. Seeing her father lose himself in time (calling Betty "Ruth," his first wife's name) or tear a strip off Don (see "Philosophy" below) makes Betty feel even more isolated than she already does.

A side note on the treatment of Gene's stroke: in many television dramas, a great deal of dramatic license is taken with such incidents, or, even worse, with characters afflicted with a retardation of intellectual growth. Luckily, Matthew Weiner is wise enough to avoid using Gene as an innocent oracle, cursed with impediment but blessed with supernatural insight. In the scene where he assaults Don for his secrecy, it does not play like an eerily correct crystal ball speculation but the utterance of a long-held secret, or the kind of observation married couples share with each other and no one else.

Time and again Weiner uses *Mad Men* like a knife to peel back the layers of intimacy, collusion, mystery, and betrayal that drape across each day of married life — whether between a divided Betty and Don ("pretending" over the course of their stay with the Hofstadts) or the stroke-afflicted Gene and his dead wife.

In this episode the audience also inherits multiple references to the first season. Betty fires off a subtle zinger to Don when she says, "I know how you feel about mourning" (referred to by Don as "extended self-pity" in "Babylon"). Harry Crane receives well wishes on his soon-to-be baby from first-season fling Hildy ("Nixon vs. Kennedy"). And there is a brief return of Glen, Helen Bishop's odd duck son, who moves into the Draper's backyard playhouse to escape his parents' plans for him and to save Betty.

The ick factor in the Betty and Glen relationship reaches a summit here; not only does he first try to hide out in the playhouse, but once found he looks quite comfortable in the Drapers' home. His earnest declaration to Betty ("I came to rescue you") is overshadowed by the overall creepiness of their connection. At least Glen's fantasies toward Betty are easily answered by his age and unsteady home life. However, Betty's motivations aren't as freely dismissed. She likes Glen's attention as there is safety in it (and no chance for betrayal), but as an adult she should seek that kind of affirmation from someone *close* to her age. She may swallow the bitter grown-up pill and call Helen Bishop to come pick up her missing son, but not until she has already given Glen a shirt of Don's to wear, furthering the uncomfortable "playing house" facet of their afternoon together. If her therapist opened his files to the ghost of Freud, I'm sure the master would suggest that Betty has inherited more than a propensity for strokes from her father, namely something along the line of a feminine Oedipal attitude.

In life, inheritance may have profit and loss, but for fans of this show, attention to the details pays off every time.

The Philosophy of *Mad Men* — Gene Hofstadt: "He has no people! You can't trust a person like that."

Period Moment: Before Don takes his seat, Paul Kinsey tells his girlfriend, Sheila, he wants to attend the Rocket Fair in California before he has to "face Mississippi, and those people screaming at me, and maybe getting shot."

In the case of Boynton vs. Virginia, the Supreme Court ruled that segregated interstate travel is unconstitutional. The landmark ruling was one that only hints at deep-seated racism throughout the country, and in the American South in particular. Congress of Racial Equality (CORE) decided to test the ruling by arranging for inter-racial bus trips across state lines. CORE director James Farmer inaugurated the first "Freedom Ride," enlisting seven blacks and six whites in a journey in two buses that was to cross through Virginia, the Carolinas, Georgia, Alabama, and Mississippi with the final stop of New Orleans, Louisiana.

On May 15, 1961, in Anniston, Alabama, over 100 members of the Ku Klux Klan attacked the Freedom Riders, beating them bloody. The mob set the first bus on fire while holding the doors closed. An undercover Alabama State Trooper onboard pulled his revolver and led the riders off the Greyhound, helping all escape just as the gas tank exploded.

The second Trailways bus suffered a similar attack with CORE member and magazine editor Jim Peck receiving enough abuse to require over fifty stitches to close his wounds. Peck later launched a lawsuit against the FBI, claiming they knew in advance of the KKK's plan to attack the bus, did nothing to prevent it, and would not enforce the Boynton vs. Virginia ruling. Before later dying of a stroke, he won his case.

Long known as champions of civil rights, the Kennedy White House did not immediately jump to the aide of the Freedom Riders. The administration asked for a "cooling off period" after the assaults, and declared the Riders "unpatriotic" as this bus tour (and those that followed) embarrassed the United States on the international stage. Attorney General Robert Kennedy was quoted at the time as saying the he did not "feel that the Department of Justice can side with one group or the other in disputes over Constitutional rights" despite the Supreme Court ruling that made desegregated interstate travel the law of the land.

Manhattan Real Estate: While mourning the loss of their birthright, Pete and Bud review their father's lavish expenditures. "What about all that money Dad gave to Lincoln Center?" Pete asks. "Get that back."

The Lincoln Center for the Performing Arts (a 16.3 acre area bordered by Amsterdam and Broadway Avenues, West Sixty-second and West Sixty-fifth Streets) was an urban renewal initiative shepherded by John D. Rockefeller III and Robert Moses in the 1960s. A building complex that is comprised of many cultural centers (including the Metropolitan Opera House, Alice Tully Hall, the Vivian Beaumont Theatre, the Walter Reade Theater, and Avery Fisher Hall), and designed by numerous architects (Max Abramovitz, Eero Saarinen, Gordon Bunshaft, Pietro Belluschi, and Wallace Harrison), the Lincoln Center has served as the epicenter of artistic endeavors in New York since its inception in 1961.

Cultural institutions housed at the center include Jazz at Lincoln Center, the Julliard School, New York City Ballet, New York City Opera, and the New York Philharmonic.

Civil Rights Movement —
Dr. Howard Thurman's *Jesus and the Disinherited* and its Influence on Dr. Martin Luther King

The specter of civil unrest haunts *Mad Men* in a subtle manner. Other than Paul Kinsey's girlfriend, Sheila, African-American characters are pushed to the fringes of this apparently "civilized" North, but their peripheral presence is always noticeable. Either in the form of the Drapers' housekeeper, Carla, trying in vain to offer marital advice to Betty ("Six Month Leave"); the Sterling Cooper elevator operator, Hollis, and his quiet mourning of Marilyn Monroe's death (same episode); or the Hofstadt family housekeeper, Viola, giving stern but loving matriarchal support to Betty after her father's stroke ("The Inheritance"), the characters are always drawn as thoughtful and caring but relegated to servile positions.

The image of New York as leading cosmopolitan light of America receives an over-painting in *Mad Men*. The American South was a bubbling cauldron of racial hatred and violent reprisals, but that does not necessarily mean that the North welcomed African-Americans and other visible minorities into their homes and offices as equals. Matthew Weiner does well to remind us that while the beginning of racial equality occurred in the Yankee states, whites who lived and worked there benefited from the inequality that prevailed.

While gender politics, inequality, and outright sexual discrimination take center stage, Weiner has always kept his eye on civil rights and introduced reminders of the burgeoning movement throughout the series. Those who say that later developments with African-American characters are a response to criticisms of exclusion might do well to remember the very first scene of the pilot episode. Don tries to glean the reason for a black waiter's cigarette preference only to have a thuggish white waiter intrude and ask if Sam is bothering him ("He can get a little chatty"). If the position of the African-American wasn't a prime concern, why would Don engage the waiter in conversation and shut down the bigoted waiter's effort to curtail their discussion?

The Civil Rights movement had a charismatic, passionate leader in Dr. Martin Luther King Jr., a man who preached non-violence as a response to violent oppression. But as the efforts of the movement simmer throughout *Mad Men* it can lead one to consider the forces that conspired to create this revolutionary ideal. Among the many inspirations, one stands out among others,

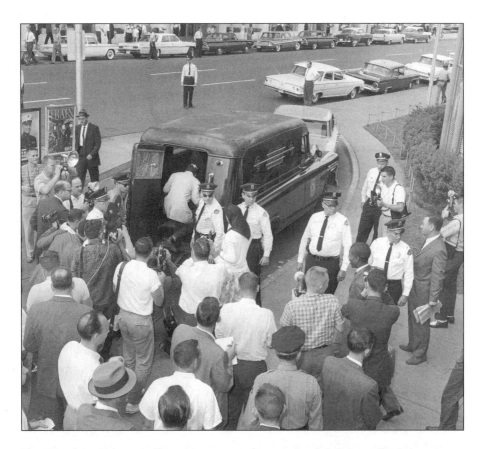

The Freedom Riders challenged some southern states' defiance of a Supreme Court ruling that desegregated interstate travel. (AP Photo/Horace Cort)

one whose writings provide a direct channel between Dr. King and the non-violent protest ethos of Mahatma Ghandi. Dr. Howard Thurman, a noted theologian and philosopher, embarked on a "pilgrimage of friendship" through Ceylon (now Sri Lanka), Burma (now the Union of Myanmar), and India in 1935 and wrote about his experiences and appraisal of Christianity in 1949. So moving was Thurman's relation of Christ's teachings through the hardship of the oppressed and the non-violent response to such oppression, King read and re-read the book many times throughout his life. And while Thurman's teachings and inspirational contribution to King's life may not be well known, the verification of it comes not only in the pacifist core of the latter's campaign, but also in the stark assertion that the book King carried with him on the day of his assassination was Thurman's *Jesus and the Disinherited*.

Saul and Alice Thurman welcomed their son Howard in Daytona, Florida, one year before the dawn of the twentieth century. Saul died from pneumonia by the time Howard reached seven years of age. Mother Alice earned money for her family (including two siblings of Howard's) by washing and cleaning for affluent white Floridians. As a result, his grandmother provided most of Howard's rearing.

A former slave who lived and worked on a plantation in Madison, Florida, up to the Civil War, Nancy Thurman passed her deeply held spiritual beliefs on to young Howard. One of his chores growing up was to read passages of the Bible to his grandmother (who held a great knowledge and recall of the book despite her illiteracy), in particular the gospels and psalms she so dearly loved. Only in later years did Howard ask his grandmother why she instructed him to never recite Paul's epistles to her (with the exception of Corinthians 13: "If I speak in human and angelic tongues but do not have love, I am a resounding gong or a clashing cymbal"). She explained that in church services conducted on the plantation, the attending minister would invoke Paul's first letter to Timothy ("Let as many servants as are under the yoke count their own masters as worthy of honor," 6:1) as evidence that the suffering of slaves under the heel of their masters was God's will. Once emancipated, Nancy never wanted to hear the words of the Apostle Paul again.

While Howard may have been out from under the yoke of slavery, he knew very well the brutality of ignorance. The Ku Klux Klan held sway over the politics of Daytona and the surrounding areas of Florida, which meant that beatings, lynchings, and burnings were an ever-present threat for African-Americans of the time and that contact with whites was always dangerous and sometimes deadly. Almost as scarring as the routine cruelties visited and witnessed at the hands of bigoted whites was the perpetual *threat* of violence, which could make the stoutest man or woman tremble, to say nothing of a sensitive boy and stellar student like young Howard Thurman.

A dedication to academics proved a respite from the sweltering environment of hatred. He showed great promise in school and garnered the attention of one James Gamble, part owner of Procter and Gamble, head of a Northern family who vacationed in Daytona and provided one of the few and earliest positive experiences Thurman ever enjoyed with whites. Through financial aides supplied by Gamble, Thurman attended the Florida Baptist Academy in Jacksonville and graduated as valedictorian. This distinction helped Thurman gain a scholarship to the prestigious Morehouse College where he studied vigorously and widely, emerging in 1923 at the top of his class. He then studied at Rochester Theological Seminary (as one of two black students admitted each year), where he interacted with whites on a regular basis, and, to his surprise, was treated as a friend and Christian fellow among his colleagues.

After a brief spell as a church pastor and a semester of study under Quaker theologian Rufus Jones, Thurman taught courses on self-worth as related through the teachings of Jesus at both his alma mater Morehouse and Spellman College in 1929. Three years later, the World Student Christian Federation invited Thurman to tour India on a "pilgrimage of friendship." The opportunity to travel through an exotic land that was the seat of a faith like Hinduism intrigued Thurman, but he did not immediately jump at the chance. He did not want to appear as ambassador for an imperialistic American Christianity, viewed this way internationally both through the subjugation of blacks in the United States but also in zealous missionary quests of conversion abroad. Once convinced that the trip's aim was to foster open communication between faiths, and that it contained the possibility of meeting the renowned activist Mahatma Gandhi, Thurman agreed to the adventure.

The concern over how India would receive the envoy proved well-founded; while Thurman and his travel mates never encountered anything but unfailing civility throughout their speaking tour, many post-seminar conferences with teachers and students revolved around the incomprehensible sight of an African-American academic speaking for a Christianity thought to have been built on the backs of his forbearers (a sensitivity heightened by an India still bristling under British control). There were not only theological pitfalls to contend with: hosts provided Thurman and his wife with flashlights at their bedside so that they could preface a twilight trip to the bathroom with a quick scan of the floorboards for scorpions; and a fellow traveler's quarantine due to scarlet fever threatened to derail any post-speech conversations with students until it was decided to relocate such discussions to an open-air setting — each party facing each other across the net of a tennis court.

The culmination of the trip was an audience with Mahatma Gandhi, internationally known figurehead of the Indian Independence movement. Thurman had much to ask the "little brown man" who pioneered the use of *satygahara* (or, the advancement of political change through civil disobedience and complete non-violence). He found that it was Gandhi who asked most of the questions. In particular, he wanted to understand why African-American slaves would choose to become Christians and not Muslims, the former being the faith of the slave masters and one that confirmed social inequality, whereas the latter drew no lines between men in matters of worship. Before his departure, Thurman asked Gandhi what he thought the biggest obstacle in spreading the message of Christianity abroad. Gandhi's answer has been boiled down to an epigrammatic bumper sticker over the years ("The problem with Christianity? Christians"), but it seems close to the spirit of his remarks, and — along with the mild accusations of treachery at being a black man preaching a "white" religion — pushed Thurman to consider the teachings of Christ and the impact they might have on faith and freedom for African-Americans.

In *Jesus and the Disinherited*, Dr. Thurman argued that the life Jesus must have led as one of the masses with his "back against the wall" contributed greatly to the religion he espoused but also connected his teachings with the state of blacks in America (and, indeed, to marginalized people the world over). Thurman examined the life of Jesus as an outsider — a poor Jew without the protection of Roman citizenry — and noted that his reaction to violence and oppression was not an attempt at equal force, but to respond with peace. Thurman discovered that a violent reaction against violence not only emboldened the oppressors, it corroded the soul of the oppressed. To love one's enemy was in itself an attack on their power and status.

The publication of *Jesus and the Disinherited* heralded a new way of approaching Christianity for African-Americans and provided a building block for the Civil Rights movement. Dr. Martin Luther King Jr. re-read the book many times during the course of the Montgomery bus boycotts in 1955, and the viability of non-violent protest it propounded — starting with Gandhi and refracted through Thurman's analysis of Jesus as one of the legion of "poor" and "disinherited" — clearly took root in the struggle he lead.

Howard Thurman's connection to Martin Luther King Jr. was less direct. Thurman knew Martin Luther King Sr. through his student days at Morehouse College, but knew of King Jr. by reputation as the young man pursued his Ph.D. Thurman and King Jr. managed to meet a few times, with time for only one serious conversation. They first met during King's last days as a doctoral student, when he visited Thurman at home and the two watched the World Series on television. The serious conversation they had was during King's convalescence after a delusional woman stabbed him with a seven-inch letter opener at a 1958 book signing in Harlem. Thurman referred to the meeting as a "vibrant session."

The two never met again. Many influences conspired to set Martin Luther King Jr. on his path, but even a cursory look at the central tenets he championed raises the words of Dr. Thurman higher than many others.

No less a figure than Dr. Walter Fluker, executive director of the Leadership Center at Morehouse College, has said, "Leaders like King do not arise out of a historical vacuum. There are movements and there are personalities who actually sow the seeds. Thurman is one of those persons who sows the seed. In fact, I don't think you'd get a Martin Luther King Jr. without a Howard Thurman."

2.11 THE JET SET
· · · · · · · · · · · · · · · ·

Original air date: October 12, 2008
Written by: Matthew Weiner
Directed by: Phil Abraham

> "To the world-weary, the cocktail-bored,
> here is a hypodermic of distilled joy."
> — Cholly Knickerbocker, May 12, 1955

Don and Pete arrive in California for the aerospace convention. Don abandons Pete to join a group of jet-setters in Palm Springs. When a request to make partner is rebuffed, Duck Phillips sets in motion a merger that would provide him with a much loftier title.

New Yorkers like to think they have a monopoly on refinement. The nature of sophistication for the monarchs of the Eastern Seaboard is affluence but, Knickerbockers aside, they don't know anything about a cosmopolitan lifestyle when compared to the old-world style of international members of "café society." Various definitions of sophistication are covered, but it is suggested that the greatest display of social grace is how one reacts to unexpected behavior instead of simply engaging in it.

Manhattanites forget that the cause of their worldliness is commerce. The city is an entrepreneurial one, built to maximize trade and profit; any trappings of cultural equipoise are by-products of this urge. No wonder Europeans dismiss Americans as vulgar and believe their far-reaching bloodlines and sartorial finesse are the motor of true sophistication (witness the derisive sniff Don receives when he suggests these upper-crust vagabonds must be "well-off").

This episode also marks the first time that the sleek wardrobe of the *Mad Men* looks fusty and out of place. Maybe it's the heat, but Don has never looked uncomfortable in a gray flannel suit until now, particularly when he meets a group of vaguely European jet-setters who, despite having names like Willy, Joy, and Rocci, manage to teach Don one or two things about effortless bar-side pickups and frothy badinage.

Forgive a quick excursion into etymology, but the root word of all this carefree urbanity is "sophistry," the art of making a clever and plausible argument that is ultimately misleading. While it leads to the kind of empty conversation Gene Hofstadt once fined his children for (see "The Inheritance"), the charms of this fizzy dialogue are difficult to dismiss. Either in the puffery of the Jet Set's dinner game, "Places" (naming all the cities they've visited, one imagines), or the world-weary lingua franca they use to discuss travel plans ("You don't need a passport . . . unless you're going to follow us to Capri") could irritate, but this motley crew of nomads dole out charm as required. If they are to take full advantage of the global "open door policy" offered to them, they couldn't wear out their welcome. And no one ever grows weary of a good conversationalist.

Meanwhile, the rest of the junior sophisticates left behind at Sterling Cooper have their veneers cracked by Kurt Smith's admission that he's gay (as if his one-piece mechanic's jumpsuit wasn't enough to single him out at the office). The shock of the admission is like a bolt of ice water, and one cannot help but look at Sal, whose kaleidoscope of emotions swirls from disbelief to admiration to terror and back again. The advantage of hindsight aside, it is difficult to believe that no one in the office picks up on Sal's occasional lapses into fabulousness, in particular how he coos over donuts just before Kurt's admission ("Mmmm . . . lemonaires!"). But this was before the sexual revolution stormed the Bastille of social mores, so perhaps it is not surprising that Harry Crane denounces Kurt as a "pervert." Kurt's creative partner Smitty announces his own proclivities by ogling Joan, who looks like she could eat the little man up in one bite, but he also covers for his friend by claiming that he's from Europe and things are "different there." Smitty also hits Cosgrove with, "What? He's the first homo you've ever met in advertising?" Sal looks like he wants to climb into his lemonaire.

Duck Phillips tries his hand at sophisticated wrangling. His effort to broker a sale of "third tier" Sterling Cooper to an old advertising crony from London requires his own brand of sophistry, laboring to convince each side the other is the one interested in the transaction. Duck adds the caveat that all creative members must report to him (a chance to harness Don), with Duck as head of International Business. The only way for Duck to summon up the courage to try such a tactic is to fall quietly off the wagon; not only is alcohol the fuel the advertising business seems to run on, but it is much easier to appear suave with a martini glass in hand.

As always, we end with Don, making a phone call from a Palm Springs pad announcing himself as "Dick Whitman." Is it any surprise that the final shot of Don is a mirror image of the show's iconic silhouette? Only, instead of a black-suited right arm draped across the back of a chair, it's a naked left arm draped across the back of a couch: Draper and Whitman, two sides of the same coin.

The Philosophy of *Mad Men* — Don Draper: "Who are these people?"
Period Moment: The term "jet set" is indicative of the time — Don and Pete attend a "Rocket Fair" to solicit business, and they face the fear of rockets delivering multiple nuclear warheads at the twitch of a finger.

Coined by gossip columnist Igor Cassini while writing under the pseudonym "Cholly Knickerbocker" (the first name a take on an upper-crust accent version of "Charlie," the latter courtesy of Washington Irving), the term was meant to describe a new echelon that took advantage of innovations in jet engine technology to trot across the globe. A jet-setter might fly to Paris for a party or Monte Carlo for a baccarat game.

Cassini knew of what he wrote, himself a crumb off the upper-crust of Russian royalty. His mother was Countess Marguerite Cassini, whose father Arturo served as a diplomat to Czar Nicholas II. Igor Cassini's father, Alexander Loiewski, worked as a Russian diplomat and adopted his wife's prestigious name (shades of Pete's father and the Dyckman dynasty). As a columnist for the Hearst syndicate, Cassini boasted 20 million readers at the height of his popularity. During his tenure, he hired a young firebrand from Texas to help research and compose these missives on society's betters, a woman named Liz Smith who would go on to serve as the *New York Post*'s "Diva of Dish" for over thirty years.

An interesting side note: Cassini's brother, Oleg, was a fashion designer who gained worldwide attention for dressing Jacqueline Kennedy during her reign as First Lady.

Ad Pitch: Pete Campbell marvels at the plans for future warfare in a way that makes Don chuckle.

"It's American Aviation Rocketdyne," Pete says. "It's no joke."

Rocketdyne developed and created liquid propelled rockets, including the F1 engine used in the Apollo missions, the Redstone engine that carried the first crewed flights for NASA's Mercury project, and a latter stage of the Minuteman III missiles.

If, as Don stated in the previous episode, part of their hope was to appeal to congressmen who sought help bringing such contracts to their states, someone must have done good work for California at this Rocket Fair. By 1965, Rocketdyne employed over 16,000 people in southern California.

Manhattan Real Estate: Kurt Smith raves about seeing "the Bob Dylan" at Carnegie Hall. Designed by architect William Burnet Tuthill with an Italian Renaissance–style terra-cotta façade with iron-spotted brick, Carnegie Hall (881 Seventh Avenue) opened in the spring of 1891, and has retained a place at the center of the New York music scene ever since. The very best of New York families attended the opening night — you couldn't swing a dead cat without hitting a Whitney, Sloan, or Rockefeller — which featured performances by New York's Symphony Society and Oratorio Society, under the direction of Walter Damrosch and Pyotr Ilyich Tchaikovsky.

The patron of the building, millionaire industrialist Andrew Carnegie, was already a known philanthropist but was urged to help with the creation of this luxurious home for the arts by his young wife, Louise Whitfield. It opened under the name "The Music Hall founded by Andrew Carnegie" but soon became known by the current title.

While it opened as a showcase for the best in high culture — that is, classical music — the hall has shown a great generosity with the stage for jazz, pop, and folk music.

Cocktail of Note: Duck pitches the sale of Sterling Cooper after draining a Gibson martini which, in truth, is like any other martini with a pickled cocktail onion substituting for an olive.

Guest Stars — I Know That Face . . .

A number of familiar actors populate roles throughout the series, but rarely anyone with enough "star power" to overwhelm the story or come across as stunt casting. For those who know the face but are not sure from where, here is a handy reference:

Anne Dudek ("Francine Hanson"): Appearances in *Six Feet Under*, *Friends*, *Desperate Housewives*, and *Bones* make her recognizable, but Dudek became known through her recurring role in the fourth season of *House, M.D.* as Amber, girlfriend to Robert Sean Leonard's character, James Wilson (and "Cutthroat Bitch" to the cantankerous Dr. House). While playing Betty's sisterly next door neighbor Francine, Dudek has also had a featured role on HBO's *Big Love*.

Rosemarie DeWitt ("Midge Daniels"): Before burning up the screen as Don's hipster mistress in the first season, DeWitt made one-time appearances in *Sex and the City* and *Law & Order: Special Victims Unit*; held a supporting role in Ron Howard's *Cinderella Man*; and played one of the lead hostage negotiators in the short-lived FOX series *Standoff*. Post–Midge Daniels, DeWitt co-starred in the critically acclaimed *Rachel Getting Married* (alongside Anne Hathaway) and secured a recurring role as Toni Collette's sister in Diablo Cody's Showtime series *United States of Tara*.

Melinda Page Hamilton ("Anna Draper"): Contrary to popular belief, Hamilton did not play the part of a wooden-legged Russian prostitute having an affair with Tony on *The Sopranos*, but has made several appearances in shows such as *Nip/Tuck*, *Numb3rs*, *Everwood*, *Desperate Housewives*, and *Ghost Whisperer*.

Colin Hanks ("Father John Gill"): Hanks is probably the most known name to land a role on *Mad Men*, although it is more for his famous surname than anything else. Other than being the son of Tom Hanks, Colin has chipped out a career for himself as a reliable working actor, appearing in shows like *Band of Brothers*, *Roswell*, and *The O.C.*, along with roles in the films *Orange County*, Peter Jackson's *King Kong*, *Untraceable*, and *The House Bunny*. Father and son appeared on-screen for the first time together in 2008's *The Great Buck Howard*, alongside John Malkovich.

2.12 THE MOUNTAIN KING

Original air date: October 19, 2008
Written by: Matthew Weiner, Robin Veith
Directed by: Alan Taylor

> "When I was a boy, I soared in a cloud chariot across the
> sea, in dreams . . . It says somewhere 'Win all the world,
> but to yourself be true, or count your glory but a wreath
> on an empty skull' . . . That's not just words. It's true."
>
> — Henrik Ibsen, *Peer Gynt*

Don visits an old friend and further details about his life after the war are revealed. Despite Don's absence, Bertram, his sister Alice, and Roger vote on the merger. Peggy brings in the Popsicle account and considers her status in the office. Pete's marriage starts to buckle under the strain of infertility and his father-in-law's meddling.

The struggle for identity is akin to navigating choppy waters. It can sometimes take a long trip away to find your true self and where you belong. Don has engaged in just such a voyage all season and while he seems to agree with Ibsen character Peer Gynt's belief in being true to oneself, Don does seem to have realized only now that it leads to uncharted waters — discovering who that person is.

Bertram Cooper might be right when he quotes the Japanese saying "A man is whatever room he is in" ("Nixon vs. Kennedy"), and unlike Don, Cooper is in the room for the discussion about selling Sterling Cooper, a decision made with his sister Alice and Roger Sterling. Alice is the only one concerned about not having Don's input in the sale ("I'd like to know what he thinks . . . he's very savvy"). Roger believes that the financial gain Don will see is enough of a cushion for not being consulted, and Bert reminds them that Don's 12.5 percent makes him mathematically irrelevant (although his presence will become much more relevant as the sale proceeds . . .).

Don is just as identifiable by the rooms he is not in. Without a word he has disappeared from his office at Sterling Cooper, his room at the Roosevelt, and, still, his house in the suburbs. While those around him are concerned, none are surprised. Don Draper is a master of the disappearing act, and the

Joan Holloway (Christina Hendricks) discovers that marriage may not be all she hopes for. (AP Photo/Jennifer Graylock)

irony that this mystery is his best-known trait is lost on none of them. Don may seem quite lost, but he has moved toward a destination for the entire season. He follows the copy of *Meditations in an Emergency* that he mailed in the first episode (see "For Those Who Think Young") all the way to the West Coast and his "first" wife Anna Draper. And thwarted by accident earlier (see "The New Girl"), Don is finally able to answer a siren call. "I can smell the ocean," he says with a look of great peace.

In fact, it's almost jarring to see Don so comfortable in Anna's home — his request upon arriving to have a shower and lie down, relaxing on the porch, or idly fixing the leg on a broken chair. This last act harkens back to a scene in "A Night to Remember," when Betty complains about a wobbly leg that Don won't fix, only to come upon the chair later and smash it into splinters. The ease with which Don helps Anna around the house in a manner he won't do for Betty is unsettling and odd for a man who worries that he's messed up so badly with his wife that he might not get her back.

Through the flashbacks, we learn that Don and Anna have found kindred spirits in their mutual wounds. They seek stability through a myriad of wobbly legs — Anna's game leg, Don's work on the wonky chair — and they only seem able to connect with one another. Don is almost ashamed to admit that he has told Anna things he's never told Betty, and instead of expressing concern or surprise, Anna suggests that he doesn't have to tell her everything. With such a cagey view of intimacy, perhaps it's not a surprise that she hasn't remarried ("I kicked him out," she tells Don, "Even though old ladies shouldn't be picky").

The subtle allusion to *Peer Gynt* through the episode's title and the piece played by Anna's young piano student helps gives those philosophical issues heft. Henrik Ibsen meant the poetic play *Peer Gynt* — about a young man who kidnaps a soon-to-be-wed ex-lover of his and steals off into the mountains where he encounters all manner of woodland creatures along his quest for self-knowledge — to be read and not performed. But when interest in mounting a production arose, Ibsen contacted Edvard Grieg to write incidental music. "In the Hall of the Mountain King" from the *Peer Gynt Suite* is one of Grieg's best known pieces, a fact that would cause the composer no end of pain. "For the Hall of the Mountain King," Grieg wrote, "I have written something that so reeks of cowpats, ultra-Norwegianism, and 'to-thyself-be-enoughness' that I literally can't bear to hear it, though I hope that the irony will make itself felt."

Ibsen meant the play to satirize "everything vapid, maudlin, or febrile in the temper" of Norway. Gynt himself is man with a "knack for story-telling and a dominant passion for lies" who, in the course of his search for identity comes across the Old Man of the Mountain and King of the Trolls. The King embodies what Ibsen saw as Norway's myopic insularity, a hallowing of all that occurs within the borders. The foreign or new is suspect and untrustworthy.

Don is just such a Gyntish man and during his search for self comes across his own mountain monarch, but this time it's a queen. Anna does not judge him or his actions and seems to believe, much like the troll king, that the past is the only thing worth trusting, hence her belief that Don need not tell Betty "everything."

Between his sidestep adventure with the jet-setters and his journey to see Anna, Don arrives at a place where he knows what he wants but is unsure whether it will be there for him when he returns. Regardless, he finally reaches the ocean by the final scene and wades in, dunking himself and becoming, it would seem, the second man in the series thus far to emerge "new baptized" ("Marriage of Figaro").

Another element that resonates with *Peer Gynt* is the treatment of women and the fate of Joan Holloway. In the play, Peer kidnaps his ex-girlfriend from her marriage and carts her off into the mountains like a man reclaiming a possession, a view of women not all that different in the early 1960s than it was when the play was written in the late 1860s. Joan's relationship with Dr. Greg Harris is by all accounts (and Joan's reports) quite fabulous. A first hint of trouble is in this episode when an attempt by

Joan to jump-start a romantic night hits a dead-end ("You're tired . . . let me do the driving"), and the young doctor is put off by his fiancée's forward attitude. The second hint of difficulty (and indication of his sense of insecurity regarding the slick ad men who surround Joan at work) comes when Joan introduces Greg to Roger, who inadvertently hints at the intimacy they both shared ("I thought you hated French food").

All this leads to a terrible incident in Don's office, an event that Greg probably thinks of as an adventurous interlude in role-playing ("Fix me a drink, will you? . . . Pretend like I'm your boss"), which turns into a brutal rape, one made all the more disturbing due to the location — at the workplace, where Joan will be reminded of it every day — and the fact that it is someone she has loved and trusted.

One can imagine Joan trying to convince herself that what happened was not an assault at all, but other than the damage such repression could do, she also has to worry about the future; spousal rape is rarely a one-time occurrence and is often but a single element of long-term abuse.

The Philosophy of *Mad Men* — Don Draper: "I have been watching my life, it's right there. And I keep scratching at it trying to get into it . . . but I can't."
Period Moment: While staying with Anna, Don stumbles upon a couple of greased-up men bent over gleaming hot rods. "Is that a '34 sedan?" Don asks. "I used to sell them . . . used."

Kustom Kulture is a term used to describe the hot-rod subculture that sprang up in California throughout the '50s — not just the custom building of cars that leads to the vehicular amalgam Don sees ("two Fords and a Buick"), but also the surrounding comics, hair styles, clothing, vernacular, and attitude. The custom paintwork and illustrations of Kustom Kulture icons Von Dutch and Robt. Williams were synonymous with the subterranean movement, but Ed "Big Daddy" Roth's character "Rat Fink" came to symbolize all of the hot-rod culture through the '50s and '60s. All owed a great debt to Stanley "Mouse" Miller, who capitalized on the "Weirdo Hot Rod Art" movement extant since the late '40s and employed his airbrush techniques on T-shirts that he sold at custom car shows. Miller later gained great notoriety for the psychedelic art posters he created in the late '60s, in particular his work for the Grateful Dead.

It is no surprise that self-made man Don Draper would find an attraction to hot rodders who took cars that rolled off the assembly line, tore them apart, and built them up new to suit their own needs. Suddenly the Coupe de Ville he bought previously ("The Gold Violin") doesn't seem like such a perfect match.

Ad Pitch: Peggy hits a home run with her Popsicle pitch: "Take It. Break It. Share It. Love It." The Popsicle executive likes the artwork and thinks the image of the mother handing snapped Twin Pops to her kids "looks familiar," in that it strikes a recognizable approximation of 'home' that will appeal to many people.

More familiar to frozen juice consumers might be the popular Popsicle Pete mascot, created and drawn by Woody Gelman and Ben Solomon in the '40s. The redheaded scamp Pete appeared in Popsicle-driven comic books, coloring books, print ads, and television commercials, along with his pony sidekick, Chiefy. Consumers last saw Pete in 1995, when he was retired from duty without pomp or fanfare.

Manhattan Real Estate: Hildy bursts with excitement when she tells Pete Campbell of his appointment with the adoption agency Spence-Chapin. Pete is less than thrilled.

In one form or another, Spence-Chapin (410 East Ninety-second Street) has served the needs of abandoned children since the early 1900s. Independent nurseries instituted by Clara Spence and Dr. and Mrs. Henry Chapin merged in 1943 and three years later began a campaign that challenged the notion that African-American families did not adopt. Through their continued hard work, and with the help of supporters like Eleanor Roosevelt and Mrs. Jackie Robinson, Spence-Chapin became and remains operators of one of the most highly respected programs that championed African-American adoption of black children in the country.

Cocktail of Note: Bert Cooper's sister and fellow board member, Alice, asks for sweet vermouth while discussing the possibility of selling Sterling Cooper to Putnam, Powell, and Lowe.

Sweet vermouth is a key ingredient to a well-made Manhattan:

> 1 ounce Bourbon
> 1/2 ounce sweet vermouth
> 1 dash bitters
> 1 dash maraschino cherry juice
> Stir well with ice cubes, strain into a cocktail glass, and decorate with a cherry

Notable Writers and Directors from *Mad Men*

Matthew Weiner knows a thing or two about hiring good people to his small circle of fellow creators.

Alan Taylor (director): A veteran of high-quality television dramas, Taylor has directed *Homicide: Life on the Street, Oz, Sex and the City, Deadwood, Lost, Six Feet Under, Rome,* and *The Sopranos.* He also directed the quirky crime drama *Palookaville* in 1995, starring Vincent Gallo and William Forsythe.

Tim Hunter (director): While Hunter has directed numerous television shows over the past twenty years, he started out making feature films, the most memorable of which may be *River's Edge,* a stark and disturbing tale of teenage alienation that received high praise when released in 1986.

Paul Feig (director): A veteran of sitcoms may not seem an obvious choice for a show like *Mad Men,* but when the credits are critically acclaimed comedies like *Arrested Development,* the beloved *Freaks and Geeks* (which he created), and a dozen episodes of *The Office,* then it doesn't seem like much of a leap at all.

Rick Cleveland (writer): He penned eight episodes of *Six Feet Under* and two of *The West Wing* and was one of four credited writers responsible for the adaptation of John Grisham's *Runaway Jury,* which starred John Cusack, Dustin Hoffman, and Gene Hackman.

Marti Noxon (writer/producer): Not only is Noxon a TV journeywoman with shows such as *Prison Break, Grey's Anatomy,* and *Private Practice* on her résumé, she can also lay claim to the unassailable geek cachet of being head writer and producer on *Buffy the Vampire Slayer* and *Angel.*

2.13 MEDITATIONS IN AN EMERGENCY

Original air date: October 26, 2008
Written by: Matthew Weiner, Kater Gordon
Directed by: Matthew Weiner

> "In this atomic age it's wise to be prepared.
> The best advice your government can give
> you is Alert Today, Alive Tomorrow."
>
> — David Wiley, *If the Bomb Falls: A Recorded Guide to Survival*

Don returns to Sterling Cooper and finds it has merged, and despite the financial windfall he will enjoy as a partner, he considers his future with a company run by Duck Phillips. Betty learns of an unexpected family development. Peggy tells Pete the true nature of her weight gain of two years ago.

The threat of launched bombs from the Cuban Missile Crisis hovered over the autumn of 1962, but in the world of *Mad Men* it is background anxiety to the barrage raining down on multiple targets in Manhattan. The flare-ups range from long-gestating tensions to more recent ones, but they all strike with deadly accuracy. And if there is any reason to prefer the blast of an H-bomb it is that, if you stand at ground zero, you need not worry about walking through the aftermath. Daily life isn't so easy.

The clandestine merger of Putnam, Powell, and Lowe moves ahead, but the boys of Sterling Cooper lean on switchboard operator Lois (ex of Don Draper's desk) for information. Harry Crane is consumed by the delicate dance of "regime change" and more concerned with the outcome of the merger than the Kennedy-Khrushchev standoff (turning off a missile crisis radio bulletin to tell the boys that he found canapés in the refrigerator, and that they are "really good ones"). But the true bomb is the long fuse lit by the Don/Duck confrontation. Duck is certain that he can bend Don to his will due to the non-compete clause in his contract, but, like Pete near the end of the first season, Don faces a foe who hasn't thought his actions through. The constant refrain of "no contract" throughout the season comes in handy for Don, who can afford to say to the new owners of Sterling Cooper that an agency run by Duck would not include him and that "if the world is still here on Monday, we can talk."

The slowest burning fuse of them all is the conversation Peggy and Pete

The Drapers in happier times. (AP Photo/Matt Sayles)

finally have. While her admission clears up the details of their child (she gave him up for adoption and did not hand him off to her sister, who was also pregnant at the same time as Peggy), the tone of the scene is jarring and, I have to say, a little disappointing. The unvarnished dialogue almost sounds like a soap-opera confession (except for the "I could have had you in my life forever" preface) and is out of place in an otherwise elegantly constructed series. It is the modus operandi of the show to tease out information, to reveal character and plot in a turned head rather than an expository recitation of what we as the audience already know. The ultimate thrust of the scene is arriving at Pete's flustered reaction, but in a series where more power is given to a fleeting look (especially between Pete and Peggy — his brutal squint while she dances at P.J. Clarke's, her dropped chin after a glance while at the burlesque Tom Tom Club), the needless verbiage sounds like a writer's room less confident with the audience than in the previous twenty-five episodes.

Of course, some devotees of the show contend that the importance of the information was so great that anything other than a direct statement might be misconstrued or lead to a vague reaction on Pete's part. For it to work, it must be clear what happened to Peggy, her decision, and Pete's reaction to all of it. And from that perspective, the scene succeeds.

Just as important is the Drapers' fuse. Don has arrived at the conclusion that he wants his family, but Betty isn't so sure. The fallout from his infidelity is toxic, and she struggles with the news that she's carrying another child. In a neat flip, Betty engages in an anonymous tryst worthy of the Bobbie Barrett collision in Don's car during the hail storm ("The Benefactor") while he holds down the domestic end with his children at the Roosevelt. Moved to an emotional plea by letter, Don writes Betty with genuine regret. And in the kind of powerful scene we've become accustomed to, she invites him back home to drop the biggest of domestic bombs, particularly to a struggling couple. Here we see the flip side of the Peggy-Pete scene, where instead of a long speech we hear two words and a simple gesture: Don doesn't take Betty's hand, but holds out his and is so vulnerable that, despite their equally questionable actions throughout the season, we can only hope that they will hold fast and be alive tomorrow.

The two couples offer an interesting counterpoint to one another; the scene between Peggy and Pete is filled with dialogue (mostly for Peggy) whereas the final scene between Don and Betty is very quiet (a surprising turn for Don, a master of elocution). Almost all of them are left hanging, completely unsure where they are and where they are going. Don and Betty contemplate another child and the continuation of their marriage; Pete sits in his darkened office, rifle in his lap. It is only Peggy who is at ease, crossing herself after she prays, cleansed after her confession — either she has placed everything that has happened behind her and is moving on, or the effects and ramifications of her pregnancy are hiding, waiting for an opportunity to burst through her placid demeanor.

No matter which, at least one of the quartet looks ready for a sound night's sleep.

The Philosophy of *Mad Men* — Don Draper: "The world continues without us. There's no reason to take it personally."
Period Moment: Don watches President Kennedy's national televised address regarding the Soviet Union's Cuban missile buildup. "Upon receiving the first preliminary hard information of this nature last Tuesday morning at

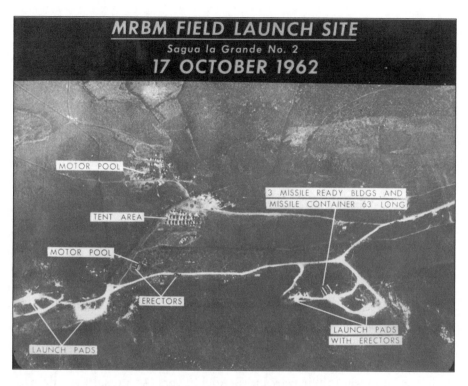

MRBM FIELD LAUNCH SITE
Sagua la Grande No. 2
17 OCTOBER 1962

MOTOR POOL

3 MISSILE READY BLDGS AND
MISSILE CONTAINER 63 LONG

TENT AREA

MOTOR POOL

ERECTORS

LAUNCH PADS
WITH ERECTORS

LAUNCH PADS

The result of "stepped-up surveillance" of missile activity in Cuba.

9 A.M.," President Kennedy said, "I directed that our surveillance be stepped up."

The information was gathered on Sunday, October 14, 1962, and passed on to National Security Advisor McGeorge Bundy the following Monday. The United States government knew of Soviet leader Nikita Khrushchev's covert shipments of nuclear technicians and weaponry from the Black Sea harbors for some time, having stepped up surveillance overflights through-out much of September and the first week of October. Khrushchev hoped that the ensuing 1962 senatorial campaign and inclement weather from hurricane season would provide cover from government scrutiny and U2 spy planes.

The plan worked until October 14 broke as a bright, cloudless day. Bundy received blown-up photographs from the overflight late on Monday, but decided to wait until his staff could compose a proper report before bringing it to the president's attention. As Arthur Schlesinger wrote in his book *A Thousand Days*, "It was better, Bundy thought, to let the president have a night's sleep in preparation for the ordeal ahead."

Thus, it was over breakfast in his pyjamas and robe that John Kennedy reviewed concrete confirmation of Khrushchev's accumulating nuclear arsenal ninety miles from the tip of Key West, Florida, on Tuesday, October 15. The next thirteen days brought the world closer than it has ever been to nuclear war.

It has not been reported whether the president managed to finish his breakfast.

Manhattan Real Estate: Before her Don Draper–esque romp in a bar manager's office, Betty indulges in a little light shopping, arriving at the bar with a pink bag from Henri Bendel (perhaps the location of the store window where she studies her reflection).

Henri Bendel (712 Fifth Avenue) is an upscale shopping destination for women, providing the very best in everything from fashionable apparel, lingerie, cosmetics, accessories, and even gourmet foods. Located at 10 West Fifty-seventh Street until 1990, the store was a Mecca for elegant women the city over. The store also featured an "Open See" event, an open call for designers to present their wares to Bendel buyers. As a result, Bendel was the first to import designs by Coco Chanel to America.

The motivating force behind Bendel's ascension to upper echelon of Manhattan's shopping food chain was Geraldine Stutz, who took over as president in the late '50s and helmed a major first floor renovation (shades of Rachel Menken?) into the U-shaped "Street of Shops" floor plan that heralded the coming shop-in-shop merchandising philosophy.

Journalist Grace Mirabella once said, "It was a store that was edited like a magazine."

Cocktail of Note: Pete appears calm as the staff of Sterling Cooper streaks out of the office, filled with H-bomb dread. Perhaps he's just that collected, or maybe it's the twelve-year-old Glenlivet Scotch whiskey he drinks. Either way, he'll need it once he finishes his conversation with Peggy.

The Glenlivet Distillery was not the first distillery in Tomintoul, Scotland, but it was the first to receive an official license to produce spirits in 1824. The Excise Act of 1823 resulted in the eradication of hundreds of illegal distilleries in the district, which by 1834 left founder George Smith in a fine position as the only purveyor of whiskey in the area.

A silky texture and a near-perfect balance of fruity and floral flavors characterize the twelve-year-old single malt. When mixed with water, the floral notes take precedence while the spices are muted. Not that many of the *Mad Men* would dare water down their whiskey.

Before Sterling Cooper — Recommended Reading: Frank O'Hara's *Meditations in an Emergency*

"It is easy to be beautiful; it is difficult to appear so."

— Frank O'Hara

By all accounts, Frank O'Hara made friends with ease. And even though his warmth and consideration of others was a constant, the O'Hara one person knew might differ from another. A fellow shipman from the USS *Nicholas* would know a sonarman who constantly read the American-based communist newspaper the *Daily Worker*. A colleague at Harvard (such as roommate Edward Gorey) would recall an earnest music student aching to become a concert pianist. Patrons of the Museum of Modern Art might remember a brittle man who worked the front desk before graduating to Assistant Curator of Painting and Sculpture Exhibitions. Readers of *ARTnews* might recall the passionate and personal reflections of associate editor O'Hara on the abstract expressionist movement of the time. Perhaps if you were among the coterie that populated the flourishing New York bohemian scene of the '50s and '60s, you would summon the portrait of a voluble, engaging, tireless party guest.

That O'Hara is best remembered as a vocal member of the New York School of poetry, a largely avant-garde set of writers (including John Ashbery, Kenneth Koch, Barbara Guest, and Alice Notley, among others) who exploded the conventions of the form, presents a paradox. There is no doubt that O'Hara's poems unleash a spring-loaded chorus of contradictory images and irregular stanzas, but, along with a colloquial style, these hallmarks cloak a craftsman's skill and affection for structure. Also, he betrayed his exacting technical elegance by an apparently diffident approach to composition that feels more like a hobby than a calling. O'Hara stole time to write between other demands — work at the MoMA, or attending movies, concerts, and, notoriously, parties — and in quick bursts with little time or desire for revisions.

Despite it all, the urgent missives that comprise *Meditations in an Emergency* indicate the depth and richness of his poetic legacy. Inexplicably ruminative and rushed, cynical but naive, a soot-covered by-product of the Industrial Revolution but infected by the same manic joy that inspired it, O'Hara's poems paint New York as a character rushing headlong from one moment into the unending possibility of the next ("capitalizing on a few memories / from childhood by forgetting them"), a reflection of his belief that poems should be about "the only truth . . . face to face."

The present-tense immediacy and first-person ruminations on New York (and identity) that populate *Meditations in an Emergency* reminds Don Draper of a world he knows but also of questions he asks. No wonder he descends on O'Hara's slender volume with a spine-buckling fervor, as if hoping to find the answers buried between the lines. That O'Hara's poems have a musical lilt is not just a result of his first love. Although what O'Hara learned at the piano could only inform his writing, the music that he transcribed in poetry rose from the crowded streets of New York. Reading the poems of *Meditations in an Emergency* in one sitting is akin to a stroll along the length of Manhattan subway car, stopping at each person to eavesdrop on the sort of thrashing subconscious current of pure thought that one suspects is eloquent despite (or in defiance) of education or breeding. The solitary observations have a truthfully informal ring that is not concerned with a scholarly "poetic" reading. Instead, each line follows the pitch and roll of breakfast table chatter, replete with the kind of innate inflections that prompted poet Robert Pinsky to suggest of every day conversation "It is almost as if we sing to one another all day."

W. H. Auden once warned O'Hara about the dangers of "non-logical relations" in his modern "surrealistic" poetry. The old master feared that it would only elicit "mere surprise and in the end fatigue," but in truth the clash of imagery in O'Hara's work is a very logical pileup of thoughts and ideas, particularly when sketching the details of a city like New York, which is itself an exultant collision of people, cultures, and philosophies. Read aloud, *Meditation* poems (in particular "On Rachmaninoff's Birthday," "A Terrestrial Cuckoo," and "Sleeping on the Wing") evoke an emotional response without a logical grounding, much like the abstract expressionism O'Hara wrote about in *ARTnews*.

More so than most, O'Hara approached his poems not simply as a literary or oral medium, but as a visual one. He performed often at parties, but these poems were of a longer form that most agree were not his finest work — gaudy strings of free-associative pearls that relied on his varied interests and activities, rather than the essential odes of a universal yet singular man. And while each poem in *Meditations in an Emergency* sculpts different stanza shapes this can also present a paradox: the full paragraphs of "Blocks" might telegraph a burst of free-form verse, but upon further inspection are tightly constructed ("she is shooting in the harbor! he is jumping up to the maelstrom!"). But the formally arranged "To the Film Industry in Crisis" spills sentiments across lines in arrhythmic fits and starts ("Sue Carroll as she sits for eternity on the damaged fender of a car / and smiles, Ginger Rogers with her pageboy bob like a sausage / on her shuffling shoulders . . .").

The most arresting visual motif in *Meditations* is autumnal; in "Poem: The eager note on my door . . . ," "Les Etiquettes Jaunes," "The Hunter," and "Jane Awake" to name a few, leaves fall as big as "pie-plates," or stun with their color "brighter than grass on the sidewalk!" The beauty of decay surrounds New York, but fails to dent O'Hara's innocent love of the city. In this, autumn takes up the metaphoric mantle of renewal often reserved for spring; it takes no great effort to love the new and fresh, but is harder to locate that same love on a season of decline. To recast a line of O'Hara's, it is easy to love the beautiful; it is difficult to love a fading beauty.

Is it any surprise that Don Draper struggles with the decline of his marriage in autumn? Or that in "Meditations in an Emergency," as Don finally apologizes to Betty for his disrespect and hopes for a reconciliation, the leaves behind him burst in color "brighter than grass on the sidewalk"?

Don Draper's attraction to *Meditations* and identification with O'Hara's work are many. Draper's colloquial writing style is mentioned often, through the first season in particular (see Roger Sterling's assessment in "Red in the Face"). Don's work is successful, in part, due to the accessibility of his writing and his non-confrontational technique. This masks a deeper understanding of not only the products he sells but who is buying them and why. Similarly, O'Hara flavored his poems with a vernacular that some thought base or vulgar which in turn made them easy to dismiss. O'Hara courted such critical oversight (it didn't help that he might grant the same cultural weight to James Dean as he did to Rachmaninoff), but his poems withstand stronger inspection and reveal adherence to a classical tradition of metrical structure that questions his membership in the avant-garde New York School of poetry.

Both men root their work in an emotional and intimate truth. O'Hara thought poems were ultimately an expression directly between the poet and the reader ("the only truth is face to face" from "Ode: Salute to the French Negro Poets"). Draper echoes the same sentiment in his belief that nothing works better in advertising than a direct connection between product and consumer, sentiment without sentimentality ("You are the product. You, feeling something — that's what sells," from "For Those Who Think Young"). Given their kinship, it wouldn't be hard to see Draper drafting O'Hara to write a "prose poem to a potato chip" (Duck Phillips, "Meditations in an Emergency").

Harder to imagine is either man bumping into each other at the theater. Draper and O'Hara both love the movies, with the theater's nearly religious solitude and sense of ritual, but the movies they'd see couldn't be more different. Draper prefers foreign films, with the icy intellectualism or emotional gusto that are unavailable in mainstream American fare — they appeal to his artistic side. Conversely, O'Hara fosters a deep and abiding love for Hollywood movies and the celebrity they generate, to a star-worshipping degree that teeters on the edge of camp.

This brings up an interesting point: the two men have sexual inclinations that diverge as broadly as their taste in movies. Draper's strong-but-silent heterosexuality is at odds with O'Hara's quiet-but-evident homosexuality, but even then there are similarities. There is a noticeably gay sensibility to Don's struggle for identity, a sort that homosexual men in the early 1960s would understand all too well. But closer still is the secretive nature of Don's double life, a "closeted" existence where both sides require complete segregation, and information from one side slipping to the other could spell disaster for both.

O'Hara placed himself in an artistic universe that better tolerated an "unorthodox" man like himself, which no doubt led to an ease and self-confidence that facilitated easy friendships. Don, however, knots himself up much tighter than that. If he can ever manage to bridge the various aspects of his life, maybe (as he recites from O'Hara's "Mayakovsky" at the end of "For Those Who Feel Young"), he'll be himself again.

HOW TO PARTY LIKE THE MAD MEN

Now that all the important stuff is out of the way (Bible quotes? Peer Gynt? I thought I would never shut up), it's time for a little digressive fun. Presented for your reading pleasure, here are a couple of articles that will help you live the Mad Men *high life. While they aren't required reading for full enjoyment of the television series, they are good for extra credit (see me after class).*

The central conceit of Matthew Weiner's fantastic series — advertising as prism for tumultuous recent history — is seductive enough to encourage addictive viewing. But peppered among the deft observation and trenchant commentary on gender politics, sexuality, racial injustice, identity, runaway consumerism, unspoken class struggle, and nuclear anxiety is the revelation of a shocking anthropological fact: the 1960s were fun! Provided you were, in no particular order or combination: white, male, straight, a Madison Avenue ad executive, in possession of a flawless profile, or a borderline socio-path (ah, Don Draper — who says there are no more heroes?).

Even more startling than the casual misogyny and elevator smoke rooms is the propensity for characters in the show to throw a party I'd actually like to attend. Whether a Paul Kinsey Montclair multicultural hootenanny (with or without Mason jar cocktail glasses), a Midge Daniels Village loft Miles Davis listening party (with or without the beatnik "appetizers"), or a flaw-lessly exotic Betty Draper Trip Around the World (gazpacho *and* Heineken?), *Mad Men* knows a thing or two about entertaining. Sadly, it's an art form particular to a culture, and one that is almost lost to the ages, much like the

Mayan dance form that pre-dates Chubby Checker by thousands of years (I've seen the cave drawings . . . or I've made that up).

Fear not. Presented for your successful shindiggery, excerpts from my journal that cover the planning, execution, and cleanup of a *Mad Men* party I threw to celebrate three years of sobriety (at least that's what you should tell my sponsor if he ever calls asking about me).

RSVP

Sunday, 8:45 A.M.: I've had a great idea. During a *Mad Men*–viewing marathon it occurred to me that I should throw a full-on theme party: period music, drinks, food, clothes . . . the works!

Monday, 2:17 P.M.: The first step is the invitation. I decided to distribute the summons in a 1960s-era method, so I spent the entire morning trying to find an open Pony Express location. The otherwise amiable UPS man I stopped decried my historical facts and suggested I was off by "at least thirty years." Outwardly I defended the choice of courier and announced my knowledge of Marques of Queensberry rules, but silently vowed to consult the encyclopedia for verification. I balled my fists and adopted a full-crouch stance to preserve my good name, but by the time I got my feet shoulder-width apart, the delivery man had vanished. Coward.

Instead, I decided to focus on the invitation itself. I flipped through the fonts and clip art available in my word processing program and was able to create an approximation of Peggy Olson's pro bono work for the CYO's A Night to Remember Dance. A quick check for "dancing" clip art and a selection of the Franklin Heavy Bold font led to something much like this:

After adding the specifics, all I needed to do was run off a few hundred copies on the work photocopier. The pink paper wasn't hard to find, but explaining it to my boss was another matter. He remained immune to my pleas of "narrative cohesion" — perhaps I should have checked to see if he'd seen the episode first, or was at least a fan of the show. Nevertheless, he did not warn me to stop making copies, unless you read "consider your future with this company" as some kind of threat.

Monday, 4:14 P.M.: After correcting a spelling error (how many ways are there to incorrectly misspell the "cream" in Brylcreem?), I ran off a few hundred more copies. Boss walked by and asked what is more important, a stupid party or my career.

Monday, 4:48 P.M.: Quit job.

MAD MEN BYOP* PARTY

Bring Your Own Pomade

Music

Tuesday, 11:45 A.M.: Slept poorly last night. Dreamt the photocopier at work came alive, bit off my hands, and spat out an eviction notice. I spent the morning plotting an "accidental" meeting with my ex-boss that had two different endings: depending on my mood or timbre of the conversation, I would either ask for my job, or hit him in the back of the neck with sock full of quarters. I envisioned the latter to a bossa nova beat and realized that if this party were going to succeed, I'd need a killer soundtrack.

I decided that strict adherence to period recordings was not crucial, but rather a template from which to start. The classics are fine, but those with a classic sound will work just as well. And a party soundtrack, like a well-designed mix tape or revenge plan, requires attention to both detail and variety.

I had the good fortune to waste a chunk of my twenties in music retail, so hours spent idly flipping through CD racks is second nature. Compilations are the best bet for a jovial gathering as the variation is ready-made and will not require multiple trips to the CD player or a wet bar built overtop of the stereo. That didn't stop me from trying such an arrangement in my first apartment, but after one drunken evening turned my CD changer into a sticky $300 five-cup drink holder, I switched to various artists collections and IKEA particle board. I stand by both decisions.

The *Ultra-Lounge* series (Capitol-EMI) is twenty-eight discs of themat-
ically arranged hipster tunes that have managed to charm with their skill
and kitsch since the 1996 release of the inaugural *Mondo Exotica*. Of particular interest are the *Leopard Skin Fuzzy Sampler*, the *Vegas Baby Sampler*,
the *Tiki Sampler*, and *Bossa Novaville*. All contain music by artists featured
in episodes — Yma Sumac ("Nixon vs. Kennedy"), Jack Jones ("The
Benefactor"), Julie London ("Indian Summer") — and music that could
very well appear (Sérgio Mendes, Martin Denny, Tito Rodriguez and his
take on the theme from *The Apartment*).

These selections would do just fine, but I felt that the ironic view taken
by the series called for music that had a similar foot in past and present
eras, so I settled upon the *Verve Remixed* series from Universal Music.

Recordings by jazz legends like Billie Holiday, Ella Fitzgerald, Dinah
Washington, Astrud Gilberto, and Jimmy Smith (among many others over
four collections) were given over to DJs for remixes that manage to update
the sound without sacrificing the spirit of the original. World-renowned
spinners such as dZihan & Kamien, De-Phazz, Rae & Christian, RJD2 (composer of the *Mad Men* theme), and Lyrics Born perform astounding work
that sounds just as natural at a rave as at a cocktail party. Plus, there are versions available that include a second disc with the original song recordings.

Tuesday, 3:30 P.M.: Basic math skills were put to the test determining how
many rolls of quarters would fill up a sock. Even then, dress or gym? So
many choices. Decided I'd have a nap.

Clothes and Accessories

Thursday, 6:42 P.M.: Yesterday was a loss, overcome as I was by an odd melancholy. Can you spell "unemployment" without "ennui"? Yes, it turned out,
but it took me five hours to come to that conclusion. (Note to self: absinthe
bottle is only for emergencies, that's why it's in the glass case.)

Lesser men might allow twenty-seven straight hours in bed to sideline
a big party, but I persevered. There is no shame in admitting that this
resiliency took the form of me scuttling across the floor like a fiddler crab,
but I did find myself at the computer searching for the appropriate fashions to make this party truly swing.

I liked the idea of purchasing some items from Michael Kors' 2008 runway collection. He captured the slim lines and dapper suits of this bygone
era, but the likelihood of delivery by Saturday was remote. Just as unlikely

was the health of my Visa card, which I had already pushed to an uncle-hollering balance on frivolities like food and rent.

I feared another trip to an absinthe-stoked dreamland, but instead screwed up my courage and ventured outside to a local thrift shop. Not only was the price right, but the chance of finding a workable suit was two-fold: either the clothes donated could come from a death-in-the-family closet purge (fingers crossed!) or the well-to-do would grow tired of recent *Mad Men*–inspired fashions and drop them like a pair of acid-washed jeans.

For less than I would spend on a good meal (not including wine, gratuity and provided my date was going dutch), I managed to squire a Kors single-breasted jacket (only stained twice), a pair of ill-fitting slacks that rode over my ankle, a crisp white shirt (well, crisp for a thrift store), and a nifty thin tie (comprised of piano keys, but a Sharpie and two hours would mend that). It was the only time I walked out of the shop feeling like an old man and liked it!

I then boomeranged right back in, and not just because I slipped on an ice patch and bruised my hip. A swinging '60s party can't feature anything other than the perfect glassware. And instead of paying through the nose for yet another "homage," I went right to the source. Martini glasses and tumblers at a dollar apiece are a bargain, no matter if they are incomplete sets. Shot glasses were trickier — not that I couldn't find any, but they were all movie-themed promotional items. I worried that measuring out an Old Fashioned in a *Cocktail* or *Barfly* jigger might undermine the illusion, but at least the latter would emit a convincingly atmospheric "bar room" aroma (and smelled like Bukowski bottled it when JFK took office).

I made one last stop at the drug store in search of the perfect hair product. I flagged down a salesclerk and had the following conversation . . .

> **Me:** My good man! I'm looking for a hair application that is both time-less in its style and breathless in its efficacy.
> **Jimmy:** What?
> **Me:** I need an elegant pomade for my locks to affect a look from a classy, bygone era; one that will faithfully retain the tracks of my comb but not render my strands crisp to the touch.
> **Jimmy:** I don't know anything about hair stuff. I'm a stock boy, not a hair expert.

Me: And you never will be with that kind of attitude. Can't you even muster a feeble suggestion?

Jimmy: You could try aisle three, or just put Crisco in your hair.

I liked the sound of saving money, but instead opted for the classic Brylcreem. This is a product that fulfilled my requirements and had a pleasing perfume to boot. Plus, it took five showers to get the lard out of my hair and attracted unwanted attention from the neighborhood cats.

Booze

Friday, 10:42 A.M.: I know two things about alcohol: first, it makes me attractive to the opposite sex, and second, you can't have a successful party without it.

I called my local liquor store and requested the full *Leaving Las Vegas* treatment. For those who don't know (or live where it is forbidden by law), this is not so much a white-glove concierge-type service, but an offer to close the store and provide a shopping cart for a five-minute shopping spree, armed only with your guest list and negligible sense of self-esteem. I operated on a simple system of two bottles of liquor for each guest, plus a twenty percent contingency supply.

A quick list of what I will *absolutely* need:

- Canadian Club
- Glenlivet
- Beefeater
- Anything in a blue bottle (excluding Windex . . . I had to learn *that* one the hard way)
- Front desk number at Betty Ford

Friday, 2:45 P.M.: The booze safely ensconced in a room of appropriate size (i.e. my bedroom), I found myself gripped by a creeping dread. Everything was in place for a rip-snorting party, and yet I felt unprepared. I picked up a martini glass to see if I had remembered to wash them when I caught sight of myself in the mirror: a dumb yokel, squeezing the stem like an eight-year-old clutches a Popsicle. How could I hope to pull off a rousing good time when, as host, I have all the élan of a gap-toothed carnie pulling the lever on a rickety Tilt-a-Whirl?

I couldn't reach the absinthe because of all the booze crates (why do I keep that thing under the bed?) so instead decided to correct my hickish demeanor.

After a flurry of visual research that included *Sabrina*, James Bond films starring Sean Connery, and *anything* with Cary Grant (except *The Bishop's Wife* or *Night and Day* — seriously, a *straight* Cole Porter?), I was ready to practice. I thought it prudent to select a handful of poses that would facilitate good conversation and encourage the admiration of my attendees, or at least extract me from an awkward situation with style and grace. I have written them here for future reference, and to properly remember the six martini glasses that so gallantly gave their lives while I practiced.

The Greet: Not so important if you attend a party, but critical if you host one. Hold the martini glass in your least used hand: some like to cup the bowl of the glass, I prefer a split-finger model reminiscent of a Vulcan greeting (I broke two glasses before abandoning a single-finger hold that would have impressed for certain, but risked offending guests due to the finger employed). Place other hand in pants pocket, preferably hitching up your single-buttoned jacket in a rakish manner. Resist urge to itch anything as it will deflate the image.

When a guest arrives, detach yourself from current conversation partner with a gentle nod and a grin (and if this is the first guest to arrive, consider striking up a dialogue with a coat rack — they'll think you crazy but unflaggingly debonair). Hand comes out of pocket five steps away for a warm handshake or to cradle a woman's elbow before a salutary peck on the cheek. Punctuate each hello with a sip from your glass — this shows you are polite but also sets the tone for a serious drinking party up-front (you may omit if welcoming groups of five or more).

The Big Lean: A classic that arose from the habit of laying a crooked elbow on the bar. You want to present a cosmopolitan air of detached interest when, in fact, you are probably fall-down drunk and need to anchor yourself to the only stationary object in the room.

Like all classics, this move is open to reinterpretation and I think a personal stamp can do wonders in a social setting. I have managed to dig my elbow into a bar and use that same hand to continue drinking, which leaves the other hand free to light a cigarette for a beautiful lady or tamp out the flames if I set fire to her silk scarf.

Poseidon meets Prometheus: When trying this high difficulty move, the first instinct is to use one hand to hold the drink while the other tends to the cigarette, but if I've learned anything from the previous steps, a free hand in a social setting can mean the difference between leading the pack and having your bones picked over by vultures. I recommend holding both cigarette and drink in the same hand, which is why I prefer the split-finger approach to cradling the bowl of the glass. Those who disagree can go right ahead, but do you really want an open flame that close to a pool of alcohol?

Other options include pinching the smoke between your lips, eyelids, or beneath your arm. Ear canals make a decent cigarette holder, but choose wisely. I tried this once and plugged up my only good ear which resulted in missing the call for dinner and frantic cries about a diminishing cigarette about to burn my lobe.

The Escape Hatch: If an empty martini glass, a reversible vacuum, a Groucho Marx nose, and a flare gun can't get me out of a troubling conversation, nothing will.

The Big Day

Saturday, 5:42 A.M.: This is it! I've filled the bowls with trail mix, ashtrays with butts, and water cooler with Crème de Menthe. I decided to keep a running journal of the party so I could tell why it was such a success! (Note: the following is an approximate transcription from notes I found balled up beneath the couch, covered in what I can only hope is peppermint schnapps.)

5:22 P.M.: Finished two pitchers of Gimlets and used seltzer bottle for an impromptu nasal lavage. Nobody had arrived. I hate people.

6:27 P.M.: Twenty-two guests and they have already proclaimed it the best party of the year. I love people! PS — The Greet was a huge hit. One person said I look like Ray Milland in *Lost Weekend*. I'm so flattered!

8:10 P.M.: The party was going swimmingly until catastrophe struck. I was playing Peter Lawford in the Marilyn Monroe Murder-Suicide Mystery Party Game and just when I gave RFK a false alibi, my ex-boss walked in. He saw one of the photocopied invites around the office after I left (read: dragged out by security) and thought I meant for him to come. Why the hell would I want that? But the joke is on him — I fixed him a drink that was *all* ginger ale. Sucker!

9:44 P.M.: Ex-boss life of party and officially at the top of my Most Hated list. This required a comprehensive list reshuffle, with Gabe Kaplan dropping off completely. I started to cut my martinis with absinthe. What could possibly go wrong?

9:54 P.M.: I couldn't feel my hands.

10:17 P.M.: Ex-boss talked me off the building ledge which was, in fact, the top of the refrigerator. The party crowned him a hero and he made progress with Joan Holloway look-alike while using my Big Lean move. Where the fuck was my sock of quarters?

11:09 P.M.: I realized that my clothes were trying to eat me. Nudity struck me as the best option and this effectively ended the party. As people shuffled out, ex-boss thanked me for a great time, said he forgave me and that he'd see me at the office on Monday. He put arm around curvy knockout who made a disparaging remark about my manhood. If only I had a way out of such an awkward situation.

11:14 P.M.: The Escape Hatch did *not* work. I aimed the vacuum cleaner poorly and learned too late that it was not reversible. Instead of extracting me from awkward conversations, it most certainly led to more with the curvy woman's lawyer. Oh, well. At least I had a job again.

There it is, all the steps you need to throw a successful party — personal injury, lawsuits, and alcohol poisoning aside. You know, success is a relative thing . . .

Think you can do better, huh? Tough words coming from some schnook reading a book. I dare you to do better (all invitations to better parties may be forwarded to my AA sponsor).

THE PERFECT MANHATTAN RENDEZVOUS:

An Itinerary for Touring Locations Highlighted in *Mad Men*

Visiting a city like New York can overwhelm, even before you arrive. The multitude of attractions available for your sight-seeing pleasure is mind-boggling, greater than any vacation would permit you to see. It is best to approach the city with a specific angle in mind, such as historical or geographical. However, it is important to do your homework first. Decide on a path before you arrive, particularly if you've gained all your knowledge of this peerless metropolis from the movies. Known for a seedy underbelly that is somehow also glamorous, there is no end to darker depictions of New York. Whether the prowling, predatory camera of Alexander Mackendrick's *Sweet Smell of Success*, Stanley Kubrick's *Killer's Kiss* from the 1950s, the anti-heroes of Sidney Lumet's *Dog Day Afternoon*, or Aram Avakian's underrated gem *Cops and Robbers* which is set against the backdrop of New York as bombed-out economic wasteland, there is enough evidence on-screen to make any potential visitors to New York think twice about the trip.

Glamorized renditions of Manhattan turn it into a burnished, autumnal wonderland of bittersweet romantic travails that, somehow, never disabuse the players of their sentimental aspirations. One could argue that Woody Allen is chiefly responsible for this view of Gotham (*Annie Hall*, *Manhattan*, and just about everything else he's done), and this is certainly borne out by an endless line of filmmakers who chose to place their films in the world he created (Joan Chen's *Autumn in New York*, Edward Burns's *Sidewalks of New York*, Nora Ephron's *Sleepless in Seattle*). It is unclear why versions of this city swing so wildly between demonized and idealized, but possibly because the city is big, complex enough to contain stories from both points of view and everything in between. For most, it is the idealized version that wins out, and this can only be a result of a global view of New York as the place where people go to make their dreams come true.

The New York presented in *Mad Men* is created with a whiff of the idealized city on display in movies like *When Harry Met Sally . . .*, *Breakfast at Tiffany's*, and *Working Girl* but more restrained, more internal. The ideal mode is befitting to a series that is as much about the interior landscape as the exterior, but the choice is clearly an economic one too. Recreating the homes and offices of an era forty years past is costly but within reach, while laying out the budget for a believable street scene, complete with wardrobe, vehicles, and avoidance of telling anachronisms would be prohibitive.

That doesn't mean you can finish watching an episode without a zesty New York aftertaste left in your mouth (for the record, that would be a combination of soft pretzel, vermouth, and exhaust). A tribute to the makers of the show is how convincing the New York of *Mad Men* is — attributable to canny set design and decoration to be sure, but just as instrumental is the way in which Matthew Weiner and his writing team weave the geography of 1960s Manhattan into each episode. It is much easier to believe that the gang is going to Chumley's for an after work drink when you get a sense of how far the place is from Sterling Cooper (for the record, about a ten-minute cab ride down Park Avenue, across West Fourteenth Street, and then a hop down Seventh Avenue).

If watching Don Draper unleash his trademark charm at El Morocco or drown his existential sorrows at Larre's gives you itchy feet, first off see your doctor. Once given a clean bill of health, feel free to use this jaunty long weekend itinerary as a way to discover the Manhattan you see and hear about in each *Mad Men* episode.

Friday

Citizens of New York who walk or pedal around Manhattan may take the sights of the city for granted. For the uninitiated, it doesn't matter what mode of transport taken, a newbie's first sight of New York will invigorate the senses and fire the imagination. This may take a little longer for those traveling by bus, but you can congratulate yourself on the immediate acclimatization you endure walking through the Manhattan Port Authority (at *least* half of the people in the city are crazy, and yes it always smells like roasting garbage).

Check into your room at The Roosevelt just like Don did in "Six Month Leave" (at Madison Avenue and East Forty-fifth Street) and rest up. You're going to need it! Although you might be tempted to use one of the many stationary exercise machines in the twenty-four-hour fitness room, you might do better to avail yourself of the appropriately named rooftop lounge, mad46, which features a terrific view and bottle service. However, if you feel the need to work out and want to save time, a well-placed Benjamin Franklin could arrange for bottle service on a treadmill.

Instead, why not consider an early dinner at P.J. Clarke's (915 Third Avenue — seen in "The Hobo Code")? Or make it a late one if you like — the kitchen closes at 3 A.M. and the bar closes an hour later. Either way, P.J.'s is known for its hamburgers (go for "The Cadillac," if your heart can stand the bacon, cheese, sautéed mushrooms, and béarnaise chili), oyster bar (including the Friday Blue Point Oyster Po Boy special) and convivial service. Learn from my mistake: *don't* walk in and loudly proclaim to expect the "full Frank Sinatra service." When I did this, the entire place went silent and the waitstaff wept openly, showing that not only do New Yorkers have a soft side they also really miss a big tipper.

If the early option strikes you, a five-minute cab ride will get you to P.J.'s from the Roosevelt, but you're in New York for God's sake, take the twenty-minute route by foot. Walk west on Forty-fifth and then go north toward Fifty-fourth Street. If you take Fifth Avenue north, you'll pass Rockefeller Center (45 Rockefeller Plaza), the GE Building (30 Rockefeller Plaza), and St. Patrick's Cathedral (460 Madison Avenue) before going east on Fifty-fourth and north on Third Avenue to number 915.

Otherwise, you could go up Sixth Avenue (or Avenue of the Americas) and pass by Radio City Music Hall (1260 Sixth Avenue) along the way. You could also take the opportunity to visit the Museum of Modern Art (11 West Fifty-third Street). The MoMA is where Frank O'Hara worked while penning the verse that so enraptures Don Draper in season finale "Meditations in an Emergency." You can drop in for a quick peek at some of the avant-garde painting and sculpture that O'Hara might have acquired during his time at the museum and wonder what Don would think of Vladimir Baranoff-Rossiné's discordant sculpture *Symphony Number 1*, or Juan Gris' cubist *Still Life with Flowers*. Depending on how quickly you want to get the table at P. J. Clarke's, you may want to consider Draper's appraisal in advance — the museum is closed Tuesdays but is otherwise open 10:30 A.M. to 5:30 P.M., except on Fridays when it is open until 8 P.M.

Saturday

Do you need an invigorating splash to get yourself moving today? Forgo the Roosevelt's serviceable amenities and take a ten-minute walk to the University Club (the site of Duck Phillip's American Airlines overture in

"Flight 1," West Fifty-fourth Street and Fifth) for a quick squash game and steam bath. If Duck Phillips can get in why can't you?

I'll tell you why — only members may enter and the club collects dues from only the finest blue-blood stock. A strict coat-and-tie dress code is in effect for men (elegance is assumed for the ladies, allowed in the University Club's hallowed halls since 1987), and members have reported that if they arrive dressed for squash, they are often asked to use the service entrance. For the afternoon, stroll by Carnegie Hall (154 West Fifty-seventh Street) to take in a show. It's unlikely you'll catch Bob Dylan like Peggy and Kurt did ("The Jet Set"), but there are Saturday matinees ranging from jazz to classical to world music. Tickets are on sale the day of any show, but Carnegie Hall also offers a few cost-saving options: rush tickets (not for all events), student and senior discounts (up to one hour before showtime), and a $10 ticket program open to all (but with limited availability).

You can marinate in the old-school glamour Don and Bobbie Barrett enjoyed ("The New Girl") when you have dinner at Sardi's (234 West Forty-fourth Street). While some of the main courses can run between $30 and $40 apiece, they do offer a prix fixe menu just shy of $50 that includes an appetizer, entrée, dessert, and (non-alcoholic) beverage.

Sunday

Last day and what you need is a great buffet to fill your sails. How about the Most Luxurious Brunch in New York?

At $95 a pop, Peacock Alley's Sunday Morning Brunch (mentioned in "Kennedy vs. Nixon") at the Waldorf=Astoria (301 Park Avenue) should fit the "luxurious" bill. You select your food from twelve themed displays arranged around the hotel's famous Lobby Clock Tower all to the gentle sounds of live piano music. A ten-minute walk from the Waldorf=Astoria (west on Fiftieth Street, north on Fifth to Fifty-sixth Street) will take you to Henri Bendel's (712 Fifth Avenue; "Meditations in an Emergency"), a perfect place to spend an afternoon shopping for fashion, cosmetics, jewellery, or luxury "lifestyle" products. As advertised, it is "a girl's playground for trendsetting young women," but it is also a great place for a fella to find a white jasmine and gardenia candle. You know, for those really rough days.

Perhaps the best place to wind up your stay is at the hotel where you started. The Madison Club Lounge at the Roosevelt features lighter fare such as Black Angus Beef Kabobs and thin-crust pizzas, and you can choose from a top-drawer menu of martinis. Whether you are there for playfully closeted banter ("Hobo Code") or just to watch the streetlights stream into the bar through the stained glass windows, you could hardly choose a better place to put a period on your time in Gotham. Don't worry, you'll be back. For now, sink into the deep leather chairs and allow the decadent mahogany paneling to wrap around you and slowly iris your vision into a slender dot bleeding with light.

But that could have been just me . . . and the eight Sambuca Con Moscas.

Sources

"71-1 (The Food and Drug Administration warned today...)."
American Medical Association's Historical Health Fraud &
Alternative Medicine Collection. January 14th, 1971.

Angelou, Maya. *I Know Why the Caged Bird Sings.* New York: Bantam
Books, 1993.

Arendt, Hannah. *Eichmann in Jerusalem: A Report on the Banality of
Evil.* New York: Viking Press, 1963.

Arsenault, Raymond. *Freedom Riders.* New York: Oxford University
Press, 2005.

Atlas, Riva D. "Bernard Geis, Celebrity Publisher, Dies at 91." *The
New York Times.* January 10, 2001.

Bailey, Blake. *A Tragic Honesty: The Life and work of Richard Yates.*
New York: Picador, 2003.

Blakeslee, Sandra. "Medical Devices; F.D.A. Warns Against Misuse of
Electric Muscle Stimulators." *The New York Times.* April 7, 1988.

Blumenthal, Ralph. *Stork Club: America's Most Famous Nightspot and
the Lost World of Café Society.* Boston: Back Bay, 2001.

Bowman, David. "When Nudists Swung." *Salon.com.* April 11, 2003.

Brantley, Ben. "Do You Speak Hollywood?" *The New York Times.*
October 24, 2008.

Brantley, Ben. "Mourning a Child in a Silence That's Unbearably
Loud." *The New York Times.* February 3, 2006.

Breslin, James E.B. *Mark Rothko: A Biography.* Chicago: University of
Chicago Press, 1998.

Buckley, Michael. "Stage to Screens: Robert Morse of 'Mad Men'."
Playbill. July 29, 2007.

Burrows, Abe. *Honest, Abe: Is There Really No Business Like Show
Business?* Boston: Little Brown & Company, 1980.

Byrne, Fiona. "'Mad Men' Star Jon Hamm on Smoking Clove
Cigarettes." *New York Magazine.* September 4, 2008.

Carlson, Peter. "Another Race to the Finish." *The Washington Post.*
November 17, 2000.

Chambers, Whittaker. "Big Sister Is Watching You." *National Review.*
December 28, 1957.

Chan, Sewell. "The Mayor's Tall Tales." *The New York Times.* December 4, 2006.

"Cigarettes vs. Lollipops." *Time Magazine.* December 11, 1964.

Clausager, Andres Ditlev. "Ivan Hirst." *The Guardian.* March 18, 2000.

Coontz, Stephanie. "Feminine Mystique revisited." *The Guardian.* August 24, 2008.

Dawdziak, Mark. "'Mad Men' set is Robert Morse's Place to Hang Out." *The Plain Dealer.* July 24, 2008.

De Bertodano, Helena. "Sex and the Octogenarian." *The Telegraph.* June 25, 2003.

Diamond, Edwin; Bates, Stephen. *The Spot: The Rise of Political Advertising on Television.* Cambridge: MIT Press, 1992.

Dorrien, Gary J. *The Making of American Liberal Theology: Idealism, Realism, and Modernity, 1900-1950.* Louisville: Westminster John Knox Press, 2003.

Dunlap, David W. "New Team, Old Look for Saloon; P. J. Clarke's Changes Owners, Who Plan to Retain Atmosphere." *The New York Times.* February 15, 2002.

Dutch, Von, Ron Turner, Ed Roth, and Robert Williams. *Kustom Kulture.* San Francisco: Last Gasp, 1993.

Dwyer, Kevin. "Blasts from the Past." *New York Magazine.* June 5, 2005.

Ebert, Roger. "Another Day in Paradise." *Chicago Sun-Times.* February 26, 1999.

Ed. Halliwell, James Orchard. *The Merry Tales of the Wise Men of Gotham.* London: John Russell Smith, 1840.

Egan, Michael. *Henrik Ibsen: The Critical Heritage.* London: Routledge, 1997.

Elliott, Stuart. "Pepsi Shifts to a New Ad Agency." *The New York Times.* November 17, 2008.

Elsworth, Catherine. "Christina Hendricks: A Fine Figure of a Woman." *Telegraph UK.* January 19, 2009.

Evans, James H. *We Have Been Believers: An African-American Systematic Theology.* Minneapolis: Fortress Press, 1992.

Ferguson, Russel; O'Hara, Frank. *In Memory of My Feelings: Frank O'Hara and American Art.* Berkeley: University of California Press, 1999.

Fitzgerald, Nora. "Chipless in Paris, L.A., N.D." *Adweek*. May 18, 1998.

Freeman, Lucy. "The Feminine Mystique." *The New York Times*. April 7, 1963.

Friedan, Betty. *The Feminine Mystique*. New York: W.W. Norton & Company Inc., 1963.

Goodrum, Charles; Dalrymple, Helen. *Advertising in America — The First 200 Years*. New York: Abrams Books, 1990.

Greenburg, David. "Was Nixon Robbed?" *Slate.com*. October 16, 2000.

"Greenroom with John Slattery." *The Charlie Rose Show*. July 28, 2008.

Grimes, William. "Vincent Sardi Jr., Restaurateur and Unofficial 'Mayor of Broadway,' Dies at 91." *The New York Times*. January 5, 2007.

Gross, Matt. "The Bowery." *New York Magazine*. July 26, 2005.

Gross, Terry. "Get on the Bus: The Freedom Riders of 1961." *Npr.org*. January 12, 2006.

Guthrie, Marissa. "From Ad Man to 'Mad Men'." *Allbusiness.com*. July 21, 2008.

Hanson, Dian. *Naked as a Jaybird*. Taschen, 2003.

Hantman, Melissa. "Helen Gurley Brown." *Salon.com*. September 26, 2000.

Harris, Bill. "'Mad Men' Star Plays Pitiable Jerk." *Sun Media*. October 9, 2008.

Henkel, John. "Sugar Substitutes: Americans Opt for Sweetness and Lite." *FDA Consumer Magazine*. November–December 1999.

Higgins, Dennis; Bernbach, William. *The Art of Writing Advertising*. New York: McGraw-Hill Professional, 2003.

Hogan, Phil. "The Interview: Elizabeth Moss." *The Observer*. January 25, 2009.

Hollingsworth, Jan Carter. "Dr. Leila Daughtry-Denmark — A life of service to children." *The Exceptional Parent*. August 2007.

Horowitz, Simi. "Vincent Kartheiser — 'Slag Heap' Play." *Backstage.com*. April 30, 2005.

"How to Succeed in Business Without Really Trying." *Variety*. January 1, 1967.

Ibsen, Henrik. *Peer Gynt*. Mineola, New York: Dover Publications, Inc., 2003.

Iley, Chrissy. "The Interview: Jon Hamm." *The Observer*. April 27, 2008.

Irving, Washington. *Knickerbocker's History of New York*. Chicago: W.B. Conkey Company, 1809.

Irving, Washington. *Rip Van Winkle, a posthumous writing of Diedrich Knickerbocker* and *The Legend of Sleepy Hollow*. New York: P.F. Collier & Son, 1917.

Jamieson, Kathleen Hall. *Packaging the Presidency: A History and Criticism of Presidential Campaign Advertising*. New York: Oxford University Press US, 1996.

"January Jones (Mad Men) Interview." *lastbroadcast.co.uk*.

Karni, Annie. "Private Clubs: Hideouts of the Rich and Shameless." *Page Six Magazine*. January 18, 2009.

Knickerbocker, Cholly. "Cholly Knickerbocker Says." *New York Journal American*. May 12, 1955.

Lawton, Kim. "The Legacy of Howard Thurman — Mystic and Theologian." *Religion & Ethics Newsweekly*. January 18, 2002.

Lowenthal, David. *The Past is a Foreign Country*. Cambridge: Cambridge University Press, 1985.

Macy, Caitlin. "Gurley Talk." *The Village Voice*. July 29, 2003.

"Maidenform Blushes." *Time* Magazine. April 25, 1983.

Maynard, Micheline. "Reliving a 1962 Crash on 'Mad Men'." *The New York Times*. August 4, 2008.

McGrath, Charles. "Kate! Leo! Doom! Can It Work?" *The New York Times*. December 12, 2008.

Morgan, Bill. *The Beat Generation in New York: A Walking Tour of Jack Kerouac's City*. San Francisco: City Lights Books, 1997.

Natividad, Angela. "Mad Men Hit Runway on Michael Kors' Dime." *Adrants.com*. July 7, 2008.

Newman, Clayton "Q&A — John Slattery." *Amctv.com*. October 14, 2008.

—. "Q&A — Robert Morse (Bertram Cooper)." *AMCTV.com*. September 8, 2008.

Nussbaum, Emily. "Square Peggy." *New York Magazine*. July 20, 2008.

O'Brien, Michael. *John F. Kennedy*. New York: Thomas Dunne Books, 2005.

O'Hara, Frank. *Meditations in an Emergency*. New York: Grove Press, 1957.

O'Nan, Stewart. "The Lost World of Richard Yates." *Boston Review*. October/November 1999.

Offit, Paul A. *The Cutter Incident: How America's First Polio Vaccine Led to the Growing Vaccine Crisis*. New Haven: Yale University Press, 2007.

Osterman, Jim. "Utz Lets Chips Fall MGH's Way." *Adweek*. November 16, 1998.

Ouzounian, Richard. "Musings on Mamet and Mad Men." *The Toronto Star*. November 16, 2008.

Perloff, Marjorie. *Frank O'Hara, poet among painters*. Chicago: University of Chicago Press, 1998.

Plotz, David. ""Helen Gurley Brown." *Slate.com*. April 7, 2000.

Prato, Alison. "Some Like it Hot: Christina Hendricks." *Page Six Magazine*. October 12, 2008.

Prial, Frank J. "Énrico Donati, 99; sculptor considered last of the Surrealists." *The New York Times*. May 2, 2008.

Ravo, Nick. "Ivan D. Combe, 88, Marketer of Clearasil and Just for Men." *The New York Times*. January 17, 2000.

Rochlin, Margy. "Those Were the Good Old Days? Hardly." *The New York Times*. September 30, 2007.

Rodman, Sarah. "Oh, *That* Guy." *The Boston Globe*. August 17, 2008.

Rooney, David. "Rabbit Hole." *Variety*. February 2, 2006.

Schlesinger Jr., Arthur M. *A Thousand Days*. Boston: Houghton Mifflin Company, 1965.

Schuessler, Jennifer. "The Humane Flophouse." *The New York Times*. December 10, 2006.

Schwartz, Ralph. "A Mill that Shaped a Nation." *Archaeology*. November–December 1999.

Severo, Richard. "Igor Cassini, Hearst Columnist, Dies at 86." *The New York Times*. January 9, 2002.

Shaw, Hollie. "Back to the Future." *The National Post*. August 22, 2008.

"Sicknicks, The." *Time* Magazine. July 13, 1959.

Simon, Alex. "Christina Hendricks Drives 'em Mad." *Venice Magazine*. July/August 2008.

Sivulka, Juliann. *Soap, Sex and Cigarettes: A Cultural History of American Advertising*. Belmont: Wadsworth Publishing Company

Somers, Christina Hoff. "Reconsiderations: Betty Friedan's 'The Feminine Mystique'." *The New York Sun*. September 17, 2008.

Stailey, Michael. "Interview: 'Mad Men' star Elizabeth Moss." *TVverdict.com*. July 15, 2008.

Steinberg, Jacques. "In Act 2, The TV Hit Man Becomes a Pitch Man." *The New York Time*. July 18, 2007.

Stern, Ellen. "Drawing a Crowd." *Playbill*. November 27, 2007.

Sullivan, Patricia. "Earl Mazo, 87; Richard Nixon Biographer." *The Washington Post*. February 18, 2007.

Thurman, Howard. *Jesus and the Disinherited*. Boston: Beacon Press, 1996 (reprint).

—. *With Head and Heart: The Autobiography of Howard Thurman*. Orlando: Harcourt Brace & Company, 1979.

Tungate, Mark. *Adland*. UK: Kogan Page Publishers, 2007.

Vallance, Tom. "Obituaries: Oleg Cassini." *The London Independent*. March 20, 2006.

Vic, Trader. *Trader Vic's Bartender's Guide, Revised*. New York: Doubleday & Company, 1972.

Walker, Nancy A. *Women's Magazines, 1940–1960: Gender roles and the Popular Press*

Wappler, Margaret. "'Mad Men': All Together Now." *The Los Angeles Times*. October 12, 2007.

—. "'Mad Men': Production designer Dan Bishop." *The Los Angeles Times*. September 28, 2007.

White, Theodore H. *In Search of History*. New York: Harper & Row Publishers, Inc., 1978.

Wieselman, Jarrett. "'Mad' About Vincent Kartheiser." *New York Post*. July 24, 2008.

Wilson, Benji. "Jon Hamm: Why Mad Men Was an Instant Star." *The Telegraph UK*. March 14, 2008.

Wilson, Eric. "Geraldine Stutz Dies at 80; Headed Bendel for 29 Years." *The New York Times*. April 9, 2005.

Wise, David; Ross, Thomas B. *The Invisible Governement*. New York: Random House, 1964.

Witchel, Alex. "Mad Men Has Its Moment." *The New York Times*. June 22, 2008.

Wolcott, James. "Miss January." *Vanity Fair*. February 2009.

Yates, Richard. *Disturbing the Peace*. New York: Delta, 1975.

—. *Revolutionary Road*. Boston: Little, Brown & Co., 1961.

Online sources:

"A Brief History of Kodak Slide Projectors."
slideprojector.kodak.com/archives.shtml

"A Cup of Joe." *www.bbc.co.uk/dna/h2g2/A1300410*

"A New Waldorf Against the Sky."
www.oldandsold.com/articles08/waldorf-astoria-17.shtml

"After Months of Anticipation — New Maytag® Repairman
Announced.
investors.whirlpoolcorp.com/phoenix.zhtml?c=97140&p=irol-newsArticle_print&ID=980748&highlight=

"Another Day in Paradise" review.
www.passionecinema.com/imdbphp/imdb.php?mid=0127722

"Broadhurst Theater." *www.newyorkcitytheatre.com/theaters/broad-hursttheater/history.html*

"Candid Camera." The Museum of Broadcast Communications.
www.museum.tv/archives/etv/C/htmlC/candidcamera/candidcam-era.htm

Cesarani, Professor David. "Adolf Eichmann: The Mind of a War
Criminal." *www.bbc.co.uk/history/worldwars/genocide/eich-mann_01.shtml*

"Chapter 36 — Cigarette Labeling and Advertising." *www.law.cor-nell.edu/uscode/15/ch36.html*

"Combe Inc." *www.fundinguniverse.com/company-histories/Combe-Inc-Company-History.html*

"Forging America: The History of Bethlehem Steel."
www.mcall.com/news/specials/bethsteel/all-bethsteel-c0p1,0,4389048.story?coll=all-bethsteel-nav

Gribben, Mark. "The Giggling Grandma." The Malefactor's Register.
markgribben.com/?p=250

"Hobo Code." *www.hobo.com/hobo_code.htm*

"Holy Innocents RC Church." *holyinnocentsbrooklyn.org/history.htm*

Horsley, Carter B. "The New York Athletic Club."
www.thecityreview.com/cps/cps180.html

Kelly, Prescott. "The Automotive Century: Most Influential People — Ferdinand Porsche." www.autohistory.org/feature_6.html

"Immediate Trial — What is Immediate GIK?" www.immediatetrial.com/NewFiles/whatisgik.html

"Inventor Chester F. Carlson Biography." www.ideafinder.com/history/inventors/carlson.htm

"New York City Athletic Club." www.nyac.org

"P.J. Clarke's: History." pjclarkes.com/history

"Peak… or 'Peak-ish'?" Today's Inspiration. todaysinspiration.blogspot.com/2008/04/peak-or-peak-ish.html

"Penelope Hughes Baker Wade McGuire Cunningham." www.soapcentral.com/atwt/whoswho/penelope.php

Phillips, Irna. The Museum of Broadcast Communications. www.museum.tv/archives/etv/P/htmlP/phillipsirn/phillipsirn.htm

"Popsicle Pete." scoop.diamondgalleries.com/public/default.asp?t=1&m=1&c=34&s=264&ai=44693&ssd=12/6/2003&arch=y

"Rocketdyne Division." www.boeing.com/history/bna/rocketdyne.htm

"Scarred faces: Girl, Interrupted." www.themakeupgallery.org.uk/disfigured/burnt/girlint.htm. December 18, 2005.

"Tanquerary." www.diageo.com/en-row/ourbrands/ourglobalbrands/tanqueray

"The Broadhurst Theater." www.shubertorganization.com/theatres/broadhurst.asp

"The Bunker Revisited." www.boweryboogie.com/2008/12/bunker-revisited.html

"The Defenders." The Museum of Broadcast Communications. www.museum.tv/archives/etv/D/htmlD/defendersth/defendersth.htm

"The Mad Men Guide to New York." gridskipper.com/62605/the-mad-men-guide-to-new-york

"The Man in the Light Gray Flannel Suit." www.whedon.info/Vincent-Kartheiser-Mad-Men-Tv,23772.html. September 5, 2007.

"The Roosevelt Hotel." www.history.com/content/nyc/the-roosevelt-hotel

"The Waldorf Astoria." www.nyc-architecture.com/GON/GON017.htm

"University Club." *www.nyc-architecture.com/MID/MID048.htm*

"Utz Quality Foods, Inc." *www.fundinguniverse.com/company-histories/Utz-Quality-Foods-Inc-Company-History.html*

"Waldorf=Astoria Hotel." *www.earthdocumentary.com/waldorf_astoria_hotel_new_york_city.htm*

"William Bernbach." Adage.com. *adage.com/century/people001.html*

"Winning Tradition." *www.snopes.com/politics/ballot/redskins.asp*

"Xerox 914 Plain Paper Copier." Smithsonian Institute. *www.american-history.si.edu/collections/object.cfm?key=35&objkey=191*

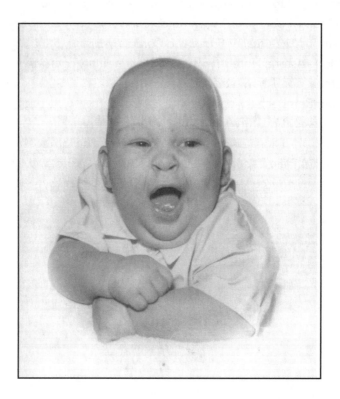

Jesse McLean has written film and television criticism for PopMatters and numerous humor pieces
for Yankee Pot Roast. He lives in Toronto. He can be
quite fussy around dinnertime but no longer poops
while he sleeps.